THE GROUND OF CERTAINTY

Other Books by Donald G. Bloesch
Centers of Christian Renewal
The Christian Life and Salvation
The Crisis of Piety
Christian Spirituality East and West
(with J. Aumann and T. Hopko)
The Christian Witness in a Secular Age
The Reform of the Church

THE GROUND OF CERTAINTY

TOWARD AN EVANGELICAL THEOLOGY OF REVELATION

by

DONALD G. BLOESCH

Professor of Theology
Dubuque Theological Seminary
Dubuque, Iowa

Wipf and Stock Publishers
150 West Broadway • Eugene OR 97401

Wipf and Stock Publishers
150 West Broadway
Eugene, Oregon 97401

The Ground of Certainty
By Bloesch, Donald G.
©1971 Bloesch, Donald G.
ISBN: 1-57910-877-6
Publication date: January, 2002
Previously published by William B. Eerdmans Publishing Company, 1971.

*To Dr. Arthur C. Cochrane,
a theologian of the Word of God*

This at least must be clear, what we intend to be: Christian theologians or philosophers. To be unclear on this point means that we in any case are not Christian theologians. For the Christian theologian must know the proper and stable premise of his whole thinking which the philosopher does not recognize: the premise of the revelation of God in Christ, or, on the subjective side, faith in this revelation.

— Dietrich Bonhoeffer

FOREWORD

With the new interest in natural theology and the philosophy of religion, it has become necessary to restate the relationship between theology and philosophy from a biblical perspective. Attempts are being made to bring the Christian faith into alignment with such philosophies as existentialism, evolutionary naturalism and syncretistic mysticism. Instead of subjecting the claims of the various philosophies and religions to the scrutiny of the Word of God, theologians are more often appealing to a common religious experience. Tillich and Schleiermacher are looming ever more significant in the theological world.

In this book we sharply diverge from much traditional thinking on the relation between theology and philosophy and suggest an alternative that is solidly anchored in biblical faith. Instead of seeing this relation in terms of synthesis or correlation or even simple subordination, we call for the conversion and transformation of philosophical meanings in the light of the biblical revelation. Philosophy can be of considerable aid to theologians, but they must take care not to let philosophical concepts determine the meaning of faith. Reason can be enlisted in the service of revelation, but it cannot establish the truth of revelation.

Against the irrationalism of contemporary existentialist theology and the rationalism that has pervaded both scholastic orthodoxy (Catholic and Protestant) and liberal philosophical theology, what is here proposed is an evangelical theology of revelation that seeks to employ reason in the task of understanding the faith. What we uphold is not an autonomous reason but an obedient reason, and as will be seen this ideal has support in the history of theology as well as in the Bible.

Our principal criticism is directed not at philosophy but at a theology that has turned away from its own criterion. Even an evangelical theology is constantly tempted to bind rather than herald the truth. The theologian should be an ambassador of the truth, but too often he seeks to be its master. His condemnation might conceivably be greater than that of the philosopher, for though enlightened by the truth, he does not always abide in the truth (cf. Luke 12:47, 48). It is well to remember our Lord's admonition that even the sons of the kingdom might be cast into the outer darkness (Mt. 8:12; 13:41, 42).

Some no doubt will conclude that what I call "theology" is in reality a Christian philosophy of life. I could accept this in a qualified sense, but then I must go on to point out that Christianity is not just another way of looking at life but a revelation of God. Nor is it a position one has arrived at through historical analysis or abstract reflection, but rather a concern or passion that has gripped one and that directs one's thinking and acting. Theology is not rationalistic philosophy but reason in obedience to revelation.

I wish to thank my colleagues in the Dubuque Theological Seminary for their criticisms and suggestions regarding the chapter "The Meaning of Truth," which was read at one of our faculty forums. I also acknowledge the help of my wife in the proofreading and correction of this manuscript.

CONTENTS

Foreword	7
Introduction	11
I. The Contemporary Debate in Theology	15
II. The Theological Encounter with Philosophy	26
III. A New Role for Philosophy of Religion	51
IV. The Ground of Certainty	68
V. Theology and Philosophy	78
VI. The Problem of Evil	105
VII. The Meaning of Truth	126
VIII. Faith and Mysticism	140
IX. Philosophy, Myth and Culture-Religion	156
X. Faith and Reason	176
Index of Subjects	204
Index of Names	207
Index of Scripture	211

INTRODUCTION

Christian theology, which is faith's reflection on the Word of God in Scripture, is constantly brought into confrontation with philosophy, man's universal attempt to gain an overall view of reality. In the former case reflection is controlled by faith in Jesus Christ, and in the latter it is born out of confidence in man's own possibilities. As they endeavor to give a faithful and intelligible witness to God's Word, theologians are compelled to ask to what extent they may use the language and categories of philosophy.

In its efforts to define itself in relation to the world of secular or philosophical thought, theology has often made two mistakes: on the one hand there has been a wholesale condemnation of philosophy, and on the other an attempted synthesis of faith and philosophy. In our view theology must be open to the authentic insights that philosophy offers, but it must be critical of the philosophic bent to include all things in a conceptual framework. Philosophy has been defined as the "effort toward a maximum organization of ideas around a minimum of principles" (Haroutunian), and such an attempt is a tribute to the human spirit as well as a sign of human hubris. But theologians must resist this kind of system building because God cannot be subsumed under some higher generalization. He is not a philosophical abstraction that can be enclosed within the thought of man but the Personal Spirit who stands over against man. The true God cannot be conceived by human reason, and this is why He must reveal Himself if we are ever to know Him. But the divine revelation shatters all man-made systems and reminds us that the all-encompassing perspective is the possession only of God.

Theology should not necessarily repudiate philosophy but instead try to take seriously the challenge as well as the failings of philosophy. It should warn against the peril of idolatry in the philosophical enterprise even while taking to heart many of the criticisms that philosophers have directed against the church in particular and religion in general. To be sure, theological speculation is not immune from the temptation to idolatry, but insofar as the theologian relies upon his own wisdom and seeks to find the truth by his own resources he has forfeited his status as a theologian.

Philosophy can be said to signify the pinnacle of natural human wisdom, and such wisdom reflects both the wonder of creation and the fall of man. We as theologians should beware of any synthesis or correlation between faith and philosophy, but we should not hesitate to utilize the concepts of philosophy in the service of the Word of God. Theologians may indeed engage in philosophical reflection, but not the kind of reflection in which faith is reinterpreted by philosophical ideas. Rather our philosophical concepts must be reassessed in the light of faith. To put this in other words, our world view should be drawn from the Christian faith and not our faith from our world view.

When philosophical concepts are brought under the rule of faith, their meanings are invariably altered. Whereas the probability is that they were originally used in a literal sense as categorical principles, they now become metaphors pointing beyond themselves to the living God. Their function is no longer normative or regulative but one that is purely supportive. They are now subsumed under a structure of meaning that is itself the criterion and ground of all meaning, the revealed Word of God (meaning here not the Bible as such but the truth that it attests).

It is well to recognize that the affirmations of faith are metaphysical as well as religious, although their intention and their basis for assertion are quite different from the general pattern of metaphysical beliefs. They are incidentally metaphysical because they refer to God, but they are primarily religious because they arise out of a need for the salvation that God provides. The ground of their truth, however, lies not in human need but in the revelation of God in the history mirrored in the Bible.

Although it has a definite metaphysical dimension, Christianity is not metaphysics. Biblical religion is centered about a Person and a message, but not a metaphysical schema. At the same time the Bible contains a teaching about God, man and the world as well as a proclamation of what God has done for us. But this teaching about God and man must always be seen in relation to Jesus Christ. Sometimes the biblical witnesses will speak of the attributes or perfections of God, but it is only in Jesus Christ that we gain real knowledge of these perfections.

Introduction

Christian theology should refrain from an outright denunciation of philosophy and still less should it ignore philosophy, but it must protest against the attempt to reinterpret the faith in the light of the latest philosophical world view. Philosophical concepts can often be brought into the service of faith, but they must not be allowed to determine the meaning of faith. This is because Christianity rests upon a divine revelation and not upon human speculation. Whenever theology departs from its biblical foundations and appeals to a particular philosophy for the validation of its truth-claims, it becomes another philosophy of religion and has thereby forfeited the right to speak on behalf of the church. Theology can only retain its integrity by bringing thought into obedience to the Word of God, and this indeed is its reason for being. The need today is for the recovery of a biblical, kerygmatic theology that will herald the truth that "God was in Christ reconciling the world to himself" (II Cor. 5:19), the truth that signifies both the fulfillment and negation of human wisdom.

Theology is a perilous enterprise because it entails fidelity to a divine revelation as well as the penetration of the cultural situation. It involves being both sensitive to contemporary reality and zealous for the truth. The theologian should be sympathetic to the philosopher who is trying to make sense out of a world that can only appear absurd apart from the light of revelation. But he should also be wary of accommodating the truth-claims of the faith to philosophical speculation which can only serve to sever faith from its divine anchorage.

Karl Barth helped theology to regain its integrity, but he nevertheless opened the door to new compromises with secular thought by a certain imbalance in some of his interpretations and emphases: we need only mention here his universalism of grace, which undercuts the decisive significance of faith, and a view of inspiration that underplays the divine guidance in the writing of Scripture. There is also a question whether he takes unbelief seriously enough, since he is sometimes inclined to say that it should be ignored, whereas we hold that it needs to be overthrown by the Law and the Gospel. Conservative evangelicals have been alert to some of these inadequacies and ambiguities in Barth's thought, but they have much to learn from him in liberating themselves from a dependence on philosophical methodology and regaining a dynamic concept of revelation.

What both liberal and evangelical Christians need to recognize is that theology has its own epistemology and metaphysical stance, although it has need of philosophy to clarify its language and sharpen its insights. The hope of Christianity lies not in an accommodation to the Marxist call for revolution, nor in a Whiteheadian reinterpretation of God in terms of process, nor in an existentialist reductionism of the faith, but in a rediscovery of the biblical and catholic roots of the faith and a proclamation of the evangel of the cross of Christ in all its power to a lost world.

ONE:
THE CONTEMPORARY DEBATE IN THEOLOGY

THEOLOGIES IN CONFLICT

The point of conflict between theological schools of thought frequently lies in the area of methodology. Here we are concerned with the question of whether there is any real difference between theology and philosophy. The older theology (both liberal and conservative) was inclined to blur the lines between the two disciplines, and consequently theology became just another philosophy of religion.

The neo-orthodox movement (Barth, Brunner, Reinhold Niebuhr) should be seen as a protest against the biblical-classical synthesis which was very evident in both the old orthodoxy and liberal theology.[1] The dynamic concepts of biblical faith, the neo-orthodox maintained, cannot be subsumed under the static categories of Hellenistic philosophy without compromising the faith. They placed the emphasis not upon the vision of God (as in Christian mysticism) but upon the service of God. Their concern was not so much with divine perfection and impassibility as with divine sovereignty and holiness. In their view, the main problem confronting the church is not how the One can be reconciled with the Many (as in classical philosophy) but how sinful man can be reconciled with the holy God.

Neo-orthodox theologians contend that the church can baptize secular and philosophical insights, but it must beware of synthesizing these insights with the biblical message. It can and should listen to philosophy, but it must not suppose that philosophy presents an accurate diagnosis of the human condition. Philosophy can be useful in clarifying Christian insights, but only when it is seen in the light of the Christian revelation.

[1] Niebuhr can be regarded as neo-orthodox only with qualification, for he sees theology as the rational explication of man's faith rather than the science of God.

Partly in reaction to neo-orthodoxy, a neo-liberal movement has arisen that seeks the aid of contemporary philosophy in arriving at a valid picture of the world and man. The neo-liberals hold that faith needs metaphysical undergirding if it is to be made intelligible to modern man. A stress upon the continuity between creation and redemption characterizes this theology. Unlike their liberal forebears, the new liberals seek to avoid the over-optimistic view of man associated with the metaphysics of progress. Their answers are somewhat different from those of classical liberalism, but their methodology is quite similar. Among those who might be included in the category of neo-liberalism are Paul Tillich, Rudolf Bultmann, Frederick Sontag, Schubert Ogden, Henry Nelson Wieman, Daniel Williams, John Cobb, John Macquarrie and Gordon Kaufman.

Secular or radical theology (associated with such names as William Hamilton, Harvey Cox, Gibson Winter, R. Gregor Smith, James Pike, J. A. T. Robinson and Thomas J. J. Altizer) is more intent upon the affirmation of human values in a secular world than the fortifying of faith by philosophy. This is not to deny that some of the radicals (such as Altizer and Robinson) are deeply interested in metaphysical problems, but for the most part philosophy is treated as an aid in realizing human potentialities. There is also an emphasis in this theology upon the reform of society and the establishing of the kingdom of God on earth.

Lately there have been some new developments within secular-radical theology. One of these is the theology of revolution represented by such thinkers as Richard Shaull, Michael Novak, Dorothee Sölle, Arthur Rich, Camilo Torres and Earl Smith; here political action (including violence) is regarded as an integral element in the mission of the church. Radical theology also includes the dominant strand within the newly developing theology of hope which sees hope primarily in terms of social change. A convergence of the theologies of hope and revolution is noticeable in the thought of Jürgen Moltmann, Johannes Metz, Carl Braaten and to a lesser extent Edward Schillebeeckx and Leslie Dewart. All these scholars seek a drastic reformulation of faith in the light of the secularization of modern culture, although trying at the same time to maintain a certain continuity with the church tradition and biblical faith.

The new wave of liberal and radical theology can best be

understood as an affirmation of the world over against the seeming depreciation of human culture and values prevalent in the old orthodoxy and also in neo-orthodoxy. H. Richard Niebuhr would undoubtedly place the new theology under the category "Christ of Culture."[2] The neo-liberal and radical theologians, instead of spurning cultural philosophy, tend to strive for a correlation and even a synthesis between Christian faith and the creative thinking of the culture. Harvey Cox even looks to the secular mind for some of the answers to the questions posed by faith.[3] The German Christians, who anticipated much of the new liberalism, sought to bring the faith of the church into harmony with National Socialism. The process theologians are bent on reinterpreting Christianity through the eyes of Whiteheadian or Teilhardian philosophy. Others such as Thomas Altizer call upon theology to open itself to the thought world of the Orient. Altizer has also spoken highly of American culture as being the most conducive to theological innovation and freedom.

Even those who espouse a theology of revolution are not necessarily opposed to human culture: their aim is to bring the Christian faith into accord with the aspirations of the dispossessed or proletariat. Moreover, they advocate using the weapons of the world to usher in the righteousness of the kingdom. It is not surprising that these men are actively engaged in seeking a rapprochement with Marxism. Considerable attention is given to the writings of the Marxist Ernst Bloch, who affirms an open future and hope as a key philosophical category. In their efforts to liberate the faith from its attachments to bourgeois ideology, they have unwittingly allied it with the ideology of the revolutionary left.

The new conservative or neo-evangelical movement also merits serious consideration. This is not so much a school of theology as a general outlook that embraces various theological positions.[4] The emergence of a new conservatism signifies a reaction against both the rationalism and irration-

[2]See H. Richard Niebuhr, *Christ and Culture* (N.Y.: Harper, 1951).

[3]Harvey Cox, *The Feast of Fools* (Cambridge: Harvard, 1969), p. 176. See my review of this book in *Eternity* (April, 1970), Vol. 21, No. 4, pp. 59-60.

[4]We are including in this general category all those who seek a fresh interpretation of the faith but who at the same time desire to remain within the tradition of historical evangelical orthodoxy. Although still relatively conservative, some of these men prefer to be regarded as progressive.

alism that have marred much of the theology of the past. The neo-evangelicals are particularly critical of the subjectivism that they find rampant in liberal and neo-orthodox thought. For them revelation is propositional as well as personal, conceptual as well as experiential. Some thinkers like H. M. Kuitert, Colin Brown and James Daane are strongly critical of the dependence of theology upon metaphysics. Others, like the late Edward Carnell and Carl Henry, while fully aware of the dangers in a synthesis of faith with philosophy, see the necessity for working out the metaphysical implications of the faith. Neo-evangelicals generally see Jesus Christ as the ultimate arbiter of truth, but they seek to conjoin the self-disclosure of Christ with the inspired word of Scripture. Some evangelical luminaries like Carnell, George Eldon Ladd, Colin Brown and Bernard Ramm have demonstrated a marked openness to neo-orthodox theology. Whether the new evangelical theology will move towards a convergence with neo-orthodoxy or prepare the way for a return to fundamentalism remains to be seen.

Those on the conservative side of the theological spectrum today would be benefited by reexamining the position of Jonathan Edwards, who admittedly made use of philosophical ideas (such as those of Locke) but who steadfastly maintained that apart from the Holy Spirit man cannot have any sound or true knowledge of spiritual things. Moreover, for Edwards religion is a matter of the heart, a direct personal experience of God rather than mere intellectual assent to propositional truth. In this existential emphasis he anticipated Kierkegaard.[5]

TESTIMONY OF SOME MODERN PHILOSOPHERS

In their attempt to come to terms with the secular mind, theologians would do well to consider the opinions of some modern representatives of secular philosophy on the Christian religion. The fact that philosophers generally deride the claims of Christianity should make theologians cautious in seeking a Christ-culture synthesis.

Immanuel Kant, who has been hailed as the philosopher of Protestantism, nevertheless contended that the demands of

---

[5]See Conrad Cherry, *The Theology of Jonathan Edwards* (Garden City, N. Y.: Doubleday, 1966); and Warren Groff and Donald Miller, *The Shaping of Modern Christian Thought* (Cleveland: World, 1968), pp. 332-350.

reason contravene the claims of faith. He declared that to hold that a Supreme Being has revealed to us concepts and principles "amounts to destroying at its root the possibility of all philosophy." Kant held "that the principles of reason as applied to nature do not conduct us to any theological truths, and, consequently, that a rational theology can have no existence, unless it is founded upon the laws of morality."[6]

The existentialist philosopher Martin Heidegger, whose influence upon both Catholics and Protestants has been appreciable, has held that the biblical word cannot even be brought into relation with philosophical questions and that a "Christian philosophy" is a contradiction in terms.[7] Although averse to the historical development of Christian theology, he allowed a role for theology similar to that of poetry. At one point in his life Heidegger was amazingly open to National Socialism, although he never allied himself with the excesses of the Hitler regime. It is interesting to note that Bultmann contends that Heidegger's thought gives the correct interpretation of pre-faith existence. The theologian Heinrich Ott has even referred to Heidegger's philosophy as "secularized Christianity."[8]

Karl Jaspers, another guiding light of existentialism, has confessed that "the One of philosophy is not the One of the Bible": it is "the difference between transcendence as an intellectual idea, and the living God."[9] Yet Jaspers chose the One of philosophy because it has more clarity and demands no submission to authority. Fully conversant with contemporary Christian thought, he maintained that if the controversy between theology and philosophy is to disappear, "the things proclaimed in church would have to shed their charac-

[6]Immanuel Kant, *Critique of Pure Reason*, trans. J. M. D. Meiklejohn (N. Y.: Wiley, 1943), p. 356.

[7]Martin Heidegger, *An Introduction to Metaphysics*, trans. Ralph Manheim (N. Y.: Doubleday Anchor, 1961), p. 6.

[8]On the attempt of theologians to reconcile biblical faith and Heideggerian philosophy see James Robinson and John Cobb, Jr., eds., *The Later Heidegger and Theology* (N. Y.: Harper, 1963). For theologians who are generally negative in their appraisal of Heidegger as well as of other modern existentialists see J. Rodman Williams, *Contemporary Existentialism and Christian Faith* (Englewood Cliffs, N. J.: Prentice-Hall, 1965); and Arthur Cochrane, *The Existentialists and God* (Philadelphia: Westminster, 1956).

[9]Karl Jaspers, *The Perennial Scope of Philosophy*, trans. Ralph Manheim (N. Y.: Philosophical Library, 1949), p. 80.

ter of revealed realities, dogmas, and creeds — in other words, their proclamation would have to become a conjuration of ciphers."[10] He acknowledged that the philosopher can also speak of faith. "But this faith has no religious content that would exclude others; it is solely the faith in the possibility of unlimited mutual understanding."[11]

On the American scene those engaged in Christian education sometimes appeal to the philosophy of John Dewey to lend credence to their views. Yet Dewey recognized that faith in democracy and science, which he upheld, is antithetical to faith in divine revelation. He saw that faith in intelligence is "religious in quality" and properly understood is "a dangerous rival" to biblical Christianity.[12] A Catholic thinker argues that Dewey's naturalistic thought is probably the best philosophical form for communicating the Christian faith to the modern mind.[13] Yet Dewey himself averred: "The opposition between religious values as I conceive them and religions is not to be bridged. Just because the release of these values is so important, their identification with the creeds and cults of religions must be dissolved."[14]

Finally, attention should be given to Alfred North Whitehead, particularly in light of the fact that numerous theologians have tried to reconcile his thought with the Christian faith.[15] It must be recognized that some of Whitehead's insights lend themselves to Christian appropriation; yet this philosopher openly disavowed the principal tenets of the Christian religion. He frankly admitted that his God "is not the God of the learned tradition of Christian theology."[16] Indeed, what he upheld is a finite God struggling toward

[10]Karl Jaspers, *Philosophical Faith and Revelation*, trans. E. G. Ashton (N. Y.: Harper, 1967).

[11]*Ibid.*, p. 90.

[12]John Dewey, *A Common Faith* (New Haven: Yale, 1955), p. 26.

[13]Thomas F. McGann, "John Dewey and Vatican Council II" in *America*, Vol. CXX, No. 14 (April 5, 1969), pp. 411-415.

[14]Dewey, *A Common Faith*, p. 28.

[15]For a brilliant attempt to restate the Christian doctrine of love with the aid of process philosophy see Daniel D. Williams, *The Spirit and Forms of Love* (N. Y.: Harper, 1968). A good introduction to process theology is given in Bernard Meland, ed., *The Future of Empirical Theology* (University of Chicago, 1969). Though not the only philosopher who has exerted an influence on process theology, Whitehead should be seen as the most important.

[16]Ruth Ashen, ed., *Alfred North Whitehead: His Reflections on Man and Nature* (N. Y.: Harper, 1961), p. 170.

fulfillment with the world and not the majestic Creator-God of the Bible who is supreme over the world.[17] He acknowledged Christ as "the highest moral moment" of world history, but he was inimical to Christianity as a system of belief and even indicated a preference for Buddhism because of its understanding of the tragedies and frustrations of existence.[18] In his view Christian theology went astray by failing to incorporate the Greek notions of liberty, democracy and the horror of brutality.

The views of other modern philosophers on the claims of Christianity could be included in this survey: we might cite here Freud, Nietzsche, Marx, Russell and Santayana. We would find that these men too, as well as others not mentioned, have a decidedly negative view of the Christian revelation. The philosophers that we have referred to do not hide their faith-presuppositions: some of them even see their philosophy as a substitute for the Christian faith.

As theologians we should take seriously their frank disavowal of the Christian religion. To pretend that these philosophers are covertly Christian or that they are really seeking for the Christian answer is not to respect their integrity. There is no doubt that Russell, Whitehead, Freud or Dewey would take a dim view of any theology that sought to combine their particular philosophy and traditional Christian beliefs. In my estimation, those theologies that recognize the qualitative difference between Christian thought and secular philosophy are being most true to their own heritage as well as to the faith-affirmations of the philosophers themselves.

TOWARD AN AUTHENTIC THEOLOGY

With many of those in the general tradition of Protestant evangelicalism, I believe that the attempted synthesis between faith and philosophy has been detrimental to both religion and culture. Theology, if it is to stand on its own foundations, must renounce any "mixing" of faith and unbelief. It must try to rediscover its own integrity if it is to be of service to

[17] Hartshorne interprets Whitehead as holding to a finite-infinite God, since he is finite only in some respects, but in our terms of reference we are justified in regarding this as a finite deity.

[18] Lucien Price, ed., *Dialogues of Alfred North Whitehead* (N. Y.: Mentor, 1954), p. 162. Whitehead was sympathetic to the religion of Jesus but decried the development of Christian theology beginning with Paul.

both the church and the secular world today. It must seek to develop its own methodology, one informed by the biblical revelation.

We hold that Christian faith does not need to appeal for metaphysical support, but metaphysical speculation stands in need of the illumination and correction of faith. Faith should be wary of seeking a philosophical basis, but philosophical norms should be measured and judged by the truth of faith.[19] In our view, the truth of the Gospel stands on its own foundation and is self-authenticating.

Faith has metaphysical implications, but human thought cannot give it metaphysical undergirding. Faith exercises thought, but thought cannot build up faith. Just as faith is the ground of truly penetrating thought, so creative thought is the intellectual fruit of faith.[20]

Those who are attracted to a new natural theology should be reminded that truth is not an unfinished discovery, as religious liberals suppose, but a definitive revelation from God. Man by himself cannot find truth, but he must be found by the truth. He cannot create truth, but he must be re-created by the truth.

We must go on to affirm that man through the power of the Spirit can apprehend the truth. He cannot control it, but he can receive it as it is given to him in the moment of decision and surrender. The skeptical current in much of modern Protestant theology must be resisted, for we have been entrusted with a quite definite message to proclaim.[21] The man born of the Spirit must be able to say with Paul, "We have the mind of Christ" (I Cor. 2:16). But he must also

---

[19]It can be seen that our position is at opposite poles from that expressed by Frederick Sontag in his *The Future of Theology: A Philosophical Basis for Contemporary Protestant Thought* (Philadelphia: Westminster, 1969). It also differs considerably from that of the more conservative scholar Page Bailey, who in his *Commitments and Consequences* (N. Y.: Lippincott, 1968) espouses a "Christian rationalism" very similar to that of Leibniz and ends with a God of unrestricted power to whom moral standards are not applicable.

[20]Although the reference here is to thought carried on by Christians, the creative thinking of the wise men of the world is also generally inspired by some faith-commitment, though it is centered not in divine revelation but in a purely human or cultural vision.

[21]For a poignant critique of the skepticism in much of modern Protestant theology see Carl Henry, "Justification by Ignorance: A Neo-Protestant Motif?" in *Christianity Today*, Vol. XIV, No. 7 (Jan. 2, 1970), pp. 10-15.

acknowledge with Paul that "now I know in part" (I Cor. 13:12) and "not that I have already obtained" (Phil. 3:12). In Christ we have access to "all spiritual wisdom and understanding," but this is more a goal than a present achievement (Col. 1:9; 2:2, 3; 3:1).

Immanuel Kant gave theology an opportunity that it missed when he affirmed "that all attempts to establish a theology by the aid of speculation alone are fruitless."[22] Interestingly enough, at one place he declared: "The biblical theologian proves that God exists by means of the fact that he has spoken in the Bible." Even though this utterance was given in a derogatory way, it is more true to the faith of the Bible than the attempts of Christians through the ages to give a rational or scientific demonstration of the existence of God.

Theology today needs to sound the call to *diastasis* (separation) if it is to penetrate the secular mind with the truth of the Gospel. Our situation is remarkably similar to that of the 1930's when there were concerted efforts to amalgamate the faith with German nationalism or Western culture or American democracy. Christians would do well to heed the admonition given some years ago by Elmer Homrighausen: "When Christianity is made into a 'philosophy of religion' and its revelation made into man's approach to God, Christianity has been thereby betrayed or falsified."[23]

But theology cannot rest content with separation: it must also prepare to attack the bastions of unbelief in the culture. When it has regained its integrity and spiritual vitality, it is then able to wrestle with the principalities and powers of the world. Its goal should not be to secularize Christianity but to Christianize the secular. It should not let the world write the agenda for the church but instead should bring to the world God's agenda.

Theology, to be sure, must allow for the reality of common grace which accounts for the truth amid the untruth of philosophy. Plato's myth of the cave, for example, is not wholly erroneous, since people generally do dwell in a world of shadows. But our aim should not be to turn away from the material world, as Plato suggested, but rather to see this world in the light of the Sun of Righteousness.

I concur with such thinkers as Helmut Thielicke, H. M.

[22]Kant, *Critique of Pure Reason*, p. 356.
[23]E. G. Homrighausen, *Choose Ye This Day* (Philadelphia: Westminster, 1943), p. 82.

Kuitert, Kenneth Hamilton and Arthur Cochrane that a new expression of orthodoxy is necessary in our time, one that is freed from the scholastic rationalism that marred orthodox theology in the past.[24] At the same time the theologian must beware of obscuring the rational content of the faith. A flight into irrationalism would be equally perilous, for it represents an accommodation to another kind of secular philosophy. We must bear in mind that the "wisdom from above" is "open to reason" (Jms. 3:17), even though it opposes reason's arrogance and pretension. Elton Trueblood rightly says that today we need to reaffirm Christian beliefs as well as a Christian style of life. Christianity must not be deemed acceptable simply because it promotes community or meets human need; it also gives a true picture of the dilemma of man and the saving works of God.[25] A new orthodoxy that is both catholic and evangelical will seek the recovery of the "Christian mind" as well as of Christian spirituality.[26]

In constructing a new theology for our time we must not ignore what contemporary philosophers are saying. Philosophy is relevant even to a theology that intends to be biblical and not philosophical. Luther called philosophy the "theology of the pagans." For that very reason it must be taken with the utmost seriousness.

Although there is no common ground between secular philosophy and the biblical revelation, there is such ground between Christians and philosophers. They share a common humanity and also a common sinfulness. There can be no co-existence between Christianity and Marxism or any other philosophy. But there might be a co-existence between Christians and Marxists as persons or between America and Russia as national states. The Christian revelation, however, cannot abide with idolatry and will always stand in judgment upon both believers and unbelievers, church and world.

It is possible to speak of a confrontation and even an en-

[24]Others who are thinking in this same direction include Tom Torrance, Jacques Ellul, Bernard Ramm, Philip Watson, Lewis Smedes, Colin Brown and Jack Rogers.
[25]Despite the many sound insights of Diogenes Allen in his *The Reasonableness of Faith* (Washington, D. C.: Corpus, 1969), we cannot go along with him in basing the truth-claims of religion on whether it satisfies man's needs. Rather our faith is true because it is based on events that really happened. That it satisfies our needs is the consequence but not the ground of its claim to truth.
[26]See Harry Blamires, *The Christian Mind* (London: S.P.C.K., 1966).

counter between Christianity and philosophy, but it is erroneous to think that there can be a dialogue in this area. Dialogue presupposes a common point of departure and a general agreement on objectives or goals. The Marxist-Christian dialogue, which has lately enamored so many theologians, is a misnomer. We do not wish to question the validity of conversations between Marxists and Christians that might help to remove roadblocks to understanding. If these encounters are genuine, however, they will indubitably bring into focus the spiritual chasm between the two faiths, one that is irrevocable. The same can be said regarding the dialogue that some are actively seeking between Christianity and the world religions.

We do not deny that perceptive Christians can learn much from the world of philosophy. Some incisive criticisms have been directed against the Christian church by such philosophers as Voltaire, Marx, Nietzsche and Russell, and these must be taken seriously by men of faith. Philosophers can notice the dark flaws within the church, but they cannot perceive its light; they can know something of the goodness within creation, but they have no knowledge of the miracle of the incarnation.

In this book philosophy and theology should be considered ideal types. No particular philosophical or theological system, for example, completely conforms to the ideal or normative pattern. Barth has rightly said that Christian thinkers are always both philosophers and theologians. Nevertheless it is well to distinguish between normative philosophy and normative theology for purposes of clarification and direction.

TWO:

THE THEOLOGICAL ENCOUNTER WITH PHILOSOPHY

In this chapter we seek to explore the intricate and ever changing relationship between theology and philosophy in the history of the church. It is our thesis that theology has been strongest and most vital when it has clearly recognized the differences between itself and secular philosophy. When it has sought to establish common ground with philosophy for apologetic purposes, it has forfeited its integrity and become just another philosophy of religion.

FAITH VS. PHILOSOPHY IN THE NEW TESTAMENT

It can be said with surety that the accent in the New Testament is upon separation from the spirit and values of the world *(diastasis)* rather than synthesis or correlation. The natural man is pictured as being bound to the powers of darkness. Because of sin he has become futile in his thinking and his senseless mind has become darkened (Rom. 1:21). He refuses to understand the Gospel message because he cannot bear to have his sin exposed (Jn. 3:19, 20; 8:43). The infinite chasm between faith and unbelief is underscored by Paul:

> Do not be mismated with unbelievers. For what partnership have righteousness and iniquity? Or what fellowship has light with darkness? What accord has Christ with Belial? Or what has a believer in common with an unbeliever? What agreement has the temple of God with idols? For we are the temple of the living God . . . (II Cor. 6:14-16; cf. Jms. 4:4).

The principal philosophies that challenged the Christian faith in the New Testament period were Stoicism, Epicureanism and Platonism. We might also mention the mystery religions, each of which represented a philosophy of life as well. It was in opposition to pagan philosophy that the apostles emphasized the uniqueness and historicity of the event of the incarnation. In II Peter we read: "For we did not follow cleverly devised myths when we made known to you the power and coming of our Lord Jesus Christ, but we were eyewitnesses of his majesty" (1:16). It was against an attempted synthesis of pagan and Christian ideas that Paul warned: "See to it that no one makes a prey of you by philosophy and empty deceit, according to human tradition, according to the elemental spirits of the universe, and not according to Christ" (Col. 2:8).

Jesus was very insistent that the message of the kingdom contravenes the wisdom of the world. What keeps the wise of the world from responding to the Gospel is not doubt but sin (Jn. 8:43f.). It is only those who acknowledge the inadequacy of their wisdom and surrender as little children to their heavenly Father who receive the truth of the Gospel. He declared: ". . . thou hast hidden these things from the wise and understanding and revealed them to babes" (Lk. 10:21; cf. Mt. 11:25). To be sure, Jesus often spoke in parables, and it would appear that He sought in this way to make the truth of faith more intelligible to the man of the world. Yet our Lord Himself contended that the parables were only understandable to His disciples because to them had been given the secret of the kingdom of God. For "those outside everything is in parables; so that they may indeed see but not perceive, and may indeed hear but not understand" (Mk. 4:11, 12). According to our Lord, to know the truth is not a matter of intellectual curiosity but of obedience (Jn. 8:31, 32). Truth, moreover, is not an intellectual construct or idea but rather a Person. As He affirmed: "I am the way, and the truth, and the life . . ." (Jn. 14:6). Our Lord did not, however, condemn all natural wisdom (Mt. 7:11), nor did He regard the natural man as totally outside the compass of God's grace (Mt. 5:45), but He did insist upon the utter uniqueness and transcendence of the divine wisdom.

The apostle Paul also contended that the Gospel stands over against the philosophy of the natural man. He held that "whatever does not proceed from faith is sin" (Rom. 14:23). It is a mistake to suppose that a philosophy of religion or a natural theology can be found in the thinking of the apostle. His view is that God can be known only through God: ". . . no one comprehends the thoughts of God except the

Spirit of God" (I Cor. 2:11). The Gospel is pictured as a "secret and hidden wisdom" which is revealed by the Spirit (I Cor. 2:7-10). Paul felt free to enter into the thought-world of paganism but only for the purpose of overthrowing it (I Cor. 9:21, 22).

Paul's address at Mars Hill in Athens is often pointed to as a recourse to natural theology (Ac. 17:22f.). Yet a closer examination of this sermon reveals that it is better to regard it as a discourse on creation culminating in the proclamation of the resurrection. This indeed is the position of Karl Barth, although it is strongly contested. It is interesting to note that it is not until Paul speaks of the resurrection that the people begin to mock, but others believe. It cannot be denied, however, that Paul's address lends itself to possible misunderstanding, since he begins with a reference to the unknown god that the Athenians worshipped. That his sermon bore little spiritual fruit is attested by the fact that he refers to the household of Stephanas in Corinth and not to the Athenians as "the first converts in Achaia" (I Cor. 16:15).

When Paul arrived in Corinth he resolved to know nothing except "Jesus Christ and him crucified" (I Cor. 2:2). In order to underscore his break with philosophy he declared: ". . . my speech and my message were not in plausible words of wisdom, but in demonstration of the Spirit and power, that your faith might not rest in the wisdom of men but in the power of God" (I Cor. 2:4, 5). Paul nevertheless sometimes made use of the terminology of Greek philosophy, but he always sought to give it new meaning and direction.

THE STRUGGLE WITH PHILOSOPHY IN THE EARLY CHURCH

In the patristic period of the church a change of attitude can be detected towards philosophy. The church was now in open rivalry with various philosophical movements which were at the same time religions. This was the age of the apologists — Justin Martyr, Clement of Alexandria, Tatian and others. These men out of loyalty to the Gospel sought to appeal to the pagan mind by upholding Christianity as the most perfect philosophy or the highest religion. Theology became a Christian philosophy of religion or natural theology. Justin Martyr made use of the Stoic concept of the Logos and sought to convince his hearers that the divine Logos had be-

The Theological Encounter with Philosophy 29

come incarnate in Jesus Christ. Clement of Alexandria taught that knowledge and eternal salvation are inseparable from one another, but the former has priority. According to Harnack the apologists generally held that "grace can be nothing else than the stimulation of the powers of reason existent in man; revelation is supernatural . . . only in respect of its form."[1]

Tertullian stands out among the apologists for his sharp criticisms of philosophy, yet he too sought to vindicate the faith at the bar of reason. He wrote concerning the Gospel: "It is believable because it is absurd . . . it is certain because it is impossible." And yet reason remains the criterion of what is absurd and impossible. He often portrayed Christianity as a divine foolishness that stands in contrast to the spurious wisdom of philosophy. He is noted for his remark: "What indeed has Athens to do with Jerusalem? What concord is there between the Academy and the Church?"[2] This does not mean, however, that Tertullian abandoned the apologetic task. Rather he sought to attack philosophy on its own ground. He found the point of contact not in a "seed of the Logos" but rather in the Stoic concept of the implanted perceptive ability of the soul. He held that the soul can perceive God by its very nature. His natural theology is especially evident in his *Testimony of the Soul*, where he declared that Nature is just as competent a teacher as Scripture.

Athanasius, although greatly influenced by Platonism, did not seek to confound the philosophers of his time; instead his aim was to clarify and defend the central mysteries of the Trinity and incarnation. Moreover, his theological method was to elucidate the faith by means of revealed concepts rather than philosophical constructions. He was not opposed to philosophy in principle, but he seems to have had little use for it. In the words of one interpreter: "He converted the past more than developed it. He descended on the world, like the true preacher he was, rather than arose from it."[3] Because he did not base his case on a criterion held in com-

[1] Adolf Harnack, *History of Dogma*, trans. Neil Buchanan (Boston: Roberts, 1897), Vol. II, p. 225.
[2] Tertullian, *On Prescription Against Heretics*, in *The Ante-Nicene Fathers*, eds. Alexander Roberts and James Donaldson (N. Y.: Scribner's, 1926), Vol. III, p. 246.
[3] P. T. Forsyth, *Positive Preaching and the Modern Mind* (London: Independent, 1953), pp. 79, 80.

mon with secular thought, he is not to be numbered among the apologists.

Irenaeus also is known more as a systematic biblical theologian than as an apologist. In his view theology has its own integrity and does not stand in need of philosophical supports. In his noted work *Against Heresies* he seeks to wrestle with unbelief within the circle of faith. His principal concern was to counteract the influence of Gnosticism within the church. Gnosticism was a syncretic amalgam of the Christian faith, the Greek mystery religions, Platonism and Persian dualism. According to Irenaeus the Gospel cannot be fused or united with pagan philosophy. Clearly disdainful of the apologetic method, he pointed out that Jesus did not address His hearers in accordance with their preconceived notions, nor did He reply to them in harmony with their opinions, "but according to the doctrine leading to salvation, without hypocrisy or respect of persons."[4]

THE MEDIEVAL SYNTHESIS

Medieval theology, beginning with Augustine, sought to come to terms with the Greek philosophic tradition by subordinating it to Christian faith. At times philosophical categories, whether Platonic or Aristotelian, gained the ascendancy in theology despite the almost universal recognition of the Bible as the formal authority for faith.

Augustine, reflecting his own spiritual pilgrimage through various philosophical systems to Christianity, understood philosophy as a preparation for theology. In his view reason is both prior to and subsequent to faith. Before one believes, it is necessary to determine what one believes *(cui est credendum)*. But he also maintained that before one can fully understand, one must make the act of faith. In Augustine's thought can be seen elements of both Platonic mysticism and biblical personalism. He seeks to unite the philosophical absolute of pure being and the religious absolute of the living God of the Bible who acts in history. Like the Platonists he proceeds from self-knowledge to God-knowledge: "O God, let me know myself so that I may know you." At the same time he seeks to relate the experience of the deepest within the self to the historical revelation in Jesus Christ. His cri-

---

[4]Irenaeus, *Irenaeus Against Heresies* in *The Ante-Nicene Fathers*, Vol. I, p. 418.

terion for truth is twofold: recollection and revelation. In the
final analysis Augustine should be regarded as a philosophical
rather than a biblical, evangelical theologian, even though the
biblical basis can always be discerned in his thinking.

In the eleventh century Anselm of Canterbury reaffirmed
the Augustinian motto, "I believe in order that I might understand" *(Credo ut intelligam)*. It is not enough to have faith;
one must seek to comprehend and even to demonstrate the
meaning of faith. Anselm proffered his famous ontological
proof for the existence of God which proceeded from the idea
of perfection to a perfect being. Karl Barth maintains that
this must be understood in the context of Anselm's epistemology — faith seeking understanding *(fides quaerens intellectum)*.
It is not a scientific demonstration but rather an illumination
and even a confirmation of faith. It is well to note Anselm's
words at the conclusion of his proof: "I thank thee, good
Lord . . . that what I first believed because of Thy gift, I now
know because of Thine illuminating in such a way that even
if I did not want to believe Thine existence, yet I could not
but know it." It appears that his proof rests upon the divine
donare and is made possible by the divine *illuminare*. Fairweather argues against Barth that while Anselm begins his
argument within the framework of faith, he supposes that
the notion of God once stated is persuasive to unbelievers and
that his argument, once carried through, is independent of
faith.[5] In our view it seems that Anselm does not return to
a natural theology but instead lays the basis for a Christocentric philosophy of religion understood as theology reflecting
on philosophical themes from the standpoint of faith.

Anselm definitely stands in the neo-Platonic, Augustinian
tradition, but the biblical foundations of faith are very much
evident in his theology. He was a realist in that he believed
that general concepts refer to real universal essences or eternal
ideas. Unlike Plato, however, Anselm affirmed the highest
universal to be God and not the idea of the Good. In common
with other scholastics he saw the intellect as occupying a
middle position between faith and sight, and he envisioned
knowledge (or sight) as a level much higher than faith.

Scholasticism reached its apogee in the thought of Thomas

[5] See Eugene R. Fairweather, ed. and trans., *A Scholastic Miscellany: Anselm to Ockham* (Philadelphia: Westminster, 1956), pp. 49-53. Henri Bouillard makes a similar criticism of Barth's interpretation in his *The Knowledge of God* (N. Y.: Herder and Herder, 1968), pp. 66ff.

Aquinas (thirteenth century), who sought to make a place for both philosophy and theology, reason and faith. According to Thomas philosophy should be seen as a handmaid of theology, indeed as a preparation for theology. Reason is capable of discerning many truths about God and the world, including the existence of God, various attributes of God, the freedom of man and the immortality of the soul. But reason can take us only so far, and then faith is necessary in order to know those truths inaccessible to the mind of natural man. Reason can know some truths about God but not saving truths. As knowledge, natural reason is superior to faith, since it can make its object clear. But faith is superior to reason, for its objects have greater worth. Just as reason must be fulfilled in faith, so philosophy must be fulfilled in theology. But none of the truths of faith contradict those of reason nor does theology contradict philosophy. Thomas envisioned a time when faith itself would make way for perfect knowledge, the beatific vision of God. He saw reality in terms of a hierarchy of nature, grace and glory; in the area of epistemology he also saw three stages — opinion, faith and knowledge.

Thomas expounded the cosmological and teleological proofs for the existence of God in which the argument centers on God's effects in nature. Thomas contended that the motion observable in nature presupposes a Prime Mover; from the causal relationship in nature he stated the case for an uncaused cause; the degrees of perfection presuppose a highest perfection; contingency and possibility presuppose necessity. He also presented a proof for God on the basis of purpose or design in nature. Unlike Anselm, Thomas held that we cannot know God in Himself but only His effects upon us. Our knowledge of God is mediated rather than immediate.

Whereas Augustine and Anselm depended heavily on Plato, Thomas drew upon Aristotle. From Aristotle he derived the idea that knowledge is attainable through sense experience rather than through reminiscence. The forms are abstracted by the mind from sense experience. With Aristotle he affirmed the validity of reason in analyzing nature and morality. He also shared with the philosopher the idea of purpose in the world; everything has a form or end. Like Aristotle he envisioned a world hierarchy conceived of as Being through Becoming culminating in Perfect Being. He saw the world as a process by which potentiality is fulfilled in actuality and culminates in pure actuality. Thomas also shared with the philosopher the idea of natural law as the law that belongs to man by nature, by virtue of what he essentially is. Finally from Aristotle and also from Plato he derived the idea of the impassible God, the God who is exempt from suffering love. Here we can see how a dependence on philosophy results in a profound distortion of the biblical conception of God.

But Thomas in the light of his Christian faith also modified and corrected Aristotle. First of all he conceived of God as real existence rather than pure thought. The actuality that he envisioned was one of existence, not thought. Whereas Plato and Aristotle said "That which is," Thomas affirmed the biblical principle: "He who is hath sent you." Moreover, in Thomas' philosophy God gives existence to the world in that He is its creator. Substances do not exist in their own right but are contingent. Efficient causality does not make beings to be what they are but it makes them "to be." Again Thomas held that revelation is necessary for a saving knowledge of God. The idea of a special divine revelation was completely foreign to Aristotle and indeed to all Greek philosophers. Thomas also held in contradistinction to Aristotle and the philosophical tradition that natural law is derived from the eternal law in the mind of God and is confirmed and partly transcended by the divine law revealed in the Bible.

What characterized later medieval scholastic philosophy was a profound and ofttimes almost irrepressible confidence in human reason. Many of the revealed truths were transformed into self-evident truths. Sin was understood as a loss of the supernatural gifts of blessedness rather than a corruption of the natural state of man. The man in sin is in a weakened condition, but his reason is still to a considerable extent capable of apprehending spiritual or metaphysical truth. Some schoolmen like Abelard ventured to maintain that reason can even prove the supernatural mysteries of the faith. Reason was also regarded as the judge of Scripture rather than vice versa. Thomas Aquinas declared: "No one should decidedly adhere to an exposition of Scripture that with sure reason is ascertained to be false . . . in order that, from this, Scripture not be derided by the infidels." In his view because Moslems and pagans do not accept Scripture "it is necessary to have recourse to natural reason, which all are obliged to assent to."[6] Yet he acknowledged that "in the things of God natural reason is often at a loss." Thomas, it should be noted, was more circumspect regarding the claims of reason than some of the other schoolmen.

The scholastic theologians constantly sought to incorporate the insights of Greek philosophy into their thinking, and sometimes at the expense of biblical truth. The desire for happiness *(eudaemonia)* was accepted as legitimate except that this desire was said to be fulfilled only in communion with the living God. The concept of love in medieval theology was essentially that of the Greek Eros, man raising himself up to God, rather than of the biblical Agape, God descending to the level of man. The eternal truths in Greek philosophy became in medieval thought the eternal truths in the mind of God. As with Leibniz later, these truths were believed to exist independently of the will of God. Thomas Aquinas, Duns Scotus and even Occam said that "what includes in itself a contradiction does not fall under God's omnipotence."

This is not to overlook the fact that some theologians in the medieval period were deeply critical of an alliance with philosophy. Peter Damian was one who railed against the dependence on Greek philosophy. He affirmed that *cupiditas scientiae* (lust for knowledge) was for men "leader of the flock of all vices." William of Occam openly questioned the capacity of reason to prove the existence of God or the validity of His revelation. The truths of faith must simply be accepted on the arbitrary authority of the church and even more of Scripture. Occam was more a philosophical skeptic than a theologian of revelation, but he helped to prepare the way for a positive theology anchored in the divine revelation alone. The mystics, Meister Eckhart, Henry Suso, and Johann Tauler among others, also held that divine truth transcends reason, and that the way to truth lies in divesting oneself of all mental images. Yet the mystics returned not so much to the biblical sources of faith as to Neo-Platonic philosophy which in the name of reason posited truth beyond reason. At the same time both the nominalism of Occam and the mysticism of Eckhart and others served to break up the medieval synthesis of Christian theology and Greek rationalism. The

---

[6]Thomas Aquinas, *Of God and His Creatures*, an annotated translation of *Summa Contra Gentiles*, ed. Joseph Rickaby (Westminster, Md.: Carroll, 1950), p. 2.

question arose in the minds of many that if reason could not give valid knowledge of God, could this be procured by faith alone?

REBIRTH OF FIDEISM IN THE REFORMATION

The Protestant Reformation of the sixteenth century marked a definite break with the medieval scholastic tradition. In the view of Luther and Calvin, authority lies not in the teaching office of the church, nor in the rational speculation of the theologians, but in the divine revelation given in Holy Scripture. Moreover, Scripture is self-authenticating; it does not need to be buttressed by human reason or churchly power. Faith alone lays hold of the revelation of God, but faith seeks an ever deeper understanding of the divine truth; therefore a role is still allotted to reason, but this is reason in the service of faith.

The Reformers protested against the biblical-classical synthesis that characterized the Catholic theological tradition. Both Calvin and Luther affirmed the total depravity of man, and this meant that man's reasoning is also infected by sin. Natural reason may be reliable on purely secular matters, but in matters pertaining to salvation it is "stone-blind" (Luther). Theology, which is based on liberated reason, always stands in opposition to philosophy, which is the work of natural reason.

Luther was especially vehement in his criticisms of human reason and philosophy. He called reason an "enemy of faith," a "beast," and "the greatest and mightiest enemy of God." In his words: "Faith kills reason and slays that beast which the whole world and all creatures cannot kill." Faith is characterized more by confidence and trust than rational assent. For him, "Faith . . . is a certain obscure knowledge, or rather darkness which seeth nothing, and yet Christ apprehended by faith sitteth in this darkness. . . ."[7] Theology, unlike philosophy, rests upon the promise and truth of God rather than conscience, reason or experience. Instead of beginning with the world of particulars, as did the Nominalists, or the eternal ideas, as did the realists, Luther began with the self-revelation of God in Scripture and sought to interpret all of reality in the light of this revelation. He allowed for a natural knowledge of God as well, particularly in his *Commentary on Gene-*

---

[7]Martin Luther, *A Commentary on St. Paul's Epistle to the Galatians*, trans. Philip Watson (London: Clarke, 1953), p. 134.

sis, but this is sufficient only for condemnation, not for salvation.

Luther was not averse to the study of philosophy so long as this was carried on within the perspective of biblical faith. Yet he cautioned against any synthesis of the Christian religion and philosophy:

> Let philosophy remain within her bounds, as God has appointed, and let us make use of her as of a character in a comedy; but to mix her up with divinity may not be endured; nor is it tolerable to make faith an "accidens" or quality, happening by chance; for such words are merely philosophical, — used in schools and in temporal affairs, which human sense and reason may comprehend.[8]

Calvin sometimes referred to the need for a Christian philosophy, but by this he simply meant a theological world view rather than a philosophy of religion that would serve as a preparation for theology. He allowed for apologetics or the rational defense of faith within the circle of faith, but he insisted that there can be no purely rational foundation for faith. Reason can confirm and illuminate revelation, but it cannot prepare the way for revelation. Calvin's antipathy towards natural philosophy and rational apologetics can be seen in these words: "We seek not arguments or probabilities to support our judgment, but submit our judgments and understandings as to a thing concerning which it is impossible for us to judge."[9] According to Calvin the natural man yearns and longs for God, but he does not seek God apart from the irresistible grace given through the preaching of the Gospel. Calvin expresses himself quite strongly on this point: "Human reason . . . neither approaches, nor tends, nor directs its view toward this truth, to understand who is the true God, or in what character he will manifest himself to us."[10] The philosophers, he says, have tried "with reason and learning to penetrate heaven," but the truths that they uncover prove upon close inspection to be only "fleeting unrealities."

Calvin's opinions on philosophy were not wholly negative,

[8]Martin Luther, *The Table Talk of Martin Luther*, ed. T. Kepler (Cleveland: World, 1952), p. 30.
[9]John Calvin, *Institutes of the Christian Religion*, trans. John Allen (Grand Rapids: Eerdmans, 1949), 8th ed., Bk. I, Ch. VII, Sec. V, p. 91.
[10]*Ibid.*, Bk. II, Ch. II, Sec. XVIII, p. 299.

however, since he recognized that the Spirit works among all peoples, though not necessarily in a saving manner. Man may reject God, but he cannot escape from God. The light of divine truth may therefore be displayed even in the writings of the heathen, albeit in a distorted form. While a philosophical system as such must be repudiated, one must always be open to the truth itself no matter where it appears.

Despite their warnings against a Christ-culture synthesis, it can be shown that both Luther and Calvin were at least partially influenced by secular philosophical thought. They frequently utilized Aristotelian and Platonic terminology in order to clarify their theological positions, but they always sought to bring this terminology into the service of the biblical revelation. Calvin, for example, made use of Aristotle's four causes in order to explain the plan of salvation, but he concluded that this plan is basically a mystery and that it is finally to be understood more in terms of paradox than strict logic. With the Greek philosophers the Reformers acknowledged that sin is partly due to ignorance, but they contended that this is a guilty ignorance. Calvin was also influenced by Stoicism, particularly in his doctrine of the Christian life; yet instead of the impersonal love of humanity as advocated by Stoic philosophers, he stressed that Christians should have an infinite preference for their neighbor's welfare. Some critics have said that Calvin compromised with Stoicism in his doctrine of predestination; but it should be pointed out that against the determinism of the Stoics he asserted freedom from necessity and the responsibility of man in the fall.

An impartial observer will acknowledge that at times the Reformers tended to accept philosophical ideas uncritically and that their training in philosophy sometimes resulted in their succumbing to such unbiblical notions as the impassibility of God and the body as the prison of the soul. Yet for the most part they used philosophy to clarify biblical truths, and only occasionally did their philosophical tools obscure the truth of biblical revelation.

Melanchthon, unlike the mainline Reformers, gave a positive role to philosophy, and it is his theology that has had the greatest impact upon the subsequent development of Protestant orthodoxy. By viewing the act of faith as primarily intellectual, Melanchthon lost sight of the truth that faith is possible only by a total conversion of the will by the Spirit. Faith became in his system intellectual assent to propositional truth, though the dimensions of trust and confidence were never absent; they were seen, however, to follow upon the persuasion of the mind. The logic of his position resulted in the belief that it is possible to bring about faith by appealing to man's reason. He saw philosophy as a propaedeutic device by which men can be led to the Gospel. He even sought to prove without the aid of revelation that God is powerful and just. His attempt to use Aristotle to validate theological propositions paved the way for the introduction of that philosopher into Protestantism.

CONFLICTING CURRENTS IN MODERN PROTESTANTISM

The scholastic orthodoxy that sought to build upon the theologies of Luther and Calvin marked a return to the dependence upon philosophy that was characteristic of Christian thought in medieval times. Melanchthon rather than the mainline Reformers was the real guiding spirit of Protestant orthodoxy.[11] Philosophy of religion was viewed as a means to convince the world of the credibility of the faith. Apologetics came to be regarded as a necessary preparation and even foundation for dogmatics. The traditional proofs for the existence of God once more gained respectability. The faith was also defended on the basis of the trustworthiness of the Bible and the plausibility of the biblical miracles. Christianity was seen as the highest religion or as the supreme philosophy.

Many of the Protestant scholastic theologians were affected by the rationalistic philosophy that they sought to combat. Leibniz, who exerted a profound influence upon the theologian Christian von Wolff, echoed the thinking of some of the older orthodox theologians in his remarks: "Faith must be grounded in reason . . . without this why should we prefer the Bible to the Koran or to the old books of the Brahmans?" David Hollaz (seventeenth century) held to a natural as well as a revealed knowledge of God. In his view unaided reason could accept both the creation of the world by God and the resurrection of Christ. Not only the method but much of the content and significance of this natural knowledge of God

[11]See Jaroslav Pelikan, *From Luther to Kierkegaard* (St. Louis, Mo.: Concordia, 1950), pp. 24-75.

are derived from Aristotle. In Hollaz, as in many orthodox theologians, there is no difference in kind between revealed and natural truths. The former are believed to be objective, necessary and universally valid, and are persuasive to any rational being. The primary role of the Holy Spirit in scholastic orthodoxy was to authenticate the doctrines of Scripture rather than to testify that we are children of God (Rom. 8:16).

Pietism and Evangelicalism signified a marked reaction against the wooden orthodoxy of the scholastics. For the Pietists faith is heartfelt confidence and trust in God and not merely intellectual assent to metaphysical propositions. Salvation is a living experience of Christ and not simply knowledge of His person and work. The only apologetic deemed worthy of espousal was the personal testimony of what God has done for man in the life and death of Jesus Christ. The Moravians Zinzendorf and Peter Böhler rejected every idea of God which was derived, however indirectly, from any general principle of human reason. "He who wishes to comprehend God with his mind," said Zinzendorf, "becomes an atheist." Both these men repudiated all ethics that did not take Jesus Christ and His love as the starting point.

The Pietists and Evangelicals took seriously the sinful bias in human reasoning. John Wesley held that sin is manifested not only in pride and love of the world but also in a deviation from truth: "All natural men will, upon a close temptation, vary from or disguise truth. If they do not offend against veracity, if they do not say what is false, yet they frequently offend against simplicity. They use art; they hang out false colours; they practice either simulation or dissimulation."[12] The Puritan theologian John Owen contended that there "is a natural impotence, through the depravity of the faculties of the mind, or understanding, whereby a natural man is absolutely unable, without a special renovation of the Holy Ghost, to discern spiritual things in a saving manner."[13]

The evangelical revivalists did not, however, deny the possibility of a natural knowledge of God. Spener opened the door to natural theology by affirming a divine light within man that enables man to seek God. But he warned that saving knowledge cannot be obtained in this way but is given only

[12] Philip Watson, ed., *The Message of the Wesleys* (N. Y.: Macmillan, 1964), p. 99.
[13] John Owen, *The Holy Spirit: His Gifts and Power* (Grand Rapids: Kregel, 1967), p. 159.

through the preaching and hearing of the Gospel. Wesley held to a prevenient grace which enables man to seek Christ without a crisis experience of conversion whereby he is turned in an altogether new direction. Jonathan Edwards postulated a seeking for salvation that is prior to the receiving of salvation, but he contended that this seeking is rendered possible by a preliminary work of the Spirit. He did hold to a general light of nature, but he cautioned that this light does not afford even the possibility of obtaining that higher knowledge of the true God.

Fundamentalism, which had its beginnings in the later nineteenth century, signifies a synthesis of Pietism and scholastic orthodoxy. In addition to the emphasis on personal religious experience there is a stress upon correct doctrine and rational proofs for the faith. Biblical prophecy and miracles also play a role in the apologetics of many evangelical conservatives. The older Pietist distrust of reason (shared by the Reformers) is much less pronounced in the modern fundamentalist movement.

Protestant liberal theology, which has its roots in the Enlightenment of the seventeenth and eighteenth centuries, has sought to validate the truth of faith by appealing to the findings and insights of secular philosophy and science. Lessing set the direction of liberal theology in his remark, "Accidental truths of history can never become the proof of necessary truths of reason." The criterion of authority in liberal theology was no longer a revelatory act of God in history but some universal principle or idea that was manifested in Jesus to a supreme degree. The philosopher Immanuel Kant exerted a formative influence upon modern liberal theology in his view that reason is incapable of penetrating ultimate reality and that contact with this realm lies only in the area of the moral will and feeling. Many modern liberals have adopted Spinoza's position that whereas faith pertains to piety and obedience philosophy has to do with truth. Others, similarly influenced by the Enlightenment, have held that theology concerns the realm of myth and symbol; philosophy, on the other hand, deals with the realm of knowledge and truth. It is no wonder that in the mainstream of liberal theology philosophy of religion came to signify the fulfillment of theology. Hegel reflected the viewpoint of a great many theologians in his dictum: "The true content of Christian faith is to be justified through philosophy." The concern in liberal theology is no longer faith seeking understanding but how the understanding can accept faith.

Friedrich Schleiermacher (d. 1834) exemplifies Protestant liberal theology at its best, for he attempts to relate an earnest commitment to Christ with the self-understanding of modern culture. In his *Addresses to the Cultured Despisers of Religion* as well as in his monumental *The Christian Faith* the vital role of Platonic and Spinozistic as well as Kantian philosophy can be discerned. His theology signifies a marked departure from Christian supernaturalism, and this is due partly to his attempt to come to terms with modern secular thought. The divine is no longer a personal deity but the ground of all finite being; moreover, it comes to self-consciousness in human nature. Christ is no longer God incarnate but rather the exemplar of perfect manhood. Christianity is not a unique revelation but rather the highest point in man's religious development. Doctrines are accounts not of God's dealings with man but rather of religious affections set forth in speech. Continuity, not crisis, marks his doctrines of God and creation. Nature and grace are co-extensive; God is simply the ground or depth of nature. Sin is not conscious rebellion against a personal God but instead the resistance of the lower nature to God-consciousness within us. This is no longer evangelical, biblical theology but a philosophical theology or, better, a theologically oriented philosophy.

Schleiermacher had insisted upon the independence of dogmatic theology from philosophy, but he was unable to maintain this posture because his theology presupposed a particular philosophical view of the world. Moreover, he viewed philosophical theology as the fulfillment of theology because by it we can link theology to the theoretical sciences. Later liberal theologians such as Ritschl and Troeltsch were also wary of a dependence upon philosophy; yet they could not prevent Kantian (and in Troeltsch's case Hegelian) insights from obscuring the Christian message.

Søren Kierkegaard, the nineteenth-century Danish religious thinker, stood out among his contemporaries in his protest against the attempted synthesis of Christian faith with secular philosophy. According to Kierkegaard Christianity consists not in a rational conclusion but rather in an existential decision. The tension between time and eternity cannot be resolved in a rational synthesis but only in a leap of faith. He spoke of the "infinite qualitative difference between God and man," which cannot be bridged by human reason. The chasm that separates God and man has its source in both human finitude and sinfulness and can be overcome only by the initiative of God. The object of faith is not a universal idea or principle but rather the God-Man, Jesus Christ, whom he also calls "the Absolute Paradox." This can be grasped only in the passion of faith and not in the speculation of reason. He asserted: "Truth is inwardness; there is no objective truth, but the truth consists in personal appropriation."[14] And again: "If I am capable of grasping God objectively, I do not believe, but precisely because I cannot do this I must believe."[15]

He was especially vehement in his denouncements of Hegelian philosophy, which in his mind distorted rather than confirmed the truth of the Christian faith. "The behavior of speculative thought in mediating Christianity is not unlike the behavior of a rebellious ministry which has seized the reins of power and now governs in the king's name while keeping the king himself at a distance."[16]

Kierkegaard, however, was not willing to abandon the apologetic task. In place of the older rationalistic apologetics he advocated a new kind of apologetics, one that seeks to undercut the self-confidence of man and remove the illusions that keep him from accepting the Christian message. The principal illusion that must be shattered is the belief that one is already a Christian. The point of contact between the natural man and the Gospel is the temptation to despair, the consciousness of guilt. By reminding man of his guilt and despair we can prepare him for the salvation which Christ offers. According to Kierkegaard apologetics must finally be superseded by direct witnessing, since men cannot be moved toward a decision until they are confronted with the biblical Gospel itself.

THE NEW MEDIATING THEOLOGY

Since the great depression of the 1930's and particularly since the second world war, scholars have been accustomed to speak of our present age as the post-modern or even post-Christian era. The confidence in man and particularly in human reason has been shattered. The emphasis is no longer

[14]Søren Kierkegaard, *Kierkegaard's Concluding Unscientific Postscript*, trans. David Swenson (Princeton, N. J.: Princeton University, 1944), p. 71.
[15]*Ibid.*, p. 182.
[16]*Ibid.*, p. 336.

on moral progress towards a this-worldly utopia but on survival amid a balance of terror caused by the nuclear stalemate. The breakdown in sexual mores has prompted contemporary novelists and playwrights to focus attention upon psychic sickness and perversion. The dominant philosophies that have arisen generally reflect the disillusionment and despair of our times. This is particularly true of existentialism and Zen Buddhism. Samuel Beckett has cogently described our age as that of "the death of man."

Theologians are no longer satisfied with the old apologetics. Brunner has echoed the views of many in his contention that neither revelation nor faith can be proved. Some theologians have sought to come to terms with the new mood of relativism and nihilism and thereby have given up any notion of absolute truth. Those thinkers who have tried to bring the Christian faith into a fruitful dialogue with the new climate of secular opinion can rightly be called "the new mediating theologians."

Paul Tillich has sought to restate the relationship between theology and philosophy in terms of the method of correlation whereby the creative existential questions of the culture are answered by the Christian faith. Philosophy springs from the "mystical apriori," the universal experience of the ground of being, whereas theology is oriented about the appearance of the New Being in Christ. Philosophy deals with the structure of being in itself; theology is concerned with the meaning of being for us. Philosophy, says Tillich, is in quest for revelation, and this is why its questions and formulations can find their fulfillment in the message of the Christ revealed in the Bible. What was "formerly called natural theology and the philosophy of religion should be transformed into an analysis of the questions implied in the structure of human existence and existence generally."[17] A Christian philosophy of religion will be roughly identical with an existential analysis of man and his culture. It is in the service of apologetic theology, since it points beyond itself to the Christian answer.

Reinhold Niebuhr is more critical of the contributions of secular philosophy. He often contrasts the biblical personalistic view of reality with the ontological philosophical view. Indeed, his principal method is to unmask the contradictions

[17] Paul Tillich, "The Present Theological Situation in the Light of the Continental European Development" in *Theology Today*, Vol. VI, No. 3 (Oct., 1949), p. 305.

and antinomies in secular philosophy in order to show that the Christian faith alone makes sense out of life. A Christian philosophy of history seeks to prove that alternatives to it fail to do justice to the totality of human experience. Yet he acknowledges that there is truth in secular philosophy on the basis of general revelation. Original sin is the source of the error in both philosophical and theological formulations. The point of contact between the Gospel and the natural man lies in his uneasy conscience, and those philosophies which take into consideration the despair and ambiguity in the life of man more nearly approximate the Christian understanding of man. The natural knowledge of God, Niebuhr contends, is a stepping-stone to faith, but it cannot induce faith.

Rudolf Bultmann is also to be numbered among the new mediating theologians of our time. He maintains that there is a basic continuity between the secular philosophical analysis of man and his predicament and the Christian analysis. Existentialist philosophy can accurately describe the fallenness of man, but it cannot bring to man the right solution. Only the grace of God given in the Christian message can enable man to gain authenticity and freedom. The Christian answer can be made a theoretical possibility for the natural man, but it becomes a practical reality for him only in the decision of faith and repentance. For Bultmann philosophy of religion is primarily an analysis of pre-faith existence from the standpoint of faith.

Finally attention should be given to Karl Rahner, the ecumenical priest-theologian of Austria, who has made a significant impact upon contemporary Catholic thought. Although standing within the Thomistic philosophical tradition, he has drawn heavily upon the philosophy of Martin Heidegger. Rahner posits a universal prevenient grace which creates within men an openness to God and Christ. Man's nature is such that it must look to grace for its fulfillment. Secular philosophy reflects this longing and seeking on the part of the natural man for the glory of God. Rahner speaks of the "anonymous Christian," by which he means one who, although not having a conscious knowledge of Christ, nevertheless lives up to the highest within him. Any man who accepts completely his own humanity has accepted the Son of Man, because in Him God accepts man. Reflecting the thought of Heidegger,

Rahner maintains that the capacity to perceive the poetic word is the presupposition of hearing the Word of God.

THE THEOLOGY OF REVELATION

There are some theologians today who seek to eschew any kind of synthesis or correlation with secular philosophy. They do not deny the validity of wrestling with the questions of the secular man, but they are dubious about the apologetic enterprise as this has been traditionally understood. They view theology not as a rational explication of man's faith (as do Niebuhr and Tillich) but rather as an explication of the meaning of the biblical revelation. Among these theologians are Dietrich Bonhoeffer and Karl Barth.

Bonhoeffer stands in the line of Paul, Irenaeus, Luther and Calvin. He sees the relation between theology and philosophy as one of conflict rather than collaboration. In his view philosophy of religion in the old sense must be supplanted by a theology of revelation. Our criterion and authority cannot be human reason but only the divinely given Word of God. There is, however, a place for a new kind of philosophy of religion which is simply theology examining the thought-world of modern man from the standpoint of revelation.

Bonhoeffer contends that philosophy by its very nature excludes any appeal to a divine revelation. The *cor curvum in se* (the heart turned in upon itself) is what prevents philosophy from perceiving final truth. "Even a critical philosophy is powerless to place the philosopher in truth, because its criterion issues from itself, and the seeming reality is still subservient to the . . . claims of the *cor curvum in se*."[18] Man can be in truth and reality only in faith through the grace of the Lord Jesus Christ. "True reality is reality seen through the truth of the Word of God, so that whoever is in reality is also in truth and vice versa."[19]

Yet although theology must be anchored in the divine revelation, it must at the same time be related to the cultural and existential situation in which men find themselves. Bonhoeffer upholds an incarnational theology over against what he calls "revelational positivism" (which he associates with Karl Barth). The Word of God is the means by which men

[18] Dietrich Bonhoeffer, *Act and Being*, trans. Bernard Noble (N. Y.: Harper, 1956), p. 89.
[19] *Ibid.*, p. 88.

are converted from unbelief to belief. But this Word must be incarnated in the human situation. We are called to preach a concrete, specific word, one that enters into the cultural experience of our hearers. Our proclamation should be geared to the unbeliever rather than the believer, but this does not mean that it should be correlated with the ideological system of unbelief. Rather it should address itself to the problems and needs of the unbeliever.

Bonhoeffer advocates a non-religious interpretation of the Gospel in order to establish the necessary relation between revelation and the world. By this he means involvement in the sufferings and trials of our fellowmen and speaking out of this involvement on concrete issues. It also signifies the eschewing of metaphysics and a supernatural or otherworldly orientation. Bonhoeffer did not have time to spell out the full implications of a religionless Christianity, but he did not have in mind the substituting of existential philosophy for the New Testament myth (as in Bultmann), since he regarded the revelational myth as practically identical with the Gospel message itself. What Bonhoeffer was attempting was to break through the division between the secular and the sacred and claim the whole of life for Christ.

He was deeply critical of apologetics because it exploits the weaknesses of man and does not recognize man in his maturity. God is not to be found so much at the boundary of life as in the midst of life. He is to be encountered where man is strong, not where he is weak. Faith should not be defended but lived. The most potent witness to the cross of Christ is a life lived under the cross.

Karl Barth is perhaps the foremost representative in our time of a consistent theology of revelation. He understands theology as an explication of the biblical revelation, one that is related to the world of sin and death and yet not correlated or conjoined with the ideologies of modern man. He declares: "When faith makes alliance with philosophies, it moves into this unspiritual sphere. But its confession has no true basis in this sphere. Hence faith cannot have any other relation with philosophies but an external, provisional, non-committal and paradoxical one."[20]

According to Barth theology must take an agnostic attitude

[20]Karl Barth, *Church Dogmatics*, eds. G. W. Bromiley and T. F. Torrance (Edinburgh: Clark, 1960), III, 2, p. 11.

The Theological Encounter with Philosophy 47

regarding the specific nature of ultimate reality. The Christian message is not a world view, a *Weltanschauung*, but the heralding of a new creation that brings into question all world views. Theology "is not concerned to penetrate to the foundation of things. It can only bear witness to the foundation which all things actually have, and which has actually been revealed as such."[21] The fundamental question is not "What is the real?" but rather "What does God require of me?"

There is no place in the Christian scheme of things for philosophy of religion or natural theology, but the study of philosophy is very necessary for the Christian. According to Barth,

> ... the function of philosophy should be to present a sincere *history of philosophy*, that is, to give a review of what man has thought. Philosophy should produce a broad picture of the different thinking of man down through the ages, but always with the presupposition that philosophy can never answer the ultimate question.[22]

One of the tasks of theology is the analysis of secular philosophical thought, not for the purpose of convincing secular thinkers but for the purpose of better understanding the message of revelation and interpreting it in such a way that philosophical meanings are either negated or subordinated to the meaning of the Word. We should not seek to appeal to a criterion held in common with secular thought; rather our task is to bring the criteria of speculative thought under the scrutiny of divine revelation.

The theological approach to philosophy, in Barth's view, should be primarily utilitarian. Philosophical terminology and insights can occasionally be used by the theologian for the strengthening and clarifying of the Christian message. Other terms and ideas in philosophy must be repudiated, particularly if they are too deeply rooted in ideological meanings that stand in contradiction to the Christian faith. Barth explains that the children of Israel were permitted to take with them jewelry of silver and gold from Egypt for their own personal use, but they sinned when they used these things to make a molten image for the purpose of idolatrous worship. Philosophy

---

[21]*Church Dogmatics*, II, 2, p. 536.
[22]Karl Barth, *Karl Barth's Table Talk*, ed. John D. Godsey (Edinburgh: Oliver and Boyd, 1963), p. 20.

can be a servant of theology, but the danger arises when it seeks to become master and dictate both the form and content of the Christian proclamation.

Barth himself has made use of Kantian as well as Platonic philosophy. It has been said that his philosophical heritage is the realism of Anselm and the modified idealism of Kant. He has for the most part been aware of his dependence on certain strands of philosophical thought, and he has constantly sought to bring philosophical concepts into the service of the evangelical proclamation. The revelation of Christ was described in his earlier writings as the epiphany of the eternal present. His early use of such terms as "eternal spirit" and "substance" of the Bible shows a tendency towards uneschatological and unhistorical thinking. In his later writings he has sought to correct this imbalance by becoming more consciously historical and by making a place for futuristic eschatology.

Kantian philosophy is particularly important in the development of Barth's thought. From Kant he has derived the distinction between "phenomenal" and "noumenal," but in contrast to that philosopher he sees the unity of the phenomenal and noumenal in Jesus Christ. Like Kant Barth maintains that man is only free when he brings his actions into conformity with the good, but this is not to be identified with the categorical imperative within but with the will of the sovereign God. Again, Barth views Christ as the living Lord and "Commander" rather than an archetype within consciousness or an immanent moral law. He shares Kant's view that human reason is gravely limited in its power and scope and that it is unable to attain metaphysical knowledge. On the other hand, Barth insists that although man by his own power and reason cannot attain valid knowledge of God, God can reveal Himself, His will and purpose, to man, and He has done this in the person of Jesus Christ.

In contradistinction to the Reformers, Barth sees philosophy not as an instrument of the devil *(advocatus diaboli)*, something to be guarded against, but rather as an advocate of man and the world *(advocatus hominis et mundi)*. The philosophers make known to us the self-understanding of the culture, and we must acquaint ourselves with this self-understanding but not succumb to it. The theologian should be thankful for the philosopher who is the truly wise man of the world, even though he is severely limited in his view of the world and reality.

Barth holds that theologians and philosophers should discuss and debate, and they can do this because of their common humanity. They are all men, and this means fellowmen *(Mitmenschen)*. They are also virtual brothers, since the natural man is claimed by Christ and indeed stands under His grace. Yet there is no fruitful encounter if the two sides seek a neutral standpoint. There can be no real exchange if we seek to disengage ourselves from our presuppositions. He asserts: "Even philosophers will not listen to a theologian who makes concessions, who is half-philosopher himself. But when you ring the bell of the Gospel, philosophers will listen!"[23]

Barth can perhaps be criticized for not giving enough recognition to the temptation to idolatry in the philosophical enterprise. Does not a reason that is not bound to the Word of God become vulnerable to demonic powers outside the control of man? If reason is not a servant of the most high God, does not it invariably become a vehicle of man's sinful pretension and lust for power? Barth would undoubtedly answer that all men even while in sin are under the grace of God and that although their reasoning is continually being misdirected because of sin, they are nevertheless related to God at the very center of their being. He would also rightly point out that the sinful bias is present in theological as well as philosophical thinking. Although some of Barth's views may be open to criticism, it cannot be denied that he has enabled theology to regain its integrity in a time when modern relativism is subverting the very foundations of our theological and philosophical heritage.

Helmut Thielicke accuses Barth of uniting the Christian faith with a monistic philosophical world view.[24] He bases his criticism on Barth's conception that humanity is both created and redeemed in Christ and that sin and darkness are only negative realities excluded from the creation. According to Thielicke the biblical dualism between light and darkness, salvation and sin, faith and unbelief is obscured and even overcome in Barth's theology. There is some justification for this criticism, but we believe that it is a misunderstanding to regard

[23]*Ibid.,* p. 19.
[24]Helmut Thielicke, *Theological Ethics,* ed. Wm. Lazareth (Philadelphia: Fortress, 1966), Vol. I, p. 107.

this as a capitulation to philosophy or even to call this "Christomonism." Barth, to be sure, reflects the modern world perspective in his affirmation of a universal salvation, but he seeks to ground this not in the idea of the unity of all things in God but in the incarnation of God in the Jesus Christ of history. Barth has been noticeably influenced by modern secular thought, particularly that stemming from Kant and the Enlightenment, but his own theology sharply contradicts the principal thrust of modern philosophy. The modern vision of the inevitable triumph of the good is subordinated to the biblical idea of the triumph of grace revealed and fulfilled in the cross and resurrection of Christ. In our opinion Barth is a biblical theologian who has not always succeeded in holding in balance the various emphases in the Bible but who has steadfastly refused to succumb to either the spirit or the world view of secular philosophy.

THREE:

A NEW ROLE FOR PHILOSOPHY OF RELIGION

PHILOSOPHY OF RELIGION IN HISTORICAL PERSPECTIVE

The discipline of philosophy of religion has been under a cloud in contemporary Protestantism. In seeking to determine its possible future role, one must first consider how it has been understood in theological history.

First philosophy of religion has been viewed as a preparation for theology. This position is especially prominent in Roman Catholic scholasticism. In the Catholic scholastic tradition philosophy of religion is not simply an ancillary of theology but its precursor.[1] It is even held to furnish the groundwork for theological thinking. Whereas philosophy remains within the sphere of nature, theology is concerned with supernatural or revealed dogmas. The light of nature is valid in its own sphere, but it must be completed or fulfilled by the light of grace. Natural wisdom is the pathway to that higher spiritual wisdom made possible by grace just as the latter wisdom is the perfection and goal of the former. This basic orientation is reflected in varying degrees in the thought of such scholars as Thomas Aquinas, Albertus Magnus and John Duns Scotus, although they differed on many specific points. Philosophy of religion becomes in this pattern of thought a natural theology and also a philosophical theology.

Karl Rahner has sought to rethink the relation of theology and philosophy in such a way as to maintain continuity with the Thomistic tradition. Philosophy of religion, although basically independent of theology, nevertheless points beyond

[1] The term "handmaid of theology" was first used by an opponent of scholasticism as a derogatory characterization of its understanding of philosophy. Some schoolmen in accepting the term held that philosophy is a free handmaid and that her duties are not simply ornamental but essential, for she carries the light that is to guide the footsteps of theology.

itself to the questions that are answered only by theology. The role of philosophy of religion is to investigate the nature of man and demonstrate that he has an openness and readiness for revelation. Rahner holds that only that philosophical inquiry can be deemed "intrinsically Christian" which concerns itself with how man can be a subject or "hearer" of a revelation of God. The divine word can be heard and can elicit an affirmative response, for there is in man, "at the very foundation of his nature, a reaching out of finite love towards God."[2] Because philosophy of religion introduces man to the possibility of a divine revelation, this discipline can legitimately be viewed as a *praeparatio evangelii* (preparation for the Gospel).

Within the circles of Protestant orthodoxy and to a lesser extent in some strands of Protestant liberal theology, philosophy of religion is treated in a similar manner — as a propaedeutic leading to the study of theology proper. In the neoliberalism of Paul Tillich one can discern this same general approach. According to Tillich philosophy of religion investigates the questions implied in the human situation; theology deals with the biblical answer to these questions. Philosophy of religion is made possible because of the "mystical apriori," the universal awareness of the ground of being. Theology, on the other hand, is oriented about a special historical revelation.

A general criticism of this first view of philosophy of religion is that it presupposes that reason can gain valid knowledge of God apart from divine revelation. It does not take seriously enough the ideological taint of reason, the infection of our reasoning by sin.

A second approach is that which understands philosophy of religion as a branch of theology. Philosophy of religion becomes in this view an apologetic defense of the faith and sometimes also a natural theology. This position can be discerned in the older Protestant orthodoxy (such as that of Edward Carnell) and also in some types of Protestant liberal theology (such as that of Schleiermacher). It also is present in the neo-orthodox theology of Reinhold Niebuhr, who sees the Christian faith as a philosophy of history which he contrasts with secular world views such as the classical and the modern.

This general approach can be criticized on the grounds that

---

[2]Karl Rahner, *Hearers of the Word*, trans. Michael Richards (N. Y.: Herder and Herder, 1969), p. 101. See also his *Theological Investigations* (Baltimore: Helicon, 1969), Vol. VI, pp. 71-81.

it tends to conceive of Christianity as only another type of philosophy or world view. In the circles of Protestant orthodoxy Christianity becomes a "rational theism" or "classical supernaturalism." In some strands of neo-orthodoxy the Christian faith is equated with "biblical personalism" or "Christian realism." The door is thereby opened to the autonomy of reason, that is, the capacity of reason to discern spiritual truth independently of divine revelation and authority. The case for Christianity is made on the basis of whether it can be validated rationally; little attention is given to its inherent power of convicting men of sin and leading them to repentance.

Still another approach to philosophy of religion regards it as the fulfillment of theology, the heir to theology. Here we can mention the idealistic philosophical theologies of William Hocking and George Adams and the neo-naturalism of Wieman, Meland, Hartshorne and Daniel Williams. Schleiermacher might also be placed in this category in that he regarded philosophical theology as the culmination of theological endeavor; he even indicated that it takes its stance "above Christianity." The personalist school of philosophical theology (Edgar Brightman, Albert Knudson) should also be included here.

In this pattern of thought philosophy of religion is held to be more inclusive than theology. It considers not merely the idea of God but also the meaning and value of the whole development of religion. Theology is seen to be a branch of philosophy of religion. It is commonly said that whereas religion concerns the realm of myth and symbol, philosophy deals with the realm of knowledge. Faith is often spoken of as something less than knowledge, and the Christian religion is therefore said to stand in need of philosophical undergirding. As Whitehead put it, Christianity is a "religion seeking a metaphysic."

Our objection to this approach is that it denies an authoritative divine revelation. Instead of witnessing to the truth that has become incarnate in Jesus Christ, it prefers the universal quest for truth. It seeks to find God in religious experience or in rational speculation rather than in His revelation in Holy Scripture. This kind of philosophy of religion signifies a surrender to autonomous reason.

Finally philosophy of religion has been understood as an

independent discipline allied to theology. It can be of service to theology, but it has its own area of investigation. These thinkers generally uphold a Christian philosophy which they contrast with secular philosophical systems.

Herman Dooyeweerd, a Dutch jurist and philosopher, is one representative of this line of thought. According to Dooyeweerd, a Christian philosophy is independent from theology but inseparable from religion.[3] It is that discipline which investigates the whole of reality in the light of revelation. It is distinguished from theology in that the latter focuses upon the meaning and truth of Scripture. He rejects speculative natural theology because it takes for its point of departure the autonomy of reason. The gulf, he says, is not between faith and reason but between a Christian and a non-Christian conception of reason. All philosophy is grounded in a religious faith of some kind, thereby pointing to the truth that the starting point of theoretical thought is not to be found in thought.

Emil Brunner in his later period also understands philosophy of religion as being a discipline in its own right, to be distinguished but not divorced from theology. In Brunner's view philosophy of religion is a bridge between theology and secular thought. Theology and Christian philosophy are different in respect to their subject matter, but they are mutually complementary. Christian philosophy is a reflection on the principles of being in the light of revelation whereas theology deals with the biblical revelation. In an earlier period Brunner pictured philosophy of religion as being a branch of theology, although the rationale for the later distinction can already be discerned then.[4]

Among the criticisms that I have of this position is that it tends to subordinate theology to philosophy. Philosophy is seen to be more inclusive, whereas theology is depicted as being narrow or limited in its scope. I make this criticism despite Brunner's allegation that theology is the more important discipline. What those who champion a Christian philosophy of this type do not always see is that theology itself must

[3] See Herman Dooyeweerd, *A New Critique of Theoretical Thought*, trans. David Freeman and William Young (Philadelphia: Presbyterian and Reformed, 1953), Vol. I. Also see his *In the Twilight of Western Thought* (Nutley, N. J.: Craig, 1968).
[4] See Emil Brunner, *The Philosophy of Religion*, trans. A. J. D. Farrer and Bertram Lee Woolf (London: Clarke, 1958).

be metaphysical; it cannot limit itself to the Bible and the confessions of the church, but it must go on and interpret the whole of reality in light of the biblical revelation. It should be noted that both Dooyeweerd and Brunner appeal not to an autonomous reason but to a reason in the service of faith.

A further danger in the above approach is that a conceptual synthesis may be arrived at which claims too much in the light of the biblical witness concerning the limitations of human reason. Christianity must never be tied to a particular world view, even though it can be brought into agreement with certain world views while definitely excluding others. Its interpretations of the nature of the world should be seen as provisional; the "theoretical total-view" (Dooyeweerd) is an eschatological goal rather than a present possession. Perhaps it is better to regard it as one of the fruits of that higher goal which is the glorification of God by conformity to His will. When we are united with God in perfect love, then we shall see the world through His eyes. We shall have a vastly extended horizon, for then we shall know even as we are known (I Cor. 13:12); yet this must not be taken to mean that we shall know literally everything.

One other approach should be mentioned, although it is to be included in that division which treats philosophy of religion as a discipline independent of theology. I have in mind the analytic philosophy of religion. Among its representatives are Willem Zuurdeeg, Paul van Buren, Ian Ramsey, Nels Ferré, Frederick Ferré and probably also William Hordern.[5] These men seek to come to terms with the secular movement of analytic philosophy or logical empiricism associated with such names as Wittgenstein, Ayer and Braithwaite.

According to this position the function of philosophy is not normative but analytical. It deals with the clarification of meanings, not the search for ultimate meaning. Logical analysis and semantics replace metaphysics as the chief concern. Philosophy of religion is viewed as a supplementary aid to theological work. Its role is the clarification of religious language, whereas the concern of theology is with the communication of Christian values or the biblical story, depending upon one's theological stance. Philosophy of religion in this

[5] See especially Willem F. Zuurdeeg, *An Analytical Philosophy of Religion* (Nashville: Abingdon, 1958); and Ian T. Ramsey, *Religious Language* (London: SCM, 1957).

sense is an independent discipline that can, though, be of immense service to theology. Belief in God is said to be a matter of faith, a matter which eludes scientific analysis. Statements about God and the soul can be perfectly meaningful, but they are beyond empirical verification. Here we see the influence of Kant, who contended that belief in God is in the area of practical, not pure reason. In his view belief in God and in the future life rests on the subjective ground of moral sentiment.

Unlike the Thomistic and also the Tillichian schemes, which envisage the relationship between theology and philosophy as one of interdependence, in the analytic philosophy of religion there is no integral relationship between the two disciplines. Theology is not the completion or fulfillment of philosophy nor does it answer the questions posed by philosophy. Whereas theology is based on personal convictions or faith-affirmations, philosophy's role is to analyze and clarify the terminology used in theological (and also philosophical) discourse. In one sense theology does have a need for philosophy of religion, but not as a theoretical support or foundation but rather as a tool or instrument that aids in clarifying religious language.

Several criticisms can be directed towards this type of philosophy of religion. First of all this approach masks a kind of metaphysical relativism. In contrast to the analytic philosophers I maintain that there cannot be a completely impartial investigation even of such things as language. There is no neutral standpoint, and an inquiry into what terms are most meaningful is surely largely determined by a prior commitment to meaning. In our view the role of philosophy of religion is not only analysis but also evaluation.

Again, in analytic philosophy and the philosophy of religion that it has spawned faith is divorced or at least separated from knowledge. We see faith as prior to and conditioning experience; analytic philosophy of religion sees faith as something additional to what is generally experienced.

Third, analytic philosophy substitutes subjectivity for true objectivity. It claims to give an objective judgment upon the meaningfulness of language, but its criterion is woefully subjective — that which can be empirically verified. True objectivity sees the object as it is: it consists in an openness and conformity to the object. We can see the objects of experience as they really are only when the Word of God illumines our experience and masters our reason. In other words, logical analysis must be subordinated to the logic of obedience (Torrance).

Analytic philosophy and analytic philosophy of religion can also be accused of reductionism. For this type of philosophy the principal question is not "What is truth?" but "What do you mean?" It reduces philosophy to semantics, and theology to religious or moral conviction. But the root of philosophy is metaphysics, and theology is always at the same time ontology, since God is to be equated with the ultimately real.

Finally, at least one strand of analytic philosophy of religion can be viewed as a capitulation to scientism. This criticism does not apply to those in this camp who find that religious language can be meaningful but not in the same sense as language in ordinary discourse, which has an empirical reference. At the same time when our language of God is reduced to mere symbolism and when it is said that we cannot have conceptual knowledge of God but only a true awareness of Him, then scientism is again in the picture. Some analytic philosophers, such as Braithwaite, contend that theological discourse has a use but not a cognitive meaning. In the view of Willem Zuurdeeg one should refrain from using the terms "cognitive" and "knowledge" when referring to religious convictions. Ian Ramsey holds that the function of theological statements is to lead one into situations of discernment and commitment rather than to give objective knowledge of the being and purpose of God. According to van Buren the language of faith has reference not to metaphysical reality but to the Christian way of life. The emphasis of a great many Christian analytic philosophers is that religious language has an emotive rather than a cognitive meaning. But the Christian theologian must insist upon the cognitive character of theological language if he wishes to preserve the integrity of his discipline.

The bane of scientism is that it equates all knowledge with scientific knowledge: the truth is what science guarantees. Some theologians who have been attracted to analytic philosophy (such as Frederick Ferré and William Hordern) are very much aware of the pitfalls of scientism and seek always to guard against it.[6]

[6]See Frederick Ferré, *Language, Logic and God* (N. Y.: Harper, 1961); and William Hordern, *Speaking of God* (N. Y.: Macmillan, 1964).

A NEW UNDERSTANDING OF PHILOSOPHY OF RELIGION

In our view philosophy of religion should be seen as an integral part of theology. It is not a preparation or foundation for faith but rather a supplementation of faith. Its role is not to persuade the unbeliever of the credibility of the faith but rather to help the believer to understand his faith better. Like theology itself it should be seen in the context of faith seeking understanding.

Philosophy of religion, properly understood, is an investigation of philosophy from a Christian perspective. It is that part of theology which carries on a discussion with the common consciousness of truth, the world of philosophy. Its purpose is twofold: to guard against heresy and to deepen theological understanding.

The theologian as a philosopher of religion engages in conversation with secular philosophers in order to clarify his own position, but he should take care not to let this turn into a correlation with secular thought: he seeks to let the philosophers speak for themselves. His immediate purpose is to learn through conversation, not to demonstrate the inherent superiority of the Christian view over philosophical views; at the same time by listening to the philosophers he is thereby enabled to see the pitfalls in their positions. He does not seek to hide his own presuppositions; rather he brings into the picture time and again the evangelical proclamation, the story of the Gospel, which alone can awaken within the philosopher a yearning for salvation.

The theologian as a philosopher of religion seeks an encounter with philosophy but not from a neutral standpoint. Indeed, can there be a fruitful encounter if we seek to disengage ourselves from our presuppositions? Such encounter and conversation must not be confused with dialogue, however, since there is no viable common ground between the revelatory meaning of the Gospel and the ideological constructs of secular philosophy. Dialogue indicates that the participants are not only willing to listen to one another but also to come to some kind of agreement. It even presupposes a willingness to move towards a possible synthesis if this appears feasible. Theologians and philosophers have a common concern, namely, to arrive at a true picture of reality, to integrate personal convictions and the facts of experience. Yet because their criteria are so vastly different, there is no possibility for ultimately meaningful dialogue. Our conversation with philosophers may entail debate, but its primary purpose is the clarification of the issues at hand. Vigorous debate between Christian theologians and philosophers is awkward because there is no mutual criterion. In the one case reason is in the service of faith; in the other it is in the service of unbelief.

Barth has said that discussion and debate are possible between theologians and philosophers because of their common humanity. Yet it should also be pointed out that theologians, being thinking Christians, participate in the new humanity that stands in opposition to the old humanity still enslaved to sin. According to Barth reason apart from faith is limited in scope and partially blind, but he does not always consider that it is also perverse, that it is an instrument of the lust for power. Barth is correct that a discussion and debate can take place between the two groups because they belong to a common humanity. But we must hasten to add that meaningful and fruitful dialogue cannot take place except on the basis of a common faith in Jesus Christ.

It is better to speak of a Christian in philosophy rather than a Christian philosopher. The Christian indeed is a stranger and exile in the world of philosophy, since that world expressly denies a unique divine revelation in history. We would do well to bear in mind that even theistic philosophy is not yet theology. Indeed, the God of rational theism is not the God of the Christian faith. There is, of course, a biblical theism that stands in contradistinction to philosophical theism, but we are thinking here of the theism of the philosophers that has so often been a temptation to Christian theology. Forsyth points to the anthropocentric character of this kind of theism:

> Theism . . . starting from reality as an object of knowledge transfers to it our moral qualities, and regards it as not only personal but humanely personal. It discards the remote and mechanical associations of Deism, it is more ethical; but it still begins with ourselves as the subjects of knowledge, and treats God as its object; only knowing Him as conscience knows, and not in the way of either science or art.[7]

[7]P. T. Forsyth, *The Principle of Authority* (London: Independent, 1952), p. 151.

Philosophy of religion in the context of a kerygmatic theology seeks not only to analyze secular philosophical thought but also to evaluate, to make judgments. It is not so much whether the language of philosophy or theology is meaningful but whether it is faithful to the biblical revelation: this is the standard of a theological judgment.

Philosophy of religion in the sense in which we are describing it can be viewed as a theology of the secular or even as discursive theology (i.e., theology which enters into a discussion with secular thought). It is certainly not natural theology, since the criterion for judgment is derived not from the light of nature but from the biblical revelation. It is also not to be confused with philosophical theology, which represents a conceptual synthesis of philosophy and theology. Philosophical theology seeks a dialectic between faith and unbelief whereas the dialectic that we propose is one between Christ and the believer. In this dialectic man seeks to ask questions with Christ and to appropriate the answer in Christ. He judges mistaken answers and fallacious questions with the mind of Christ.

The kerygmatic philosopher of religion examines unbelief in order to understand better the unbelief in the world and the self and to see belief ever more clearly. He does not try to link the questions of culture and the Christian answer but instead to find in what way the cultural questions reflect and also obscure the questions of faith. This kind of philosophy of religion can be viewed as both a prolegomenon of and a supplementation to theology proper, that is, to dogmatics. It is that side of theology which wrestles with and explodes the unbelief of the world outside the church. In this way such a philosophy of religion serves the dogmatic enterprise and prepares the way for an evangelical proclamation that is intelligible but not respectable, understandable but not palatable to the natural man.

WHY A KNOWLEDGE OF PHILOSOPHY?

For our witness to the world to be intelligible we must understand not only the content of our faith but also the cultural or ideological situation to which we are speaking. We must also have some awareness of the cultural situation in which the faith has been delivered to us. The cultural situation signifies the philosophical context, the creative thinking of the natural man. The immediate reason why a Christian should be acquainted with philosophy is that he can understand his faith better. The ultimate reason is that he can make an intelligible and compelling witness to his faith before the world.

Let us now consider in what way a knowledge of philosophy can contribute towards a deeper understanding and appreciation of our faith. First it should be said that there can be no full understanding of belief until we see it in contrast to unbelief. The great theologians from Paul and Augustine to G. C. Berkouwer and Karl Barth have had a deep insight into secular thought, and this is why they have been able to explain what the faith does not mean as well as what it means. In this same connection a study of philosophy makes the Christian alive to the heresy that has infiltrated into the church from secular culture. Heresy is a result of the fusion of belief and unbelief. All Christians, to be sure, are slightly heretical in their thinking, but a real danger appears when philosophical values and insights become normative. Out of his wide scholarly background Paul warned his hearers to see to it that no one would lead them astray by philosophy (Col. 2:8). That a knowledge of heretical and pagan thought is necessary for the Christian is also indicated in the book of Titus: "He [a bishop] must hold firm to the sure word as taught, so that he may be able to give instruction in sound doctrine and also to confute those who contradict it" (1:9). The early church fathers were masters of Greek philosophy, and this is why they were able to save the church from Gnosticism, Arianism and Manichaeism.

It should be recognized that the study of philosophy can also contribute in a positive manner to the Christian's understanding of his faith. Because of the common grace of God, grace given to all men irrespective of their spiritual state, the Christian is able to appreciate certain insights of the philosophers, and he is even permitted to incorporate such insights into his theology. God indeed also works in the secular order, sometimes even against the will of a rebellious humanity. Common grace is not the grace that saves but rather that which restrains men from sin and thereby enables them to survive in the world.

Some secular insights and values can be accepted by the Christian, but they must always be subordinated to the Word of God. Secular categories need to be transformed or "baptized" if they are to serve the Christian witness. Just as God entered into secular history in Jesus Christ and made use of human language, so the Christian can also use the categories and thought-forms of secular culture. It is well to note that both Calvin and Luther occasionally quoted from Plato and Aristotle, but they constantly reinterpreted these insights from a biblical perspective. The New Testament itself often transformed secular categories. For example, *kairos* for Aristotle signified the good in the category of time; in the New Testament it signifies the fulfillment of time itself. For the Greeks *metanoia* meant to change one's mind; its meaning in the New Testament is a complete change of life.

The reader might agree that a knowledge of modern philosophy is helpful, since we are addressing our message to present-day culture. But he might ask why a study of ancient philosophy is so important. It is well to recognize that contemporary philosophy has its roots in ancient philosophy. Also we should seek to know not only the tradition of faith but also the tradition of unbelief. Whitehead has made the cogent remark that the history of philosophy is a series of footnotes to Plato. The history of theology is a history of the conflict between Greek philosophic categories and Hebraic biblical categories.

The Christian will be on guard against philosophy, but he will have a respect and appreciation for the genius and profundity of the philosophers. He will see the glory of the creation in philosophy, but he will also discern therein the fall of man. He will give serious attention to the words of Christ that the children of darkness are often wiser than the children of light (Lk. 16:8). But he will also have a compassion and concern for the philosophers because in their quest for truth they fail to find it.

Theology has need of philosophy, but not as a foundation nor as a superstructure. Theology also should not regard philosophy as a partner in marriage nor even as a handmaid (if this connotes any kind of independent role). But theology does have need of philosophy as a valuable instrument or means by which it can refine and deepen its grasp of the meaning of faith. Theology may also seek out philosophy as an adversary, since this gives it the opportunity to wrestle with unbelief. And faith always emerges stronger when it boldly meets the challenge of unbelief. Again philosophy is a reminder to the Christian of the darkness that is behind us and also of the darkness that is yet to be overcome.

Barth has given the example of the children of Israel leaving Egypt with many ornaments and implements made in that country. It was permissible for the Israelites to use these tools and ornaments, but they sinned when they sought to make out of them a golden calf. So it is with Christian theology. It may use the terminology and insights of philosophy, but it forsakes its calling when it elevates these things into objects of veneration.

The Christian may and sometimes must use philosophical categories and concepts. But he should take care not to construct a philosophy of life out of these things. He must not even try to create a philosophy of religion that can serve as the substructure or basis of theology. He must humbly confess that the comprehensive perspective of reality belongs to God alone, and that philosophical ideas can at the most be an aid in witnessing to what God has done for man in Jesus Christ.

In my view the Christian should not even try to construct a Christian philosophy which would seek to discover the Christian significance of the traditional philosophical questions. There is a place for trying to understand the origins of the world and the nature of ultimate reality in the light of the biblical revelation, but this is the task of theology, not philosophy. To be sure, this is no longer biblical theology in the narrow sense of the word, but neither is it philosophical theology nor even apologetic theology except in a very special sense. It is theology examining the created world and philosophical interpretations of this world through the eyes of biblical faith: we can therefore speak in this context of a theology of the world or a theology of culture. It is also permissible to refer to this particular enterprise as a kerygmatic or biblical "philosophy of religion," so long as it is conceived as a branch of theology proper. What we must be on guard against is confusing this particular brand of theology with a spiritually enlightened philosophy that works in conjunction with theology but which is to all intents and purposes an independent discipline.

The philosopher Martin Heidegger naturally could not know all the ramifications of the theological task, but he did perceive the absurdity of a theology that poses as another kind of philosophy; he also recognized the incongruity of a "Christian philosophy."

> A "Christian philosophy" is a round square and a misunderstanding. There is, to be sure, a thinking and questioning elaboration of the world of Christian experience, that is, of faith. That is theology. Only the epochs that no longer fully believe in the true greatness of the task of theology arrive at the disastrous notion that philosophy can help to provide a refurbished theology, if not a substitute for theology, which will satisfy the needs and tastes of the time. For the original Christian faith philosophy is foolishness.[8]

We would also do well to take seriously this cogent observation of Dietrich Bonhoeffer:

> Philosophy remains profane science; there is *no* Christian philosophy. . . . Philosophy essentially remains in reflection; man knows himself and God only in reflection. Theology at least knows of an act of God, which tears man out of this reflection in an *actus directus* toward God. Here man knows himself and God not by looking into himself, but by looking into the Word of God, which tells him that he is a sinner and justified, which he never could understand before.[9]

In conclusion, philosophy of religion rightly understood should be seen as one side of theology. It should be viewed in the context of faith seeking understanding. Its rightful role is in the service of the evangelical proclamation. Its ultimate goal, as is the goal of theology itself, is the conversion of man to God. Philosophy of religion will recognize, however, that by itself it cannot accomplish this goal. Rather the conversion of man is dependent upon the preaching and hearing of the message of the cross of Jesus Christ.

APPENDIX TO CHAPTER III

Some of those who champion a "Christian philosophy" go on to advocate a "Christian sociology" and "Christian psychology," a "Christian biology," and even more a "Christian

---

[8] Martin Heidegger, *An Introduction to Metaphysics*, trans. Ralph Manheim (Garden City, N. Y.: Doubleday, 1961), p. 6.

[9] Dietrich Bonhoeffer, *No Rusty Swords*, trans. Edwin H. Robertson and John Bowden (N. Y.: Harper, 1965), p. 372.

politics" and "Christian economics." But this is to deny the relative autonomy of the various sciences and disciplines. Such a position tends to support those who are seeking to create an ostensibly Christian social order, whether this be a "Christian democracy" or a theocracy.

Theology is a special science, but it is also the queen of the sciences and therefore supplies the ontological ground as well as the spiritual motivation for all the other sciences. It is the trunk of the tree of knowledge; the other disciplines are the branches. Since these other sciences concern the facts of the world rather than the truth of the world (in the metaphysical sense), they have a certain autonomy. Theology gives purpose and direction to the various sciences, but it cannot supply answers to the specific questions raised by these sciences. It is not proper to speak of a Christian physics, but belief in a divine creation is likely to affect our scientific research and shape our understanding of the physical world. One can certainly conceive of a theologically informed sociology but hardly of a Christian sociology. In the realm of politics it is biblically more sound to entertain the notion of a Christian in politics or a Christian approach to politics than a Christian politics. It is perhaps permissible to conceive of a politics with Christian foundations but not of a Christian political theory. The Christian doctrine of man can inform research in the area of psychology, but no psychology insofar as it is empirically oriented can claim to be specifically Christian.

Christianity cannot offer a political or social program, although it can furnish the values that can guide such a program. The church can give direction to man in the political realm, but it must beware of issuing political directives. It must not yield to the temptation of promoting a Christian political party or a Christian political platform. Christianity then becomes another ideology rather than a divine revelation that stands over against all political ideologies and philosophies. The kingdom of God must never be confused with the kingdoms of this world, even though it provides a spiritual criterion whereby men and nations can be guided towards a higher degree of justice. This is not to deny that in certain extreme cases the church might be compelled to speak out against a particular party or person in politics and thereby give support to the opposing side: the church, for example, cannot remain silent when the freedom to witness to the Word is at stake.

It should be recognized that economics, politics and also psychology and sociology are much more open to the impact of the Christian revelation than are physics and chemistry, which are concerned primarily with the impersonal object-world rather than the area of human relations. Nonetheless Christianity is basically centered in the vertical dimension, the God-man relation, even though it is to be lived out in the horizontal dimension, man's relationships with his fellowman. The Christian understanding of man and the world will weigh heavily in the political and social areas of man's existence, but it must never be confused with a particular political or economic policy, for such a policy is informed by the experience of men in a given cultural situation as well as by religious and ethical values. When a political or economic policy becomes an ideology, however, then it enters into conflict with the Christian faith. This is to say that there can be non-Christian or even anti-Christian forms of politics and economics as well as of psychology and sociology. Even the natural sciences are not exempt from metaphysical or ideological bias.

This brings us to the point that theology will always exist in tension with the cultural sciences and disciplines. It will never oppose the genuinely empirical disciplines as such, but it does contradict philosophical world perspectives that sometimes infiltrate these disciplines. It acknowledges the rightful place of biology, but it opposes biological determinism; it sees the proper role of sociology but stands against all forms of social determinism, including dialectical materialism; it lends support to the scientific investigation of human behavior, but it contravenes behaviorism.

Christianity cannot assure its children of a systematic overview of all of reality, but it does point them to Jesus Christ, the living Word of God, who holds the keys to wisdom as well as to salvation. The Christian revelation stands in judgment over all philosophies and sciences, but it does not propose in their place a specifically Christian philosophical system or science. Rather it causes men of wisdom and culture to question the sovereignty of reason and creates within them a profound humility concerning the mystery of life and the universe. A reverent agnosticism should characterize the Christian scholar rather than the fanatical delusion that he has

A New Role for Philosophy of Religion

access to all the truth in every area of life. The Christian is certain of the One in whom he believes and of the biblical testimony concerning the creation of the world and man's salvation, but he does not attempt as a "Christian philosopher" to create a synthesis of all human knowledge, which rightfully belongs only to God. He recognizes that the knowledge of God is the foundation of all other knowledge, but he does not claim to have all this knowledge or even the key to this knowledge. The biblical revelation gives men a spiritual and metaphysical vision, but it does not delineate a specific metaphysics whereby the antinomies and mysteries of existence are resolved in a rational system. By turning to Holy Scripture man can gain the knowledge of the remission of sins and the plan of salvation, but he cannot attain a "completely unified knowledge" (Herbert Spencer), which is the object of the philosophical quest.

FOUR:

THE GROUND OF CERTAINTY

THE NATURE OF CERTAINTY

The term "certainty" signifies a firm or positive belief in something. It is closely related to "assurance," which suggests confidence but not necessarily positiveness. The term "security" implies protection or guarantee from doubt, the possession of the truth. It can be said that there is certainty and assurance in the Christian faith but not security. Calvin indicated the element of certainty in faith when he defined it as "a firm and certain knowledge" of God's benevolence towards us. Lutheranism and Methodism have stressed assurance over certainty.

The theological understanding of certainty differs considerably from that of philosophy. What philosophers generally envision is a rational or demonstrable certainty. Theology speaks of the certainty of faith, the certainty of the heart which is more existential than rational. In Hebrews 11:1 (NEB) we read: "Faith gives substance to our hopes, and makes us certain of realities we do not see."

Indeed, there cannot be any logical nor even experiential necessity for the affirmations of faith. According to Kierkegaard faith consists in subjective certitude and objective uncertainty. Luther in a sermon on the Fourth Gospel points to the nature of the certainty of faith: "A Christian is not guided by what he sees or feels; he follows what he does not see or feel. He remains with the testimony of Christ; he listens to Christ's words and follows Him into the darkness."[1]

Faith in the perspective of a biblical theology consists more in being known than in knowing (cf. Gal. 4:9). It signifies an acquaintance with Christ rather than a comprehension of Him. Faith is heartfelt trust and confidence in the mercy of Christ rather than a rational knowledge of His divine nature.

[1]Martin Luther, *Sermons on the Gospel of St. John,* ed. J. Pelikan, in *Luther's Works* (St. Louis: Concordia, 1957), Vol. XXII, p. 306.

CERTAINTY IN PHILOSOPHY

Reason, which might be defined as any cognitive faculty within man, is the philosophical ground of certainty. The natural man places his dependence on sight and understanding, not on the authority of a divine revelation. He seeks to be guided by his own intelligence and often by his senses as well rather than by an invisible and holy God.

It should be recognized that reason is understood in various ways in philosophical circles. In rationalistic philosophy reason is practically equated with the intellect. For the consistent rationalist reality and conceptual truth are synonymous. No basic distinction is made between ontological and propositional truth. The ground of certainty in rationalism is that which is logically or rationally compelling. Sometimes it is said that knowledge is dependable if it is informed by ideas that are "clear" as a whole and "distinct" in details (Descartes).[2] In this general type of philosophy rational coherence is the final norm for truth. To express it in Hegelian terms, the real is the rational, and the truth signifies the whole.

In intuitionism and mysticism immediate perception or intuition rather than intellectual clarity is regarded as the ground of certainty. In some philosophies this is conceived as a flash of insight based on reflection and in others as ecstatic or mystical experience. The point is that the source of truth lies within the depths of one's being instead of in external authority. Intuition goes under many different names: in Plato it is sometimes called memory; in Kant it is viewed as moral insight; Royce speaks of inward appreciation; Tillich uses the term "mystical apriori"; Whitehead's word for it is "prehension." In this type of philosophy the ground of certainty is that which is immediately or experientially verifiable.

The more empirical and naturalistic brand of philosophy bases its case on observation. Sensation rather than logic is made the court of appeal. Not deduction nor eduction but induction is the epistemological method in empirical philosophy. Here we can mention Hume, Locke, Dewey, Wieman and also the analytic philosophers of our day. Empiricism has often been associated with naturalism and modern realism.

---

[2]Descartes was not a consistent rationalist, since he affirmed the existence of a material world. The dualism of his Christian heritage prevented him from arriving at an idealistic monism as in Spinoza. Like many rationalists he sought to combine rational insight and logical demonstration.

The ground of certainty is the demonstrable as over against the purely logical or the mystical. An appeal is made to empirical evidence for the validation of philosophical and religious truth.[3]

The view of life based upon reason (in the broad sense) naturally varies depending upon the philosophy in question. The boldest claim that has been made by those who consult only their own reason is an absolute perspective, a comprehensive synoptic world view. Hegel even went so far as to claim possession of the mind of God. The minimal claim made on the basis of the criterion of reason is a valid or true perspective, a meaningful view of reality.

CERTAINTY IN THEOLOGY

For Christian faith and theology divine revelation, not human reason, is the basis for certainty. It is not what man can conceive or discover or accomplish but rather what God has done for man in Jesus Christ that gives the Christian his assurance. It is not the idea of God in the soul or His design in nature but the encounter with God in His Word that induces belief in Him. The Christian can become certain of the existence of the world because his eyes have been opened to the existence of God, the creator of the world.

Revelation has both an objective and a subjective pole. The former signifies the disclosure of meaning in the historical events mirrored in the Bible and also in the biblical testimony itself. The subjective pole refers to the mystical or inward illumination of the Holy Spirit. It is through the Spirit of God that we are led into the experience of faith, that we are empowered to respond to what God has done for us in Christ.

Revelation is a divine-human encounter, an encounter that took place once for all between God and Jesus and also one that takes place ever again between Jesus Christ and the believer. When revelation happens, the Christ-event of the past and the encounter of faith in the present are brought together in an indissoluble unity. To use the terminology of Kierkegaard, revelation signifies the conjunction of the moment of the incarnation and the moment of decision.

[3] The indebtedness of John W. Montgomery to philosophical empiricism can be seen in his attempt to base the truth of Scripture almost wholly upon "objective facticity" or historical evidence. See his *Where Is History Going?* (Grand Rapids: Zondervan, 1969).

The content of what is revealed is both a person and a message. Revelation is personal as well as rational, existential as well as propositional. The Reformers equated the content or truth of revelation with the Law and the Gospel. This does not mean, however, that this truth is immediately accessible to man in the Bible, for it must be disclosed by the Spirit. But the Spirit does not disclose a new truth but the revelatory meaning of the text of Scripture.

Against some of the mystics I contend that the Word of God does not entirely transcend our rational faculties. It is not sheer mystery but one that is illumined by meaning. God really does make known to us His Word, His will and purpose for our lives, but our grasp of His revelation is only adequate for salvation, not for a comprehensive understanding.

What we experience in revelation is not God in His primary objectivity but God in His secondary objectivity, i.e., in His self-manifestation in Christ. Moreover, we encounter not Christ in the majesty of His glory but the hidden Christ — hidden in the sign, veil and work of His redemptive acts in history. Faith is therefore indirect cognition; only the beatific vision beyond death can be spoken of as direct cognition.

In revelation we are confronted with the mystery of the plan of salvation, the message of Christ and His redemption. This truth can partially be known by faith, but it must be given to us ever again. Through the power of the Spirit our eyes are opened to a divine message, but one that is partly concealed in the form of human proclamation. Doctrine is the clarification of the message of the cross; it is not the reconciling of opposing elements in this message. We are called to preach doctrine in addition to a gospel, since doctrine safeguards and illumines the truth of revelation.

LOCI OF AUTHORITY

Divine revelation should be seen as the basis of authority as well as the ground of certainty. It provides the criterion of faith as well as the assurance of faith.

As has been said, revelation is essentially an encounter between the living Christ and the believer. It is not the past history of Jesus Christ but the presence of Jesus Christ as history (Pelikan). The moment of encounter occurs in connection with the reading of the Bible, the hearing of the sermon and the receiving of the sacrament. These are the outward means and signs of revelation.

When we speak of revelation as an authority, we have in mind not only the divine disclosure in past history but also the eternal ground — the mind of God, as well as the existential medium — the experience of faith. The truth of faith is mediated by experience, but its foundation is God Himself and also His self-manifestation, i.e., the Word of God.

The experience of faith should be seen as a secondary criterion instead of the absolute criterion of faith. The experience of Christ brings us inward certainty, but the basis of our certainty lies outside ourselves. Forsyth has put this very profoundly: "The verification in experience cannot be the ground of our certainty since it can only be the sequel of it. Experience is the fruit of faith, or its medium, more than its ground."[4]

Faith has a twofold objectivity — history and eternity. Its position is certain because it points beyond itself to the living God and His infallible Word. In the judgment of Luther: "This is the reason why our theology is certain; because it snatches us away from ourselves and places us outside of ourselves, lest we rest upon men, conscience, feelings, character, our own work...."[5]

Yet it is also important to recognize that the Word of God must make contact with man in personal faith and commitment if it is to be effectual for his salvation. This subjective locus of revelation is the experience of faith or the experience of the Spirit. Luther, who emphasized the objective basis of revelation, could nevertheless affirm: "I have learned not only through the Scripture but also . . . I *know* through experience that these doctrines are true."[6]

One may be acquainted with the history of the Bible but still be in the dark concerning the meaning of the cross for our salvation. The historical norm by itself is not sufficient to persuade men of the truth of the Gospel. One may even have a knowledge of the historical Jesus, but this does not guarantee a recognition of Jesus as the Christ. Peter, after he had made his confession of faith, was told by his Lord: "Flesh and blood has not revealed this to you, but my Father who is

---

[4]P. T. Forsyth, *The Principle of Authority*, 2nd ed. (London: Independent, 1952), p. 331.

[5]*Luther's Works*, Vol. XXVI (St. Louis: Concordia, 1963), p. 387.

[6]Martin Luther, *Table Talk*, Vol. LIV in *Luther's Works*, ed. and trans. Theodore G. Tappert (Philadelphia: Fortress, 1967), p. 371.

in heaven" (Mt. 16:17). To know Jesus after the flesh did not of itself bring about a saving conviction in His Messiahship. At the same time one would have to be confronted in some way with the historical facts concerning the life and death of Jesus before one could recognize Him as Lord and Savior. The facts do not bring faith, but they are the occasion by which faith is induced. Yet it is not so much the biblical facts by themselves as the gospel about the facts that can be considered the means of grace, the vehicle of divine revelation.

The Pharisees were noted for their fidelity to the Scriptures. But our Lord reproved them: "You search the scriptures, because you think that in them you have eternal life; and it is they that bear witness to me; yet you refuse to come to me that you may have life" (Jn. 5:39, 40). The Pharisees appealed to the words of Scripture, but they refused to heed the Word within the words. Although they knew the sacred writings, they did not attend to the voice of Him who spoke through these writings. They rested their case on the letter rather than the spirit of the law. They approached Scripture without faith in its Lord and therefore failed to grasp the truth that it proclaims.

Although revelation is anchored in the history and testimony of Scripture, it does not take place in our lives apart from personal decision and faith. The foundation of revelation is objective, but its realization is subjective. As the converts said to the Samaritan woman: " 'It is no longer because of your words that we believe, for we have heard for ourselves, and we know that this is indeed the Savior of the world' " (Jn. 4:42). One is finally convinced of the reality and truth of the divine revelation only when he personally experiences its saving effects in his heart. The experience of faith must always be tested by the objective criterion, the message of the Bible, but the latter must also be verified by the Spirit illumining us from within. The testimony of God is to be found in the hearts of believers as well as in a book (I Jn. 5:10). Moreover, we are able to make the decision of faith only after having made contact with the community of faith, that is, the church, and this brings us to still another locus of authority.

It can be said that there are several loci of authority for the Christian. These are illustrated in I John 5:7-10 where the apostle refers to the agreement of the Spirit, the water and the blood and also to the threefold testimony of tradition, historical revelation and the inner light. Commentators have differed on the precise meanings of these various norms, but in general it can be stated that the apostle seeks to hold together the divine inspiration of the prophetic and apostolic utterances, the testimony of the cross of Christ (the blood), the sacraments (water and blood), and the inner testimony of the Spirit.

Our position is that in addition to the self-revelation of God in Christ, which functions as an absolute norm, there are relative or dependent norms, and these include the Bible, the proclamation of the church, and the light of faith implanted in man by the Spirit. All of these when taken only by themselves, divorced from their spiritual and theological context, have to be considered fallible and deficient, but together they render a reliable and compelling witness. They both conceal and reveal the transcendent, absolute norm — the living Word of God, Jesus Christ. He alone is the truth of revelation in the full sense of this word, but we have this truth in the external signs of His redemption in history (the Bible, the cross of Christ, the sacraments) and in the internal testimony of a convicted conscience. When the living or revealed Word, Jesus Christ, unites Himself with the written word, the proclaimed word or the inner word, then these relative norms begin to assume a definitive and absolute character. Surely the visible word (the sacraments) is also a means by which the truth of the Gospel is disclosed to the believer. While Scripture, being the conceptual source of revelation, has a certain priority over the other dependent norms, none of these communicates the knowledge of salvation apart from the action of the living Christ who illumines and integrates these various norms by His Spirit.

The Bible is a trustworthy and unfailing guide because the light of God's countenance shines upon it and because the Spirit grants illumination to the community of faith. This means that the indefeasible criterion is not simply the Word but the Word and the Spirit. Our authority lies in the action of God as He speaks to us through the Scriptures and also through the proclamation of the church illumining and empowering us for service in the world.[7]

[7]Note that the Reformers also called the proclamation of the Gospel the Word of God. This view is reflected in Chapter I of the Second Helvetic Confession, which states that the preaching of the Word is "the very Word of God."

THE CIRCULAR ARGUMENT

The way to meet the questions of the unbeliever is by directing him to faith's own criterion, the Gospel of Christ contained in the Scripture and made known by the Spirit. If the unbeliever asks us, "How do you know that there is a God?", our answer might very well be, "Because Jesus Christ rose from the dead." If he asks how we know this, then we should insist that it actually happened, having been attested by historical witnesses whose testimony is found in the Scriptures. And if he wonders how we can be certain that the Scriptural witness is true, we should point to the illumination of the Holy Spirit. Finally, if he wishes to know on what grounds we can be sure that this is the Holy Spirit speaking to us (and not some other voice), then we need only to reply, "Because He tells us that Jesus Christ rose from the dead." This, of course, is a circular argument, the *circulus veritatis Dei*.[8] But only when the outsider actually enters the theological circle can he begin to understand the force and validity of this kind of reasoning.

This argument tells us that faith can only stand on its own foundation. Reason must finally abdicate; the natural man must finally make the leap of faith. Every philosophy, of course, presupposes some faith-principle, some criterion which is accepted without criticism. This is a truth recognized even by many philosophers. Reason cannot support itself, and only by surrendering its autonomy can it be free for creative labor.

The circular argument should be seen as not really an argument but rather a testimony of faith. It is simply faith making its own confession before the world. And yet it is through such a confession that outsiders are won over to the Gospel of Jesus Christ (cf. Rom. 10:17; I Cor. 1:21).

We heartily concur with the British evangelical, Colin Brown:

> Christianity must be capable of vindicating itself by itself. Our proof of the existence of God must derive from our

---

[8]It is interesting to note that theologians as diverse as Barth and Tillich hold to the circular character of systematic theology. See Karl Barth, *Church Dogmatics*, trans. T. H. Parker, *et al.* (Edinburgh: Clark, 1957), II, 1, p. 253; and Paul Tillich, *Systematic Theology* (Chicago: University of Chicago, 1951), Vol. I, p. 135. Tillich, unlike Barth, does not remain within this circle when addressing the world outside the church.

experience of God *through the whole gospel* and not be made dependent upon hypothetical abstract arguments borrowed from outside.[9]

While the rationalist seeks to base his argument on a necessary and sufficient reason, the Christian appeals only to a reason that is compelling to faith. In God's sight the cross and resurrection may be necessary, but this is not evident to the natural man. There are elements of the sacrifice of Christ and the plan of salvation that remain mysterious even to the Christian, and he must simply bow in reverence before these mysteries.

The Christian does not pretend to know all the answers to life's questions, but he does claim to know some of the answers to the final questions, those that determine the direction of one's eternal destiny. Yet he makes this claim not on the basis of his own ingenuity or intelligence but on the basis of God's revelation in the Scriptures. Moreover, he does not boast that he "possesses" these answers, for they reside in the mind of Christ which is made available to him time and again by the Spirit. He points his hearers not to his own theological system but to God's Word, which alone "has" the answers. He is also quick to confess that the answers that the Bible provides are spiritually, not naturally discerned (I Cor. 2:14).

Christianity is not so much a quest as a witness. We do not grope aimlessly in the darkness seeking for answers (which regrettably is the theme of some of the folk hymns in the new liturgy), but we unashamedly proclaim the One who is the Answer, Jesus Christ. The church must not try to accommodate its Gospel to the contemporary mind or even to its youth (for this is the surest way to lose them); rather it should boldly confront them with the challenge of the Gospel.

It has been the mistake of apologetic theology through the ages to appeal not to the norm of the Gospel but to a criterion held in common with unbelief. What apologists have often failed to see is that the Gospel cannot be taught; it must be caught through the contagion of the Holy Spirit. We can make the Gospel intelligible, but only the Spirit can make it knowable. Both faith and the condition for faith are given by the Spirit of God as He acts in the preaching of the Gospel message. Forsyth's words are very relevant:

[9] Colin Brown, *Philosophy and the Christian Faith* (Chicago: Inter-Varsity, 1969). Brown's position approaches our own at many points.

> The Gospel is not something which is there for our assent in the degree in which we can verify it by our previous experience either in the way of need or of rationality. Our very response to it is created in us before it is confessed by us. It creates assent rather than accepts it.[10]

The ground of certainty is either a spurious faith or authentic faith. It is either a leap in the dark or an awakening to the light. The basis of authority in the last analysis must be either human imagination or the mind of Christ. Those who spurn the offer of God in His Gospel are unable to resist the temptation to sell their souls to the Adversary of God in order to find meaning in their lives. Those who will not bow before the true God will end in manufacturing their own gods, which are in fact idols.

St. Paul divided the human race into the living and the dead (Eph. 2:1-5). Those who are dead in sin cannot be persuaded or convinced by rational argument. What the unbeliever needs is not rational persuasion but supernatural regeneration. Indeed, entrance into the kingdom of God is contingent upon the new birth, which the Holy Spirit alone can give.

---

[10] Forsyth, *The Principle of Authority*, p. 333.

FIVE:

THEOLOGY AND PHILOSOPHY

CONFLICTING LIFE-ORIENTATIONS

The complex and often strained relationship between theology and philosophy cannot be fully understood without taking into consideration the quite severe criticisms that theologians and philosophers have leveled at each other through the ages. It can be shown that even many of those thinkers who have been most friendly to the other side have nevertheless drawn sharp distinctions between the two disciplines.

In the history of theology repeated warnings have been given by theologians against any synthesis with secular philosophy. St. Paul anticipated the general theological antipathy towards philosophy in his remark: "See to it that no one leads you astray by philosophy" (Col. 2:8). In the early church period not only apologists like Tertullian but even those who were moderate in their approach towards philosophy like Clement of Alexandria and Tatian contended for the absolute validity and uniqueness of the Christian revelation. Medieval scholastic theology, which reached its apex in the system of Thomas Aquinas, although making a place for philosophy nevertheless allotted to theology the role of explicating the truths that effect man's salvation.

The lines between theology and philosophy were even more sharply drawn by the Protestant Reformers, Luther and Calvin. For Luther God is not an object of philosophical speculation: "Those who indulge in their own ideas and speculate about God and His will aside from Christ lose God altogether."[1] Partly in opposition to the Greek philosophical tradition Calvin declared: "I call that knowledge, not what is innate in man, nor what is by diligence acquired, but that which is delivered to us by the Law and the

---

[1] *Luther's Works*, ed. J. Pelikan (St. Louis: Concordia, 1955), Vol. XII, p. 51.

Prophets."[2] Again he complained that philosophers "set up Reason as the sole directress of man; they think that she is exclusively to be attended to; in short, to her alone they assign the government of the conduct."[3] But Christian faith "commands her to give place and submit to the Holy Spirit; so that now the man himself lives not, but carries about Christ living and reigning in him." Though philosophers can reason well up to a point, they are ignorant of the corruption of the soul, and therefore everything they say "concerning religion is not only frigid, but for the most part insipid"; it is "in his word alone that there shines forth the truth which may lead us to . . . serve God aright."[4]

In the modern period, despite various attempts to convert the Christian faith into a philosophy, voices have continued to be raised against any amalgamation or compromise with secular philosophical thought. Pascal contended that the God of Abraham, Isaac and Jacob is not the God of the philosophers. In Kierkegaard's view Christianity is not a philosophical truth but a living faith that demands passion rather than contemplation. "The highest," he said, "is not to think the highest but to act upon it." Abraham Kuyper, noted Dutch evangelical and founder of the Free University of Amsterdam, tells us that in his conversion to Christ "the warmth of the gospel began to drive out the freezing chill of philosophy. I came to the conviction that the foolishness of the cross was the highest and only wisdom."[5] Although Kuyper saw the place for a "Christian philosophy," he held that there can only be a revival of the confessional standards in theology when "it escapes from the arms of philosophy, and . . . is bent upon the recovery of its independence."[6] It was Karl Heim's contention that there are only two types of philosophy — pantheism and idolatry. Man either deifies the infinite

[2] John Calvin, *Commentaries on the Book of the Prophet Jeremiah*, 44:1, trans. John Owen (Edinburgh: Calvin Translation Society, 1854; Grand Rapids: Eerdmans reprint, n.d.), Vol. IV, p. 526.

[3] John Calvin, *Institutes of the Christian Religion*, trans. John Allen (Grand Rapids: Eerdmans, 1949), 8th ed., Bk. III, Ch. VII, Sec. I, p. 752.

[4] John Calvin, *Commentary on Psalms*, 29:9, trans. James Anderson (Edinburgh: Calvin Translation Society, 1845; Grand Rapids: Eerdmans reprint, 1963), Vol. I, p. 482.

[5] Quoted in Ernest Gordon, *A Book of Protestant Saints* (Alberta, Canada: Prairie Bible Institute, 1968), p. 36.

[6] Abraham Kuyper, *Principles of Sacred Theology*, trans. J. Hendrik De Vries (Grand Rapids: Eerdmans, 1954), p. 320.

whole of things or he gives absolute value to the forms of thought and intuition.[7] According to Emil Brunner the natural man generally begins either with the subject (as in idealism) or with the object (as in naturalism), but neither way leads to God. The other possibility is that he will posit an identity between subject and object, but this way ends in pantheism.[8]

This is not to deny that some theologians have sought to mediate between theology and philosophy. Tillich perhaps best represents this line of thinking in our time. According to him the philosophers point to the same God as that of Abraham, Isaac and Jacob, but they seek to approach this God in different ways. Whereas most philosophy appeals to the authority of autonomous reason and much traditional theology appeals to the external heteronomous authority of church and/or Bible, so Tillich points beyond both of these to the eternal ground of being. The question can be raised, however, whether Tillich's God is not in fact the primal unity of mysticism rather than the living God of the Bible. Kenneth Hamilton maintains that Tillich's theology presents us not with the Gospel but only with "the System."[9]

It should be recognized that philosophers also have been quick to deny any kind of equation between their position and that of the Christian faith. Philosophy in its history is characterized by a noticeable anti-theological orientation. It has always stood against mythology, popular religion and ecclesiastical authoritarianism. It has also displayed a marked hostility towards Christian theology, although not necessarily towards religion. The general stance of philosophy is indicated by Wittgenstein in his dogmatic assertion: "God does not reveal himself in the world."[10]

The antipathy of philosophy towards Christianity can especially be seen in the modern atheists. Feuerbach stated: "Who then is our Saviour and Redeemer? God or Love? Love: for God as God has not saved us, but Love, which transcends the

[7]Karl Heim, *God Transcendent* (London: Nisbet, 1935), p. 231.

[8]Emil Brunner, *God and Man*, trans. David Cairns (London: SCM, 1936), p. 41.

[9]Kenneth Hamilton, *The System and the Gospel* (Grand Rapids: Eerdmans, 1967).

[10]Ludwig Wittgenstein, *Tractatus Logico-Philosophicus*, trans. D. F. Pears and B. F. McGuinness (London: Routledge and Kegan Paul, 1961), p. 149.

difference between the divine and human personality."[11] Here Feuerbach is more consistent than the new theology which seeks to retain God but equates God with Love. Nietzsche boldly affirmed the death of God and voiced a desire for the "Superman" to live. In almost violent reaction against his Christian background he declared: "But we do not at all want to enter the kingdom of heaven: we have become men, — *so we want the kingdom of earth.*"[12] And in the words of Karl Marx:

> Philosophy makes no secret of it. The confession of Prometheus: "In one word, I hate all the gods," is its very own confession, its own sentence against all heavenly and earthly gods who refuse to recognize human self-consciousness as the supreme divinity — by the side of which none other shall be held.[13]

Even philosophers who are more kindly disposed towards religion nevertheless are quick to differentiate their position from Christianity. Kant upheld a "reflective faith" or "moral faith," which he contrasted with the "dogmatic faith" characteristic of Christianity. Karl Jaspers speaks of the need for a liberal faith, but he is clear that this is not the faith which biblical theology upholds. In his words: "The liberal faith needs no external props, not even a redemptive history conceived as an objective absolute event, the prerequisite of all faith."[14] And again: "Revelation has no place in our ascertainment of the modes of encompassing; in this framework of ours it is neither thinkable nor imaginable for Transcendence to find a specific incarnation as a divine reality, distinct from any other, in the world of time and space."[15] For Jaspers and existentialist philosophy in general "man is everything."

One of the main points of divergence between philosophy

[11] Ludwig Feuerbach, *The Essence of Christianity*, trans. George Eliot (N. Y.: Harper, 1957), p. 53.

[12] Friedrich Nietzsche, *Thus Spake Zarathustra*, in *The Philosophy of Nietzsche* (N. Y.: Modern Library, 1927), IV, 78, 2, p. 355.

[13] In Preface of his doctoral dissertation submitted to the University of Berlin. Quoted in Robert C. Tucker, *Philosophy and Myth in Karl Marx* (Cambridge, England: Cambridge University, 1961), p. 74.

[14] Karl Jaspers, "Myth and Religion" in Hans-Werner Bartsch, *Kerygma and Myth*, trans. Reginald Fuller (London: S.P.C.K., 1962), Vol. II, p. 164.

[15] Karl Jaspers, *Philosophical Faith and Revelation*, trans. E. G. Ashton (N. Y.: Harper, 1962), p. 100.

and theology is in the former's emphasis on the rational over the revelational and historical. Fichte maintained, "It is the metaphysical element alone and not the historical that saves us." According to Hegel: "What is rational is real; what is real is rational." Truth is what reason necessarily conceives and not what God reveals in particular events in history. As Lessing phrased it: "Accidental truths of history can never become the proof of necessary truths of reason."[16]

Some philosophers, to be sure, have sought to include Christian insights within their overall perspective. But a close examination of their thought reveals that the unique claims of the Christian faith have been compromised; the message of the Bible has been diluted beyond recognition. Kant was especially reluctant to abandon his Christian heritage, and yet he could only affirm what biblical theologians would describe as an emasculated Christianity. His criterion was not the Christ-event but the rational ideal of perfection. "Even the Holy One of the Gospels," he declared, "must first be compared with our ideal of moral perfection before we can recognize Him as such."[17] Kant's pagan orientation is especially noticeable in this statement: "It is not essential, and hence not necessary, for every one to know what God does or has done for his salvation; but it is essential to know *what man himself must do* in order to become worthy of this assistance."[18] Fichte, who was hailed by Rudolf Otto as a modern mystic, nevertheless was very clear that this mysticism rendered a historical revelation superfluous: "It was necessary not merely to change the external mediator between God and man but to require no external mediator at all, since the bond of unity with the divine is to be found within oneself."[19] Whitehead, who appeared to be open to the values of Christianity and who is much revered by the school of process theology, has by no means constructed a system that can be considered "Christian." He makes very clear that his criterion is reason and not

[16] Gotthold Ephraim Lessing, "On the Proof of the Spirit and of Power" in Henry Chadwick, ed., *Lessing's Theological Writings* (London: Black, 1956), p. 53.
[17] Immanuel Kant, *Metaphysical Foundation of Morals*, in Carl J. Friedrich, ed., *The Philosophy of Kant* (N. Y.: Modern Library, 1949), p. 156.
[18] Immanuel Kant, *Religion Within the Limits of Reason Alone*, trans. Theodore Greene and Hoyt Hudson (N. Y.: Harper, 1960), p. 47.
[19] Johann G. Fichte, *Reden an die deutsche Nation*, in *Sämmtliche Werke*, Dritte Abteilung (Berlin: von Veit, 1846), p. 349.

revelation: "Ultimately nothing rests on authority; the final court of appeal is intrinsic reasonableness."[20]

PHILOSOPHY AND THEOLOGY DEFINED

The root meaning of philosophy is love of wisdom. It has also come to mean the search for wisdom and particularly the quest for a comprehensive understanding of reality. According to Brightman, "philosophy is an attempt to discover the whole truth."[21] Aristotle put it this way: "The wise man must know not only what follows from the first principles but also the first principles themselves in order to possess true knowledge."[22]

I would define philosophy as an attempt to understand man's ultimate questions on the basis of reason. Reason here signifies any cognitive faculty within man whether this be feeling, intellect or imagination. Philosophy might also be defined as man's endeavor to find meaning in life on the basis of his own resources.

Metaphysical philosophy seeks to arrive at an ultimate, universal picture of reality. That all philosophy either springs from or tends towards metaphysics is generally recognized by philosophical scholars. In Kant's view, "Reason avidly seeks universal and necessary judgments." According to Descartes philosophy is a tree whose root is metaphysics. And in Heidegger's view: "Metaphysics is a name for the pivotal point and core of all philosophy."[23]

Some scholars today, taking into consideration the emergence of analytic philosophy, conclude that philosophy may be divorced from metaphysics. Yet it can be shown that even analytic philosophy has metaphysical roots, though they are mostly hidden. We concur in the judgment of Nicholas Wolterstorff:

[20] Alfred North Whitehead, *Process and Reality* (N. Y.: Macmillan, 1941), p. 63.
[21] Edgar S. Brightman, *A Philosophy of Religion* (N. Y.: Prentice-Hall, 1940), p. 21.
[22] Aristotle, *Ethica Nichomachea*, Bk. VI, Ch. 7, 1141b, 17. Quoted in Lev Shestov, *Athens and Jerusalem*, trans. Bernard Martin (Athens, Ohio: Ohio University, 1966), p. 304.
[23] Martin Heidegger, *An Introduction to Metaphysics*, trans. Ralph Manheim (Garden City: Doubleday, 1961), p. 14.

> Philosophy today is no different in fundamentals from what it has always been. It is indeed less "systematic" and "speculative"; but it is no less synoptic. The notion that philosophers today are mere technicians solving problems, that all they do is describe and prove, is a delusion. Philosophy is today, as always, the elaboration and defense of a *Weltanschauung;* an interpretation of our human condition. The philosopher is after the meaning and "hang" of things; today as always he has a vision of the whole structure of men's thoughts. The rise of analytic philosophy, like the rise of any other philosophy, has caused a change in the whole intellectual scene. The fact that there are today a great many things about which the philosopher does not wish to talk, topics which he regards as outside his field of competence, is part of his conception of how things hang together.[24]

Philosophy by its very nature seeks an understanding of the whole of reality. For Whitehead speculative philosophy is "the endeavour to frame a coherent, logical, necessary system of general ideas in terms of which every element of our experience can be interpreted."[25] In a similar manner James Richmond describes philosophy as "a rational examination of reality as a whole, aiming at a systematic set of universal maxims, principles or beliefs."[26]

We now come to the question regarding the nature of theology. In Barthian terms theology is a *logia* or logic or language bound to the *theos* which makes it possible and also determines it. Barth has also defined it as an attempt to correlate the language of the church with the meaning of the Word.

Without disagreeing with Barth I venture to define theology as the very human attempt to understand the truth about God, man and the world in the light of the biblical revelation. It should be borne in mind that this is truth that has a bearing on man's predicament and salvation. Consequently it is with existential rather than purely theoretical truth that theology is concerned. The theoretical element is still present, but it is now given a spiritual ground and goal.

---

[24]Nicholas P. Wolterstorff, "Faith and Philosophy" in *Faith and Philosophy*, ed. Alvin Plantinga (Grand Rapids: Eerdmans, 1964), pp. 21, 22.

[25]Alfred North Whitehead, *Adventures of Ideas* (N. Y.: Macmillan, 1933), p. 285.

[26]James Richmond, *Faith and Philosophy* (Philadelphia: Lippincott, 1966), p. 11.

Theology is faith reflecting on its object; indeed it can be defined as faith seeking understanding. Or to put it another way, theology is analytic reasoning based on revelation whereas philosophy is synthetic reasoning based on experience.

It should be recognized that theology can give only a dim and blurred reflection of the Word of God; yet this is nevertheless a true reflection. The theologian cannot attain a full understanding of God's truth, but he can arrive at an accurate understanding. The universal, comprehensive view of God and creation is outside the grasp of the theologian, but it is possible for him to have a faithful or valid perspective.

Theology has an eschatological orientation that is not to be found in most philosophy. Because the theologian is forever aware that his concepts and formulations fall short of the absolute truth which is alone God's possession, he must constantly purify his ideas and seek to bring them more in accord with this truth. The theologian recognizes that his reasoning needs to be justified as well as his heart. Therefore there is in theology a dynamic propensity, a desire always to aim at a more complete or more catholic expression of the truth of faith. There can be in this life no final conceptual synthesis; a purely theonomous reasoning is not a human possibility. The theologian is acutely conscious of the fact that he is on the way, even though he has not yet arrived. Therefore authentic theology is always a *theologia viatorum* (theology of pilgrims). We fully concur in the view expressed by Barth:

> It [theology] can never satisfy the natural aspiration of human thought and utterance for completeness and compactness. It does not exhibit its object but can only indicate it, and in so doing it owes the truth to the self-witness of the theme and not to its own resources. It is broken thought and utterance to the extent that it can progress only in isolated thoughts and statements directed from different angles to the one object. It can never form a system, comprehending and as it were "seizing" the object.[27]

In philosophy it is generally assumed that one can arrive, if not at an absolute position, then at a satisfactory position. Lessing appears to contradict this assumption when he asserts

[27] Karl Barth, *Church Dogmatics*, eds. G. W. Bromiley and T. F. Torrance (Edinburgh: Clark, 1961), III, 3, p. 293.

that the search for truth is to be preferred to the possession of truth. But for Lessing the search for truth is itself the *summum bonum,* the highest virtue possible for man. Theology also speaks of seeking the truth, but this is a seeking based upon the prior knowing of faith. For theology seeking is not a virtue but a necessity. The biblical theologian adheres not to the universal quest for God, which itself is a kind of salvation, but rather to the seeking of faith in which salvation in its fullness is still in the future.

Theology sees man's most immediate need as the forgiveness of sins. The notion of sin is nonsense to philosophy, since sin being irrational cannot be fitted into a rational system. Sin indeed is the jagged rock on which most philosophical systems have been shipwrecked. Theology recognizes this dreaded reality, even though not being able fully to explain it. But it also perceives that the power of sin has been conquered through the sacrifice of Jesus Christ on the cross. And this is why it heralds the glad tidings of divine justification and redemption.

Philosophy is inclined to speak of man's greatest need in terms of a world view, perfect wisdom or self-fulfillment. But theology sees man's need in terms of repentance and faith. The deepest need is reunion with Christ, but forgiveness and repentance prepare the way for this eschatological reality. Theology also recognizes that man stands in need of wisdom, but it goes on to insist that Christ is our wisdom (I Cor. 1:30). Wisdom, moreover, lies not in an idea but in a Person.

POINT OF DEPARTURE

The point of departure for philosophy is either reason or experience. Its authority is autonomous; it begins with the rationally and/or experientially given. If reason be defined in such a way as to include experience, then it can be said that human reason is the criterion of philosophy. Reason, of course, goes under many different names: moral insight, prehension, apperception, observation, memory, recollection, etc. Yet the point is that man's reliance is upon his own capacity, his own intellect, his innate powers. The motto of philosophy, according to Plato in his *Phaedo,* is "to believe no one except oneself." Or as Dorothy Emmet has remarked: "A philosopher . . . can speak from no authority save that of the intrinsic cogency of his thought."[28] The wise man of this world seeks to bring every claim to truth "before the tribunal of the whole mind and its grasp on experience as a whole."[29]

The autonomous character of philosophical thought is certainly apparent among the Greek philosophers. It was Protagoras who boldly declared: "Man is the measure of all things." Plato corrected Protagoras by insisting that God is the measure of all things, but this is the God conceived by reason. According to Aristotle: "A good man is the right judge in every case and that which is true appears true to him."[30] And again: "The mark of the philosopher is that he can judge about everything."[31]

The later Renaissance and the Enlightenment are also noted for having a supreme confidence in reason. For Spinoza reason is "the great gift and divine light," the only god worthy of veneration. He asked, "What altar can he build for himself who offends the majesty of reason?" John Locke asserted: "Reason must be our last Judge and Guide in everything."[32] Kant, who marked the transition from the Enlightenment to the Romantic Period, declared: "Reason must regard itself as the author of its principles independent of extraneous influences."[33]

The motto of what came to be known as the Age of Reason was given by René Descartes: "I think; therefore I am" *(cogito, ergo sum)*. The thinking ego was regarded as the ground of certainty, the center of authority. The existentialist Sartre has modified this to read: "I exist, therefore I am." Yet here again the self-enclosed ego remains the point of departure. The contemporary breakdown of confidence in man's inherent rational powers is mirrored in the statement of Samuel Beckett: "I cannot think, I do not know, therefore I am — or am I?"

Modern existentialism, like most of its philosophical predecessors, is hominocentric. Man is the center of everything; his destiny lies in his own hands. As Jaspers expresses it:

[28]Dorothy Emmet, *The Nature of Metaphysical Thinking* (London: Macmillan, 1949), p. 152.
[29]Brightman, *A Philosophy of Religion*, p. 129.
[30]Aristotle, *Ethica Nichomachea*, Bk. III, Ch. 4, 1113a, 29, 30. In *Aristotle*, ed. Louise Loomis (N. Y.: Classics Club, 1943), p. 123.
[31]Aristotle, *Metaphysica*, Bk. III, 2, 1000 4a, 34. Quoted in Shestov, *Athens and Jerusalem*, p. 304.
[32]John Locke, *An Essay Concerning Understanding* (N. Y.: Dover, 1950), Vol. II, p. 438.
[33]Immanuel Kant, *Metaphysical Foundations of Morals*, pp. 193, 194.

"Man cannot be derived from something else, but is immediately at the base of all things."[34] Jaspers makes use of the term "revelation," but he means by it something completely different from what biblical theology has always envisioned. Revelation is "a series of sudden illuminations in the history of the mind," not a divine incursion into human history. As he notes: "The fact that we use the same term 'revelation' to denote both an absolute and unique divine intervention and this process of the gradual revelation of truth, must not cause us to overlook the radical difference between the two."[35] For existentialists, even for a Christian existentialist such as Berdyaev, "The criterion of truth is in the subject not in the object, in freedom, not in authority. . . ."[36]

In summary the criterion for philosophy is man's own cognitive apparatus, particularly the thinking ego. Man begins with his own experience and then proceeds towards eternal truths. In Maritain's phraseology philosophy *"ascends* from experience towards things divine" whereas "revelation *descends* from God."[37] The measure or standard of authority is not God but man, although God may nevertheless have a role in a philosophical system. Swinburne echoes the dominant view of the natural man: "Glory to man in the highest; he is the measure of all things."

The point of departure for theology, on the other hand, is divine revelation. Moreover, this revelation has happened in a definitive way in the sacred history mirrored in the Bible culminating in Jesus Christ. Revelation signifies not only the acts of God in past biblical history but also the biblical interpretation of these acts. It also includes the inward illumination of the Holy Spirit in the present by which we become convinced of the truth of the biblical witness.

Whereas the truth upheld by philosophers can be discovered or conceived by reason, the truth proclaimed by the church has its source in an authoritative definitive revelation of God. As Paul averred: "For I would have you know, brethren, that the gospel which was preached by me is not man's gospel. For

[34]Karl Jaspers, *The Perennial Scope of Philosophy*, trans. Ralph Manheim (N. Y.: Philosophical Library, 1949), p. 59.

[35]Karl Jaspers, "Myth and Religion" in Hans-Werner Bartsch, *Kerygma and Myth*, Vol. II, p. 68.

[36]Nicolas Berdyaev, *Truth and Revelation*, trans. R. M. French (N. Y.: Collier, 1962), p. 68.

[37]Jacques Maritain, *An Essay on Christian Philosophy*, trans. Edward Flannery (N. Y.: Philosophical Library, 1955), p. 20.

I did not receive it from man, nor was I taught it, but it came through a revelation of Jesus Christ" (Gal. 1:11, 12).

Faith is the subjective pole of revelation; it is the means by which we lay hold of the truth of the Gospel. It entails the assent of the mind as well as the surrender of the will. In the words of John Mackay: "Faith in Jesus Christ is, on the one hand, an *assent* to the truth about Christ, and on the other, *consent* to the reality of Christ."[38]

It is not the act of thinking but instead the act of being apprehended by God that brings man certainty. Barth has rephrased Descartes' motto in this way: *cogitor, ergo sum* (I am known, therefore I am). An equally sound formulation is the following: God is, therefore I am. The theologian seeks to begin with God and His revelation in Jesus Christ; only then is it possible to know oneself.

Because biblical evangelical theology and secular philosophy have such different starting points, it is no wonder that they arrive at such diverse conclusions. We concur in Forsyth's observation:

> And this is the real crux. Everything does turn on our footing, on our starting-point, our notion of reality. Do we find it in the *Word* or in the *World*, in a given Revelation or in innate thought, in the super-rational or in the rational, in the experience of supernatural grace or of natural culture, in the sense of the holy or in that of the merely spiritual?[39]

Whereas philosophy begins in doubt or wonder or despair, theology begins in obedience. It can be said that in one sense theology also begins in doubt but in the doubt of ourselves, of our own powers, our own reason. One can also affirm that theology begins in wonder, but this is the wonder of the love of God in Jesus Christ.

The authority of theology is not autonomous (as in philosophy) but theonomous. Theology is not anthropocentric but theocentric and Christocentric. It views man in the light of God and not vice versa.

Theology looks backward to the events in sacred history, but it also looks forward to the consummation of world history, to the second advent of Jesus Christ. Theology also is

---

[38] John Mackay, *God's Order: The Ephesian Letter and This Present Time* (N. Y.: Macmillan, 1964), p. 110.
[39] P. T. Forsyth, *The Principle of Authority*, p. 178.

directed upward to the God who dwells in heaven and to Jesus who is at God's right hand and who makes continual intercession for us. Surely theology also has an inward dimension in that the Spirit of God dwells now within all believers. Theology must concern itself with past, present and future, since we meet our God in all these dimensions, for He is the One "who was and is and is to come!" (Rev. 4:8).

The theologian ideally gives up everything in order to subject himself to Christ. The philosopher Seneca points to an altogether different way when he says: "If you wish to subject everything to yourself, subject yourself to reason." But the Christian like his Lord recognizes this to be a Satanic temptation (cf. Mt. 4:8, 9), and instead chooses to dedicate himself and all his worldly goods to the service of the glory of God. Unlike the natural man, the disciple of Christ seeks not to gain the whole world but to lose his life for the sake of the kingdom that is not of this world (Mt. 16:25, 26).

The method or procedure of theology is reverent study undergirded by prayer. The theologian must be constantly dependent upon his Teacher as he seeks to understand the mysteries of Holy Scripture. As Anselm stated in his *Proslogion:* "Teach me to see thee and *show thyself* to me as I seek; for I am not able to seek thee unless thou teachest, nor to find thee unless thou showest thyself" (Ch. I).

It can be said that theological method is receptive more than inductive or deductive, although the latter methods are certainly employed on a secondary level. This is to say the theologian seeks always to be open to the guidance and direction of the Holy Spirit. One might also contend that theological procedure is closer to being ecstatic or pneumatic rather than eductive, since the truth is not drawn out of oneself but given to man in the moment of decision. Again theology is existential more than purely rational, although it entails vigorous reasoning. The theologian is gripped by an ultimate concern; therefore he approaches his subject matter not with cold detachment but with the passion of commitment.

PURPOSES AND GOALS

The aim of philosophy in its advanced form is to attain comprehensive knowledge, in other words, absolute truth. The by-products of such knowledge are seen to be serenity of soul, self-fulfillment and inner peace. The metaphysical philosopher seeks a transhistorical perspective, one that theology holds belongs only to God. Heraclitus contended that true wisdom "is to know the thought by which all things are steered through all things."[40] For Hegel "the content of philosophy, its requirement and interest, is also completely that of religion; its object is eternal truth, nothing else but God and the explanation of God."[41] Jaspers gives a similar interpretation when he says that the goal of philosophy is to find "the knowledge of all knowledge" or "reality in the primal source."[42]

Philosophy in its rudimentary form seeks to attain valid knowledge, a true picture of how things actually are. Modern analytic philosophy no longer speaks of attaining the absolute but is content simply to gain valid knowledge of our immediate environment.

For the mainstream of philosophy and of theology as well, knowledge is power. To gain knowledge is to gain power over oneself and ultimately over others. The quest for self-fulfillment is also one for self-mastery, and this invariably leads to an attempt at world-mastery. Wise men through the ages have rightly observed that the search for knowledge mirrors the lust for power inherent in all men.

Philosophers have not been reticent in acknowledging this dimension of power-seeking. For Plato knowledge can enable one to unite himself with deity. "But to the company of the gods," he said, "no one who has not studied philosophy is admitted, save only the lovers of knowledge."[43] And again he affirmed that there is "no release or salvation from evil except the attainment of the highest virtue and wisdom."[44] And in the words of Spinoza: "By virtue and power I understand the same thing." Engels argued that the goal of philosophy is "when man not only proposes but also disposes." Sartre put it more bluntly: "The fundamental project of man is to be God." Freud's hope for the future is that "the intellect — the scientific spirit, reason — should in time establish a dic-

[40] John Burnet, *Early Greek Philosophy*, 4th ed. (London: Black, 1952), p. 134.

[41] Georg W. F. Hegel, *Philosophy of Religion*, Lasson, I, 29. Quoted in K. Barth, *From Rousseau to Ritschl* (London: SCM, 1959), p. 293.

[42] Karl Jaspers, *Way to Wisdom*, trans. Ralph Manheim (New Haven: Yale, 1951), p. 13.

[43] *Phaedo*, 82c in B. Jowett, ed., *The Dialogues of Plato* (London: Oxford, 1953), Vol. I, p. 437.

[44] *Phaedo*, 107d in Jowett, *The Dialogues of Plato*, Vol. I, p. 467.

tatorship over the human mind." According to Santayana, the "Life of Reason" is "an ideal to which everything in the world should be subordinated"; religion, art and science all fall under its dominion.[45]

Theologians have also recognized the integral relationship between the gaining of knowledge and the striving for power, but they have seen in this the fall of man rather than his grandeur. Whereas Hegel perceived the rise of man and the birth of philosophy in man's attempt to eat of the tree of knowledge (Gen. 3), theology sees this as original sin.

The quest for knowledge cannot be separated from the sinful desire to rule or control. According to Tillich, "Knowledge as such is not a matter of concupiscence, but it is the desire cognitively to draw the universe into one's self and one's finite particularity."[46] And as Barth observes: "We are masters of what we can apprehend. Viewing and conceiving certainly means encompassing, and we are superior to, and spiritually masters of, what we can encompass."[47] This is the reason why theology insists that man does not have the capability of apprehending God; rather he must be apprehended by God. We know only as we are known, and this is sufficient to keep us humble.

This brings us to the purposes and goals of theology. The immediate aim of theology is to clarify the Word of God so that obedience might follow. Spener declared that Christianity consists not so much in knowledge as in practice. Its aim is not the meditation of the real but the transformation of the actual (Nels Ferré). Theology seeks to help men to become conformed to the will of God.

In one sense it is permissible to speak of theology's aim as knowledge, but this is knowledge of God's will and purpose. As theologians we do not try to comprehend the essence of God. The knowledge that we speak of is an existential knowledge, that which changes one, rather than a speculative knowledge. It is receiving knowledge, not controlling knowledge. It is "secret wisdom" (I Cor. 2) and not a natural wisdom (cf. Prov. 2:6; 3:5, 7). The knowledge of God in this

[45]George Santayana, *The Life of Reason: Reason in Religion* (N. Y.: Scribner's, 1922), p. 7.
[46]Paul Tillich, *Systematic Theology* (Chicago: University of Chicago, 1957), Vol. II, p. 53.
[47]Karl Barth, *Church Dogmatics*, II, 1, p. 199.

sense means union with God, a union not with His being but with His will.

Whereas philosophy says "Be yourself," theology calls one to become other than himself. As Augustine put it, "Make me to be what I cannot be, and to do what I cannot do." Rather than uphold the motto "Be what you want to be," theology says, "Be what you are called to be in Christ." Theology places the emphasis upon self-denial and self-transcendence rather than self-fulfillment. Socrates said, "Know yourself"; the Stoic maxim is "Rule yourself"; the Christian faith says, "Give yourself." Bernard of Clairvaux contended that one should seek first of all not to know oneself but to know Jesus Christ. "In a word," he said, "my philosophy is this and it is the loftiest in the world: to know Jesus and Him crucified."

The final goal of theology is a fellowship of love that redounds to the glory of God. This is sometimes also referred to as a holy community. For philosophy the goal is a complete understanding or at least a satisfactory understanding. The aim of philosophy is also spoken of at times as serenity of soul, satisfaction of mind, fulfillment of self; indeed these are the fruits of a right understanding. As Jaspers phrased it: "Peace of mind is the aim of philosophical thought."[48] The theologian places the accent not upon personal peace and inward satisfaction but upon holiness, and this is envisaged not simply as individual holiness but "social holiness" (Wesley).

Both theology and philosophy use the concept of the Good as a description of the goal of man's endeavors. For philosophy the Good is the happiness of man, although this goes under many different masks including *eudaemonia* (Aristotle), *ataraxia* (Epicurus) and apathy (Zeno). The point is that the goal of philosophy is anthropocentric, centered in the fulfillment of man. Sometimes philosophers speak of the good of the race, but the race is the self projected or externalized just as the self is the race individualized.

Theology, on the other hand, understands the Good as the glory of God. Yet included in this is the salvation of man, since man's eternal salvation is precisely what gives glory to God. This is the reason why the orientation of theology is more correctly described as "theanthropocentric" (Brunner) rather than either theocentric or anthropocentric.

Concerning the means to attain the goals, again the two

[48]Karl Jaspers, *The Perennial Scope of Philosophy*, p. 169.

disciplines differ widely. We are now of course in the area of soteriology, the doctrine of salvation.

The schema of salvation in philosophy is autosoteric. This is to say that salvation is procured by self-effort whether this be discipline, contemplation, education or love. Sometimes science or the scientific method is upheld as a means of salvation. For Nietzsche the will to power is the pathway to self-fulfillment; for William James it is the will to believe. The point is that salvation is man's own work. All that is needed, according to Santayana, is that man "have a determinative character and a sane capacity for happiness." In the words of Gautama Buddha: "Man is born alone, lives alone and dies alone, and it is he alone who can blaze the trail which leads him to Nirvana." And again from Buddha: "I myself, having attained salvation, am a savior of others."[49] Even Kant, who posited a radical evil within man, held that man's moral striving is the only hope: "But if a man is corrupt in the very ground of his maxims, how can he possibly bring about this revolution by his own powers and of himself become a good man? Yet duty bids us to do this, and duty demands nothing of us which we cannot do."[50] William Henley epitomizes the general philosophical stance in his dictum: "I am the master of my fate; I am the captain of my soul."

That philosophers generally see philosophy as revealing the way of salvation or as itself a way of salvation should be acknowledged by all observers. Plato was very emphatic that philosophy pointed the way to reunion with the world soul or the ground of being. He affirmed that such reunion is only possible for "the soul of a philosopher . . . or of a lover, who has been guided by philosophy."[51] In Hegel's view the "possibility of reconciliation rests only on the conscious recognition of the implicit unity of divine and human nature."[52] According to Karl Jaspers, "All philosophy is a transcending of the world, analogous to redemption."[53]

There is little if any place for prayer in the world of philosophy. A Buddhist hermit philosopher told Dr. Brunner: "We

[49]*Sayings of Buddha* (Mt. Vernon, N. Y.: Pauper, 1957), p. 58.
[50]Immanuel Kant, *Religion Within the Limits of Reason Alone*, p. 43.
[51]*Phaedrus*, 249a in Jowett, *The Dialogues of Plato*, Vol. III, p. 155.
[52]Georg W. F. Hegel, *Lectures on the Philosophy of Religion*, trans. E. B. Speirs and J. B. Sanderson (London: Kegan Paul, Trench, Trübner, 1895), Vol. III, p. 71.
[53]Karl Jaspers, *Way to Wisdom*, p. 23.

Buddhists do not pray. We have the command of the Master to save ourselves."[54] In most philosophy prayer is reinterpreted to signify meditation and reflection upon the meaning of life. It is not petition to a personal God but soliloquy. Plato made a place for prayer, but not the prayer for forgiveness. The aim of prayer, he contended, is "to give beauty to the inward soul."[55] In Stoicism prayer is meditation on the nature of the universe. For Jaspers "philosophical contemplation" takes the place of prayer; its aim "is no longer to achieve practical mundane results, but inward transfiguration."[56] Kant is very explicit in his opposition to prayer: "He who has made progress in the good life ceases to pray, for candor is one of its first maxims."

Friedrich Heiler, an authority on spirituality, has this to say about the role of prayer in philosophy:

> Rational philosophical thought means the disintegration and dissolution of prayer. Prayer, the spontaneous and direct expression of religious experience, is subjected to an alien authority when forced into the categories of philosophical ethics and metaphysical theories of knowledge. . . . Only petition for "the good", perfect resignation, contemplative adoration may form the content of prayer. The positive ideal of prayer which philosophic criticism sets over against living prayer seems to the religious man . . . a cold product of abstraction, a miserable substitute for the real thing. Even the purest type and most beautiful flower of philosophical prayer, Epictetus's prayer and hymn of submission, is in spite of its sound . . . but the shadow of true prayer. The prayer of the philosopher is no real communion as between persons, no intercourse with God, no personal relation, no vital communion with Him.[57]

Philosophers sometimes give God a role in the work of salvation, but where God is posited He is always seen as a means to man's self-fulfillment. For Kant God is necessary as a moral governor to help man attain the *summum bonum*.

---

[54]Emil Brunner, *The Christian Doctrine of the Church, Faith, and the Consummation*, trans. David Cairns (Philadelphia: Westminster, 1960), p. 330n.

[55]*Phaedrus*, 279c in Jowett, *The Dialogues of Plato*, Vol. III, p. 189.

[56]Karl Jaspers, *The Perennial Scope of Philosophy*, p. 82.

[57]Friedrich Heiler, *Prayer*, trans. Samuel McComb (N. Y.: Oxford, 1958), p. 102.

And in the view of Jaspers: "Our enduring task in philosophical endeavour is to become authentic men by becoming aware of being; — or, and this is the same thing: to become ourselves by achieving certainty of God."[58]

For theology man can only reach his goal by divine grace. Man is unable to procure his salvation because he has fallen into bondage to the power of sin. What man cannot do, God must do for him; moreover, God has acted decisively for man's salvation in the person of Jesus Christ, in His sacrificial life and death. In Jesus God took upon Himself the sin and guilt of the world so that mankind might be saved. Because God acted on our behalf despite the fact that we merited only His condemnation, it can be said that we have been redeemed by free grace. To be sure, man must respond to the cross of Christ in faith, but faith must be viewed as a gift of God. Both faith and the condition to receive it are given by the Spirit of God.

Philosophers hardly ever speak of divine grace, but they sometimes refer to the need for faith. Yet what they mean by faith is something far different from the Scriptural meaning. For Kant faith is the moral attitude of reason concerning that which is unattainable by theoretical cognition; this is a far cry from confidence and trust in a living Savior. For some of the existentialists faith is a venture into the future based on confidence in man's own ingenuity and foresight. In the words of Jaspers: "Philosophical faith . . . is the faith of man in his potentialities."[59]

Sometimes evangelical biblical theology is contrasted with philosophical mysticism, which places the accent upon love rather than faith. In mysticism man ascends to God upon a ladder of love; in evangelicalism God descends to man, first appearing in the person of His Son in a lowly manger and finally dying upon a cross. To be sure, once the Savior is received by faith, He enables man to rise to glory. But the symbol of ascent is not the ladder but the lift, for man is carried to final salvation by free grace.

Theology too can speak of salvation by love, but the meaning here is not man's love for God, the Eros of Greek philosophy, but God's love for man, the Agape of the Bible. As the apostle explains: "In this is love, not that we loved God but that he

---

[58] Karl Jaspers, *The Perennial Scope of Philosophy*, p. 166.
[59] *Ibid.*, p. 74.

loved us and sent his Son to be the expiation for our sins" (I Jn. 4:10).

The orientation of theology is God-centered rather than man-centered. Our hope is said to lie outside ourselves in the grace of God revealed and fulfilled in the cross of Jesus Christ. Evangelical theology calls upon men to acknowledge their helplessness and wretchedness and to throw themselves upon the mercy of God. Philosophy, even where it lacks confidence in human powers, nevertheless urges men to rely upon themselves, since this is all they have.

GOD, THE WORLD AND MAN

For philosophy the ultimate or final reality is either the world within (idea) or the world without (nature). It is either mental force (Leibniz) or the world of facts (Wittgenstein). The one other alternative is to posit an underlying unity that ties together idea and process (as does Hegel), and one ends here in either pantheism or panentheism.

Theology, on the other hand, equates ultimate reality with the transcendent God of the Bible, who is to be sharply distinguished from the world of His creation. This God is the Personal Spirit who stands above process and idea, nature and mind. He is not an impersonal ground of being but active and dynamic will. Moreover, this living God is inaccessible to both thought and the senses: therefore He must reveal Himself in order to be known. The true God is neither the idea of the Good nor Absolute Mind, but the living Lord and Savior who has identified Himself with our plight and misery. This is what moved Forsyth to declare: "The real is neither the rational nor the ethical. It is the redemptive."[60]

Philosophy in contrast to theology is oriented about an abstract idea of God. Where God is spoken of, He is subsumed under a genus such as being or process. He is the supreme being or the creative process. In Leibniz's philosophy the monad is the chief category, and God is referred to as the supreme monad. Hegel described God as "the highest being" and as "pure abstraction." In naturalistic philosophy God is sometimes envisioned as a dynamic force in nature or as "the personification of the highest social values" (Ames); more often He is simply denied or relegated to insignificance. For Whitehead God is "the chief exemplification" of the meta-

[60]Forsyth, *The Principle of Authority*, p. 182.

physical principles. Both God and the world are seen by him as being in the grip of creativity. Kant in his *Opus postumum* declared: "God is not an entity outside of me, but merely a thought within me." It can be said that theology is subordinated to ontology in most philosophical systems.

God for philosophy is generally seen to be accessible to reason and/or the senses. Henry Nelson Wieman has affirmed that God is an object that can be perceived as well as conceived. But the true God is beyond the reach of our perception and conception. He can be known only as He gives Himself to be known.

Heiler gives a true picture of the God of philosophy:

> God for the philosopher is something quite different from what He is for the ordinary religious individual. He may be conceived as "personal", "non-personal", or "super-personal", but never is He a man-like Being who feels and thinks as a dweller upon earth. God is "Being", the "Absolute", the "World-Ground", the "World-Principle", the "World-Soul", the "Idea of the True, the Beautiful and the Good", or even only a "postulate of the reason", but He is not "Lord" and "Father", whose nearness to him who prays is an immediate and undoubted certainty.[61]

Modern philosophy in its various forms denies the existence of God, but false absolutes have come to the fore even in those philosophies which deny the possibility of an absolute. Luther held that whatever man places his trust in is his god, and we are witnessing today the deification of such powers as sex, race, nation (or *Volk*) and science.

Theology is oriented not about an idea of God but about the God-Man, Jesus Christ. This is why Barth labels the theological approach "unionistic" rather than materialistic or idealistic, since it takes for its point of departure the union between spirit and matter. It can also be denominated a supernatural creationism as over against both monism and dualism, since God has brought into being both idea and nature. Shestov has rightly seen that the Bible upholds created ideas rather than eternal ideas.[62] Being the seat of

---

[61] Heiler, *Prayer*, pp. 95, 96.

[62] See Lev Shestov, *Athens and Jerusalem*, pp. 310f., 344, 345, 351. We cannot accept Shestov's existentialism but appreciate his marked biblical orientation.

Theology and Philosophy

wisdom, God conceives ideas that have universal significance; yet they do not exist independently of His mind and will.

At times theology and philosophy will use very similar language in speaking about God; for example, both idealistic philosophy and evangelical theology agree that God is immutable. Yet it can be shown that the two disciplines conceive of immutability in quite different ways. The God of classical philosophy does not change because he does not have the power to change. The God of biblical faith "does not change because, and insofar as, He does not wish to change and does not judge it good to do so. . . . Immutability does not rule God, it serves Him, as do all the other truths which, insofar as they are created, possess only an executive power and only for as long as they are of some use."[63]

In the area of cosmology philosophy maintains that God is either continuous or identical with the world. The world, moreover, is generally regarded by many philosophers as the whole of reality or the final reality. Whitehead echoes the views of many: "We know nothing beyond this temporal world and the formative elements which jointly constitute its character. The temporal world and its formative elements constitute for us the all-inclusive universe."[64] In some philosophical systems the world is viewed as a subordinate reality but still eternal; in some others it is said to be illusory.

The theological view is that God is the only final reality and He is discontinuous with the world rather than identical with it or inseparable from it. The world is seen as a secondary contingent reality. It has both a beginning and an end. God relates Himself to the world, but He remains sovereign over the world.

Marked differences between theologians and philosophers can also be discerned in the area of anthropology. Reinhold Niebuhr has correctly observed that philosophy interprets man as either essentially reason, without being able to do justice to his nonrational vitalities, or as essentially vitality, without appreciating the extent of his rational freedom. Theology, on the other hand, sees man as a unity of soul and body created in the image of God. Man is capable of transcending himself, but he remains a finite and also a fallen creature. Theology sees the heights as well as the depths of

[63]*Ibid.*, p. 345.
[64]Alfred North Whitehead, *Religion in the Making* (N. Y.: Macmillan, 1957), p. 90.

human creaturehood; it considers both man's historical tragedy and his glorious destiny. For biblical theology the key to the mystery of man lies not in his bestial heritage nor in a divine spark within him but in the revelation of God in Jesus Christ. Man can be understood only when he is seen in the light of his Creator and Redeemer, the living God.

In contrast to idealistic personalistic philosophy the Christian faith bases the dignity of man not on the intrinsic infinite value of the human soul but on the fact that every soul is infinitely precious in the sight of God. Christianity in fact denies that human personality has inherent infinite worth; rather it has a derivative value of infinite significance, for God made man in His image. At the same time the Christian is called to serve his neighbor with an infinite compassion, to have an infinite preference for his neighbor's welfare (P. Ramsey). In Christianity man does not merit infinite love, but he is the object of this kind of love by God and people imbued with God's Spirit.

Finally attention should be given to the language that is used in speaking about God and God's action in the world. Philosophers for the most part prefer univocal language in this area, but sometimes they make a place also for analogical language. But this is analogy based upon the supposed continuity between the being of man and God; it is what is now called the *analogia entis*. Theology also utilizes analogical language in speaking about God, but it is based upon the *analogia fidei*, the analogical relation between God and man discerned by faith in Jesus Christ. Whereas philosophy begins with man and then posits divine attributes, theology begins with God and then infers human attributes from the divine being. For theology man, being in the image of God, reflects but does not share the attributes of God. Gordon Clark, a contemporary Reformed philosopher, interestingly enough stands with many idealistic philosophers in arguing that human logic and knowledge can be identical with that possessed by God. In our view they are analogous but not at any point identical.

For theology the truth of faith can only be grasped in the form of paradox and symbol. The meaning of the truth of revelation is veiled in mystery. We encounter Christ through His Spirit, but this is always the hidden Christ who can be perceived only by faith. We do not meet God in His primary objectivity, but God hidden in the sign, veil and work of His redemptive acts in history.

Theology and Philosophy

Evangelical theology utilizes paradoxical language more than strictly logical language in its depiction of God. It prefers the language of the biblical myth or "the language of Canaan" (Barth) to purely scientific or univocal language in describing God's activity. Sinful reason also intrudes into theology, however, and sometimes the mystery of God is dissolved in rationalistic speculation. In Calvin's words: "All the mysteries of God are paradoxes to the flesh: and at the same time it possesses so much audacity, that it fears not to oppose them, but insolently to assail what it cannot comprehend."[65]

Yet it should be recognized that paradox and analogy can also be conveyors of meaning. Arthur Holmes correctly reminds us that "while analogy, symbol and even paradox are indeed literary devices, they are still vehicles of the understanding. They represent exploratory probes, the stretching of the mind to grasp what is unfamiliar or remote, the attempt to probe the mystery of something utterly unique, or even to capture some elusive but alluring thought."[66]

RELEVANCE OF PHILOSOPHY FOR THEOLOGY

Having delineated the principal areas of conflict between theology and philosophy, we must now ask ourselves why the study of philosophy is important for theologians. First of all, such a study enables us to appreciate and understand the truth in our own position, since we see this truth over against untruth. Again, an acquaintance with philosophy enables us to discern truth within untruth. Philosophy mirrors not only worldly wisdom but also occasionally the wisdom of God, even though such wisdom cannot be neatly assimilated into a philosophical system. It can be seen that our interest in philosophy as theologians is primarily utilitarian. A study of philosophy can serve the cause of the Gospel by throwing light upon the thinking of both the church and the world.

We now come to the question of the source of divine wisdom or Christian insights in philosophy. That there are such

---

[65] John Calvin, *Commentaries on the Epistle of Paul the Apostle to the Romans*, 3:5, trans. John Owen (Edinburgh: Calvin Translation Society, 1849; Grand Rapids: Eerdmans reprint, 1959), p. 119.

[66] Arthur Holmes, "The Philosophical Methodology of Gordon Clark" in Ronald Nash, ed., *The Philosophy of Gordon Clark* (Philadelphia: Presbyterian and Reformed, 1968), [pp. 202-226], p. 223.

insights cannot be denied. Plato, for example, in his *Phaedo* makes this remarkable statement: "I would have him take the best and most irrefragable of human theories, and let this be the raft upon which he sails through life — not without risk, as I admit, if he cannot find some word of God which will more surely and safely carry him."[67] Plato was yearning for a word of God that he never received, since the time of fulfillment (the *kairos*) was not yet at hand, but theology can surely appreciate this yearning. When Wittgenstein acknowledges that the "sense of the world must lie outside the world"[68] or when Kant recognizes the presence of "radical evil" within the heart of man, these are signs of the movement of the Holy Spirit in the world outside the church. Yet radical evil was an alien element in the Kantian system, and in the same work in which he speaks of it he is compelled to backtrack and contend that there still remains hope for man, since he possesses a good will. Karl Marx approaches the Christian position in his insight that there is an ideological taint in human reasoning, but he did not recognize that this taint springs not merely from adverse social conditions but even more from the depravity of the human heart; moreover, he was not sufficiently cognizant of the fact that not only the bourgeois mentality but also socialist thought is tainted and conditioned.

The occasional presence of Christian wisdom in philosophical works must be attributed to the *imago Dei*, which all men share, and to common grace, i.e., the general working of the Spirit, which does not save man but restrains his rapacity and pricks his conscience. Yet at the same time we maintain that because of man's sin the general awareness of the goodness and reality of God is invariably distorted and made to serve some kind of idolatry. The genuinely Christian insights that philosophers stumble upon are accidental in the sense that they are not logical components of a philosophical system. Such insights indeed are frequently a source of embarrassment for philosophers, and it is not uncommon for these insights to be ignored or even repudiated as the philosopher seeks to integrate and finalize his system.

[67]*Phaedo*, 85d in Jowett, *The Dialogues of Plato*, Vol. I, p. 441.

[68]Wittgenstein, *Tractatus Logico-Philosophicus*, trans. Pears and McGuinness, p. 145. For an admirable statement on where theology can learn from Wittgenstein see Paul L. Holmer, "Wittgenstein and Theology" in Dallas High, ed., *New Essays on Religious Language* (N. Y.: Oxford, 1969), pp. 25-35.

One must also inquire about the source of pagan insights in theology. Too often we are prone to spell out the differences between philosophy and theology in black and white terms whereas we are dealing with greys. The theologian like the philosopher is a finite creature as well as a sinner, and therefore he too is severely limited in his apprehension of the truth. Yet the theologian, unlike the philosopher, ideally seeks always to recognize his limitations and to throw himself ever again upon the mercy of God. In faith he ceases to depend upon his own wisdom and relies on the wisdom of Christ. The theologian does not claim to possess final truth, but he does insist that he knows the One who is the truth, and it is this faith-knowledge which directs his thinking and sets him apart from secular philosophers.

The Christian, it must be admitted, is not always on the side of the angels, and this is why he is a divided self. He has been born again by the Spirit of God, but vestiges of the old self still remain with him. He is at the same time a philosopher and a theologian, and this accounts for both his misery and hope. He depends on natural wisdom as well as the wisdom of God, and this is why he constantly goes astray though not necessarily falling into a new kind of bondage. In practice we are often both philosophers and theologians; yet in our fundamental loyalties and in the direction of our destiny we are either-or. Faith in God leads finally to salvation whereas reliance upon self leads finally to isolation from God and neighbor, which is a form of damnation.

In summary theology is centered in the triune God whereas philosophy is centered in man. The source and criterion of theology is God's Word declared in the Bible; the criterion of the philosopher is human reason and/or experience. The aim of theology is to herald and serve the Word of God; the accent is on service instead of mastery. The aim in philosophy is to arrive at final truth which at the same time signifies the fulfillment of self. For philosophy knowledge is usually an end in itself; for theology, on the other hand, knowledge is a means to the higher end of conformity to the will of God. The culmination of theology is a holy community whereas the culmination of philosophy is a rational system. Theology ends in a concrete fellowship of love; philosophy generally ends in the most abstract or the most universal.

In this chapter I have tried to let the theologians and philosophers speak for themselves, and I believe that only in this way can one discern the real differences between them. It should be recognized that I have given a fairer and more dispassionate presentation of philosophy than many philosophers have given of other kinds of philosophy. My purpose here has not been to condemn but to understand. Theologians and philosophers are afflicted by the same poison of sin, and they share a common yearning for the truth that redeems. But only when they stand upon the same foundation can they successfully labor together in the cause of God's truth.

It could perhaps be alleged that I have not done justice to the variety and diversity in theological or philosophical thought. When one works with any kind of typology, however, there is always the danger of oversimplification. At the same time it can be shown that there is a definite unity within the diversity of theological and philosophical systems. In the former the unity is grounded in an acknowledgment of a particular divine revelation in history, and in the latter it is to be found in an appeal to autonomous reason. The way from theology to philosophy is the way of compromise, at least in the light of the norms of faith; the way from philosophy to theology is the way of conversion.

SIX:

THE PROBLEM OF EVIL

In this chapter we shall explore the ways in which various types of philosophy as well as evangelical theology seek to grapple with the problem of evil. In the Christian tradition the question has been asked time and time again how the existence of evil can be reconciled with an omnipotent and perfect God. This question, which concerns both theology and philosophy, has baffled some of the greatest minds through the ages.

PHILOSOPHICAL THEORIES

One of the principal strands of philosophy addressing itself to the problem of evil is that metaphysical dualism which draws a sharp division between spirit and matter, the eternal and the temporal. In this kind of philosophy evil is said to have its source in nonbeing and/or matter. Aristotle defined matter as "that which exists only in potentiality," and in this respect it is equivalent to nonbeing.

In metaphysical dualism the presence of evil is regarded as rational because it is caused by a recognizable and ascertainable reality, namely, matter. Also evil is necessarily connected with finitude, the mixture of matter and form. The only way to overcome evil is to "unmix the mixture" and allow the soul to rise out of its bodily prison to eternity.

Matter or nonbeing goes under various labels in this philosophical tradition, including chaos, the receptacle, the *Ungrund*, the nothingness and the void. Matter is that which is deficient in being: it does not signify the complete absence of being. Hence one can understand why dualistic philosophers view evil in terms of privation and deprivation.

The tradition of metaphysical dualism has penetrated deeply into the history of both philosophy and theology. Among the great philosophers who stand more or less in this tradition are Plato, Aristotle, Plotinus, Hegel, Heidegger, Jaspers and Whitehead. Berdyaev might also be mentioned here in that he posits a nonbeing that is prior to being. Theologians who have been to some degree influenced by this tradition are Pseudo-Dionysius, Augustine, Thomas, Schleiermacher, Tillich and Barth; it should immediately be said that all these thinkers seek to transcend the dualistic tradition.

Metaphysical dualism is also present in several of the Oriental religions including Hinduism, Buddhism and Jainism. In the Sankhya system of Hinduism there are two eternal categories of being — matter (or the phenomenal world) and the soul. Ignorance of this distinction is said to be the cause of all misery. Platonism, Hinduism and Buddhism hold in common the view that the genuinely good must be permanent or eternal and that the world is transitory and ever changing.

Plato is probably the key figure in the tradition of cosmic dualism, at least in the West. For him evil stems from the resistance of chaotic matter to form and structure. The intractability of matter accounts for the disruption and disharmony in the visible world, which is a mixture of form and matter. The chaos is understood by him as being not sheer nothingness *(ouk on)* but rather unrealized potentiality to be some specific thing *(mē on)*. Evil lies in recalcitrance and deficiency, not in aggressive rebellion.

For Plotinus matter or nonbeing is seen as the principle of evil. As light recedes into darkness, so the One, the ground of all being, diffuses itself in the world of nature. The phenomenal world is accounted for as the product of a series of emanations from the One and therefore is considered deficient in being.

The philosophies of Gnosticism and Manichaeism, which constantly threatened the early church, stem partly from Platonism. They are both based on the dualism of spirit and matter. Gnosticism, an amalgamation of Hellenic and Oriental philosophical speculation, conceives of the phenomenal world as basically evil. Manichaeism, which includes elements of Buddhism, Judaism, Gnosticism, Zoroastrianism and Christianity, also takes a dim view of material existence.

Dionysius the pseudo-Areopagite, who was profoundly influenced by Plato and Plotinus, for the most part accepted the Platonic approach to the problem of evil. He wrote that just as the sun emits light, so God emits good, giving illumination first to the spirits and then to every kind of created thing down to matter. Evil is basically "the omission of good" — mere nonbeing.

Augustine was more patently biblical in his approach, and yet he too could not disengage himself from Platonic presuppositions, particularly in his discussion of evil. For him evil is essentially privation, a turning towards a lesser good. The evil will has no positive or "efficient" cause but only a "deficient" cause. Yet at times he recognizes that there is corruption in this privation and that evil is not only the absence of what really is but the assault upon it. In his more biblical moments he affirms that the seat of evil is the perversion of the will, and yet he sees this perversion as a turning towards nonbeing.

Thomas Aquinas also stands in the Hellenic tradition in viewing evil in terms of a *privatio boni* — the absence of good. In his thinking sin is only a kind of subtraction from original perfection. He held that whatever is not God must of necessity be imperfect and that the forms of created things constitute a ladder of descending degrees of perfection.

In the modern era Hegel shows the influence of the Platonic approach to evil, although at the same time he seeks to move beyond this to a kind of spiritual monism. For the most part he holds that evil is to be attributed to the raw material that is not yet spirit. A deficiency occurs when the Absolute Spirit separates from Himself, and hence this accounts for the disharmony in the world. Evil is overcome when man and nature are reunited with the Eternal. Hegel's dualism and Platonism are especially evident in his remark: "When Man is only as he is according to Nature, he is evil."[1]

Alfred North Whitehead, who combines aspects of idealism and naturalism, likewise sees evil in terms of deficiency and incomplete good. The disharmony in the world, he affirms, is caused by the inertia of nature. A conflict of values is necessary if there is to be a creative advance into novelty. Like most Platonists he fails to perceive the positive and dynamic character of evil.

Paul Tillich, like Hegel and Plato, sees the source of evil in "meontic" nonbeing *(to mē on)* — nonbeing conceived as some kind of negative force or reality. But in opposition to Greek thought he maintains that being is prior to nonbeing. His Platonism is especially evident when he locates the origin of evil in the transition from essence to existence. Like Plato

[1] Hegel, *Lectures on the Philosophy of Religion*, trans. Speirs, Vol. III, p. 48.

he practically equates existence and estrangement. The biblical roots of Tillich's thought are more apparent in his discussion of the demonic where he views evil as perverse creativity rather than deficiency.

Barth's position is especially interesting in that he speaks out of a profound biblical faith, yet Platonic motifs are very much evident in his thinking in this area. According to Barth evil is excluded by God, but this very exclusion gives it a kind of negative reality. Whereas the good is positive and eternal, evil is negative and temporal. It is like the chaos before creation, having in itself no potency. It is a possibility which God "ignored and left behind." He calls it the Nothingness and describes it as "insubstantial and empty." It does not pose a real threat to God, but it casts a shadow upon His creation, though it is not to be identified with the negative side of His creation. It signifies not simply the absence of good but unremitting opposition to the good. Yet since the advent of Jesus Christ its power lies primarily in the minds of men, for Christ has divested it of any real power that it might have had. Barth declares: "In the light of Jesus Christ there is no sense in which it can be affirmed that nothingness has any objective existence, that it continues except for our still blinded eyes, that it is still to be feared, that it still counts as a cogent factor, that it still has a future, that it still implies a threat and possesses destructive power."[2] In the divine plan Nothingness nevertheless continues to have a semblance of power because of man's slowness in recognizing the triumph of Jesus Christ; yet it cannot be said to have a dynamism or creativity of its own. Barth seeks to overcome dualism by affirming that God is the "ground" and "lord" of the Nothingness, but evil is not to be charged to His creation.

* * * * *

Another kind of metaphysical dualism locates the source of evil in a devil who is co-eternal with God; this position is more Zoroastrian than Christian. In Zoroastrian religion there is arrayed against God a personal evil spirit "Angra Mainyu," who existed with God from the beginning. Mithraism, a syncretistic religion that grew out of Zoroastrianism, also held to this dualistic conception. Plato posited a co-eternal

---

[2]Karl Barth, *Church Dogmatics*, III, 3, p. 363.

devil in his last major work, the *Laws,* but this idea was not basic to his overall system.

In the later middle ages the Albigenses or Cathari contended that the universe was created by two powers, one good and the other evil. God brought into being the mind or spirit; Satan was responsible for the material or visible world. The aim of man should be to cultivate the spiritual side of existence and to negate and suppress the physical. While the Cathari in Italy tended toward the idea that the evil power is a rebellious creature of God, the Cathari in France generally held that it is co-existent with God.

In our time the idea of a co-eternal devil has been given prominence by Edwin Lewis in his *The Creator and the Adversary.* Lewis posits three eternal existents — the divine (the creative); the residue (the uncreative); and the demonic (the discreative). As God acts upon the residue to mold the world, the demonic is also given an opportunity to act. "God cannot act creatively without making it possible for the demonic to act discreatively. Complete divine quiescence means that there is no evil save as dark metaphysical passivity."[3] God is compelled by creative necessity to bring the world into being, although He has a choice about the kind of world that is created. Our criticism of Lewis's theory is that God is no longer omnipotent but finite, even though it is said that He will ultimately triumph over the demonic adversary. Again Lewis fails to perceive the biblical truths that the demonic can also be creative and that this power is by no means subpersonal but highly personal and even angelic with a will and purpose of his own.

Lewis's thought has been strongly influenced by Platonism, though to his credit he seeks to do justice to the biblical concept of a demonic power that stands over against God. But what the Bible posits is a moral dualism in which a holy God is challenged by the sinful rebellion of His creatures; it does not affirm a metaphysical dualism (or pluralism) in which evil is given an eternal or ultimate status. Both the Zoroastrian and Platonic types of dualism controvert the biblical concept of the sovereignty of God.

* * * * *

[3]Edwin Lewis, *The Creator and the Adversary* (N. Y.: Abingdon-Cokesbury, 1948), p. 138.

Still another tradition in philosophy holds that evil has no objective reality, and indeed some of the views discussed in the first section verge towards this. In this approach, which is basically monistic, evil is said to arise from the universal facts of ignorance and individuality. Sin and suffering are explained as a result of each finite center of consciousness mistakenly regarding itself as a locus of abiding value and significance. In philosophical monism finitude and evil are inseparable; evil progressively disappears as finitude disappears. The source of evil is not nonbeing but error, since evil is basically an illusion. Because man's misery lies in ignorance, his need is enlightenment.

This kind of thinking is very prevalent in Hinduism and Buddhism. In orthodox Hinduism men are condemned to live in the illusions of *maya* because of *avidya* (metaphysical ignorance). The world of *maya* does not signify nonexistence but appearance, and salvation lies in perceiving the reality behind the appearance.

There are traces of monism in Hellenistic philosophy also. Sometimes Plato envisaged the material world as only a manifestation of the intelligible world. Plotinus maintained in his *Enneads* that for the gods there is only good, there is no evil. A similar view is expressed by Heraclitus, whose orientation was a naturalistic monism: "For God everything is good and just, while men consider certain things just and certain other things unjust."

Early Stoicism also tended to deny the objective reality of evil. For the Stoics the seeming imperfections of the parts of the universe are necessary and advantageous to the perfection of the whole. In the modern era Leibniz's position is similar, but he insists that evil is not simply a matter of appearance but of reality.

One who stands much closer to this general outlook is Alexander Pope, who ended in a virtual denial of the reality of evil.[4] Pope's view rested upon the all-embracing order of Nature. He held that it is only man's limited perceptions which prevent him from grasping the rational and ordered perfection of the whole. His assertion that "whatever is, is right" amounted to a dismissal of evil as a mere illusion.

Spinoza (d. 1677) is perhaps the best example of how the reality of evil is obscured in a philosophical monistic system.

[4]For the differences between Pope and Leibniz see W. H. Barber, *Leibniz in France* (London: Oxford, 1955), pp. 107-122.

According to Spinoza there is only one substance, God, but he has two sides — thought and extension. Nothing is contingent; all things are determined by the creative activity of God. It therefore follows that good and evil are not objective realities but subjective notions. Evil is that which causes pain or sorrow, but its source is simply inadequate or confused ideas. Nothing is really evil except the absence of understanding. When we come to realize that all things are included in God, the power of evil is dispelled. Imperfections and incongruities are present in the world because the universe necessarily contains as many different kinds of being as possible owing to the overflowing creative activity of God.[5] Since these imperfections are caused by God, however, one may conclude that they are only apparent imperfections and that evil is in reality a lesser good.

The denial of objective evil is also to be found in various other thinkers. For Origen evil is not eternal, so at bottom it is "nonexistent" and "unreal." In Hegel's thought there is no ultimate evil; nonbeing is necessary, since it contributes to the synthesis of becoming. In the Christian Science of Mary Baker Eddy both matter and evil are regarded as nonexistent. What appears to be evil has its origins in "mortal mind," corresponding to Spinoza's inadequate ideas.

Mention should also be made of the philosophy of the Ecumenical Institute, a Protestant religious community in Chicago, whose favorite slogan is, "All that is, is good."[6] The prevailing view is that everyone is "totally accepted," "everything is approved." The thinking of the Institute has been largely shaped by Joseph Mathews, its dean, although others have also made a contribution. Mathews espouses an evolutionary naturalistic monism in which God is pictured as emerging in a new secular culture. The only moral criterion is whether something advances or hinders the cultural and secular revolution of our time. Even while affirming the goodness of the whole world, we are to be deeply impatient with its incompleteness. Man is seen as a co-creator with God

[5] For a discussion of this idea, which Arthur O. Lovejoy calls the principle of plenitude, see his *The Great Chain of Being* (Cambridge: Harvard, 1953).

[6] See Arthur McNally, "Religion for a One-Story Universe" in *The Sign*, Vol. XLVII, No. 6 (Jan., 1968), pp. 30-34; and "Church Funds for Revolution?" in *Christianity Today*, Vol. XII, No. 15 (April 26, 1968), pp. 27, 28. See also *Image*, No. 5 (Oct. 31, 1967).

in bringing order out of chaos and building a viable future. Education and science are highly prized, for it is through these that hopefully a new humanity will be created.

A radical monistic position contradicts not only the witness of faith but also the testimony of experience.[7] To associate evil primarily with a deficiency in understanding or education is to ignore the actual experiences of sorrow, cruelty and pain. If these are considered to be illusions from an ultimate standpoint, they are still very devastating illusions. The assertion (made by Spinoza and others) that they are the necessary products of God's creativity makes them more and not less dreadful.

* * * * *

Somewhat more convincing but still not satisfactory is the position that treats evil as a preparation for the Good. Evil is not denied, nor is it viewed as only appearance, but it is seen as necessary for the realization of greater good. This view is to be found in the idealistic philosophy of Leibniz and Josiah Royce and in the liberal theology of Schleiermacher, Nels Ferré and Daniel Williams. Some evidence of it can be detected in Irenaeus and Whitehead. It is also present in Mormonism, which teaches that the fall of man prepares the way for the good, that Adam's fall was essentially a fall upwards. This general orientation, which is mainly modern, was anticipated in Stoicism and even penetrated medieval spirituality: it was pointed out that the treason of Judas made possible the redemption of Christ. One medieval hymn referred to this treason as "a happy fault" — *O felix culpa*. Supralapsarian Calvinism approaches this position by holding that God decreed the fall so that the elect might be redeemed through Christ.

Leibniz acknowledged the reality of evil, but at the same time he affirmed that this is the best of all possible worlds. Evil, which consists essentially in privation or deficiency, is necessary for the realization of the divine plan. He holds that "the little evil there is, is required for the consummation of the immense good" that is found in the kingdom of God.[8] Evil is reduced to "disorders in the parts" which "enhance

---

[7] Experience can be regarded as a secondary norm in theology but only when it is grounded in the light of faith. It can never be an independent norm.

[8] Philip Wiener, ed., *Leibniz: Selections* (N. Y.: Scribner's, 1951), p. 512.

the beauty of the whole." The metaphysical source of evil lies in an immutable destiny which fixed the choice of God concerning the elements which lay at His disposal for the formation of the world.[9] God, he says, could only choose those things which are compossible or which logically fit together. Given the limitation imposed by the compossibility of contingent truths and the inevitable imperfection of finite reality, God has made the best possible world. Leibniz held to a pre-established harmony between the realms of spirit and matter, but this harmony is not quite perfect. Yet this friction or "dissonance" between the two realms is included in the ordination of God and thus contributes to the final good.

Josiah Royce, whose philosophical position mediates between absolute and personal idealism, maintained that God has willed evil so that greater good might ensue. The goodness of God apart from evil would be the superficial goodness of innocence. Royce acknowledges the reality of evil but insists that passing evils are justified as necessary preludes to the eternal good. Evil brings to sublime fulfillment the perfect goodness of the Absolute. He also speaks of the Absolute struggling against evil and triumphing. Royce has been accused by William James and others of explaining away the harsh reality of evil. This is not his intention, and yet he is compelled to acknowledge that evil, instead of contradicting God's will, is sanctioned by God for His eternal enrichment and perfection.

The theologian Schleiermacher (d. 1834) also understood evil as willed by God for the purpose of a higher good. Sin, which is the dominance of the lower nature within us, is seen as necessary for man's redemption. Sin occurs as a preparation for grace rather than grace occurring to repair the damage caused by sin. Evil has been ordained in corporate life, he says, as a gateway to the good. It should be noted that both Schleiermacher and Royce are monistic and deterministic.

Nels Ferré maintains that evil has no ultimate validity. For him evil is real historically and existentially but not ultimately. Nonbeing is seen to be in the service of being. Evil

---

[9]Although Leibniz wishes to safeguard the freedom of God, it seems that his God is bound if not by a metaphysical then certainly by a moral necessity. Given the nature of the possibilities of existence that God had to deal with, there was only one way in which He could decide that was in keeping with His goodness. For Leibniz this is not simply the best possible but the only possible world.

contributes to the good and therefore is necessary in God's plan. It is through evil that our freedom becomes real and is actually brought under God's indirect control. Sin is regarded as "a sign of life and a precondition for growth."[10] It is also a sign of sickness, but even sickness indicates life. Again, sin is viewed as the dark shadow that sets off the brightness of God's intention of perfect fellowship with His children. "Unless there is sin, grace has no meaning. Unless there is sin, love is never seen in its fullest depth."[11] Ferré appears to view evil and sin mainly in terms of negation.

John Hick takes a similar position in his *Evil and the God of Love*,[12] although at times he seems to reflect some of the concerns of orthodox theology. He is emphatic that evil is not merely negative but that it has "a terrifying positive force in the world." Yet he maintains that evil is necessary for the realization of greater good and that it therefore serves to redound to the glory of God.

In his *God's Grace and Man's Hope* Daniel Williams advances the view that tragedy is a necessary note in the divine symphony. Tragic experience can promote moral maturing both for individuals and whole communities. Past evil, he says, "can enter into the creation of present good by qualifying our moral sensitivity, and deepening our valuation of life."[13] God's work of redemption entails "the transmutation of evil and loss into new good, and higher fulfillment."[14] Williams writes out of the perspective of a process theology.[15]

The difficulty in the above views is that evil no longer seems to stand in diametrical opposition to God's will; instead it is seen (at least by some of these men) as a necessary product of His will. Sin is viewed more in a positive light, as a gateway

[10] Nels Ferré, *A Theology for Christian Education* (Philadelphia: Westminster, 1967), p. 179.
[11] Nels Ferré, *Evil and the Christian Faith* (N. Y.: Harper, 1947), p. 50.
[12] John Hick, *Evil and the God of Love* (N. Y.: Harper, 1966).
[13] Daniel Williams, *God's Grace and Man's Hope* (N. Y.: Harper, 1949), p. 119.
[14] *Ibid.*, p. 54.
[15] In a later article Williams modifies his position slightly. He still holds as integral to the Christian hope that God's redemptive activity does not cancel the loss but takes it up "into a new structure of meaning." Yet he now says that faith does not require us to hold "that every evil is redeemable" and necessarily serves the divine purpose. See his "Tragedy and the Christian Eschatology" in *Encounter*, Vol. XXIV, No. 1 (Winter, 1963), pp. 61-76.

to salvation, rather than as a perversity and wickedness that merit divine wrath and condemnation. Man is no longer envisioned as a sinner in the hands of an angry God (Jonathan Edwards) but as a fallible and errant child of God whose failings are simply stepping stones to his own fulfillment (and in some cases also to God's fulfillment). To understand sin primarily as a precondition for growth and maturity would make it exceedingly difficult to pray as did Luther: "Shield us, Lord, with Thy right arm, / Save us from sin's dreadful harm." The truth in this general position is that God makes the wrath of men to praise Him (Ps. 76:10) and that He does time and again bring good out of evil.

* * * * *

Still another approach to the problem of evil perceives it to be in the very heart of God. A demonic or irrational element is posited within the divine. This view was already present among the Greek tragedians, who tended "to concentrate good and evil at the summit of the divine."[16] The divine malevolence was regarded as having two poles, a personal one in the will of Zeus and an impersonal one in Fate.

Various philosophers in modern times have been attracted to this general position. Boehme and Schelling have referred to an *Ungrund* or abyss in the divine nature which stands at variance with the divine reason. Brightman posits a Given or Surd in the nature of God but not in His will. He sometimes calls this a dysteleological surd, an irrational propensity which God struggles against and overcomes. Berdyaev traces the source of evil to an indeterminacy or irrational freedom which is prior to being. He seems to hold that there is indeterminacy in God Himself, although he also affirms that it is originally found outside of God.[17] For Berdyaev God exercises freedom, but He does not create it. In his *Courage to Be* Tillich speaks of nonbeing within God. John Robinson has constructed a system in which evil is "part of the face of God."[18]

[16]Paul Ricoeur, *The Symbolism of Evil*, trans. Emerson Buchanan (Boston: Beacon, 1967), p. 216.

[17]Berdyaev is probably more dualistic than his precursor Boehme, who envisioned the *Ungrund* totally within God. For Charles Hartshorne's appraisal of Berdyaev's concept of God see Charles Hartshorne and William Reese, eds., *Philosophers Speak of God* (Chicago: University of Chicago, 1953), pp. 285-287; 293-294.

[18]See J. A. T. Robinson, *Exploration into God* (Stanford, Calif.: Stanford University, 1967), pp. 115-118.

A recent work which advances this general viewpoint is Walter Stuermann's *The Divine Destroyer*.[19] In the framework of a panentheistic process philosophy, in which God and the world are depicted as mutually dependent, Stuermann locates evil within a primordial chaos. In his view "God is both Chaos and Order" and therefore includes the whole of creation. Chaos and order are seen as "co-eternal complements in deity." The ground of being is consequently divided against itself; creation is the birth of degrees of order from the womb of chaos. All events and modes of being express the encompassing being and redemptive work of deity. Stuermann boldly disavows the traditional Christian conception of a God who is transcendent and perfect; in its place he postulates an amoral "Chaos-Order."

In biblical faith God is envisioned as wholly free and not hampered by a prior freedom or by a demonic element within His own nature. The biblical God, moreover, is essentially transcendent and not bound or conditioned by His creation except as He wills to be so conditioned. He is also all-holy and all-loving, and it is blasphemous even to imply that evil or malevolence mars the face of God. The Bible is unequivocal in asserting that evil is to be found outside of God, never within Him.

* * * * *

Finally we ought to consider the philosophical views which attribute evil to the imbalance in society or to a disharmony in nature. This general position has won powerful support in the modern world, although it is to be found among the ancients as well, for example, Confucius. Such an approach is basically naturalistic; creaturely life is seen to be the product of natural causes without purpose or direction. Rousseau ascribed the perversion of intrinsically good man to the corrupting influence of human society. Civilization is his *bête noire*; in a similar manner Tolstoy attributes the ills of the world to human culture. A. C. Garnett contends that our social institutions must bear much of the blame: they stifle and distort human life by their injustices. According to Freud the ills of the world are a result of the clash between the Superego (the incorporated standards of society) and the Id (man's natural impulses). In Erich Fromm's view alienation

[19]Walter E. Stuermann, *The Divine Destroyer: A Theology of Good and Evil* (Philadelphia: Westminster, 1967).

and crime are rooted in the social matrix; the alienated person accurately mirrors the alienated condition of his society. Karl Marx traces the conflict in the world to the class struggle; the perfect brotherhood of man will finally become a reality when inequity is overcome.

Naturalistic philosophy invariably fails to discern that the source of evil is in the realm of spirit rather than nature. It cannot account for the fact that when man's bodily and even social needs are satisfied, crime and delinquency still abound. It does not see that behind poverty and inequity lies unbelief, a broken relationship between God and man. The position held by Marxists and various other secular humanists that man can be changed simply by altering his social environment even though containing a modicum of truth does not do justice to all the facts of experience. The modern welfare states are presently plagued by mounting alcoholism, suicide and crime, which are all signs of a disorder within man himself.

* * * * *

Most of the philosophical theories concerning evil that have been discussed tend to be theodicies, that is to say they are attempts to justify God; they seek to explain how evil can co-exist with a divine reality. In some cases these philosophies undertake to justify man; they tend to excuse or rationalize man's evil actions.

All these theories place the blame for evil not on man himself but on some weakness within his nature or some disharmony in the world. Nonbeing or a primeval chaos is invoked in order to account for evil. In some cases God Himself is blamed for man's predicament.

Another characteristic of the philosophical approach to evil is that it seeks to render evil fully intelligible. Evil can be adequately explained because it is a constituent element of the world; it can be traced to causes that are clearly discernible to reason.

What philosophy ends in is a finite God, an amoral God or no God at all. It cannot hold on to the Christian picture of a God who is at the same time perfectly good and omnipotent.

Man is generally seen to be basically good or at least morally neutral. His misdeeds are often attributed either to ignorance or to some deficiency or privation in his nature.

Sometimes it is said that God, not man, is the author or cause of evil. But those philosophers and philosophical theologians who speak in this way then argue that God is not responsible for what He causes. Such thinking only tends to confuse rather than clarify.

Philosophy constantly oscillates between dualism and monism in its attempt to resolve the problem of evil. Either evil is reducible to some given reality such as matter, or it is only appearance and illusion. Sometimes it is held that the world itself or even human existence is evil; at other times evil is said to lie in inadequate ideas or mortal mind. Philosophical explanations have often been exceedingly comprehensive; at the same time they fail miserably to account for the real evil in the world and most of all within man himself.

It should be recognized that many philosophers have been moved to embrace various positions, perhaps because they have perceived that no one position is fully satisfactory. What should be understood is that all philosophical positions have something in common — the attempt to explain away the harsh reality of evil and to deny the inexorable fact of human sin before a righteous and holy God.

THE VIEW OF BIBLICAL FAITH

Biblical faith seeks not so much to explain evil as to overcome it. It also confesses man's involvement in evil. It sounds the call to repentance and to the struggle against evil.

For the evangelical Christian evil is more than a defect: it is a positive, dynamic force. It does not signify a deficiency of being but its perversion and corruption. It is not the absence of what really is but an assault upon it. It consists not in the dearth of rationality but in its misuse. It is not a lack of correspondence to the ideal but a dedication to the wrong ideal.

Biblical Christianity traces evil to sin. Sin, moreover, is not a *deprivatio*, the loss of something good, but a *depravatio*, a wicked corruption. It is not a certain ignorance, as some of the scholastics and also Ritschl maintained, but a wilful transgression of the divine law. Hans Küng gives an accurate description of the biblical meaning of sin:

> Sin, as *aversio a Deo et conversio ad creaturas*, drives directly toward total death and the ruin of the creature. It means much more than deprivation of an ornamental accident or of

a white robe or grace. It means an attack on substance and heart.[20]

Evil springs from anti-being rather than from nonbeing. It is a defect for which we are personally responsible. If we speak of ignorance in the realm of moral decision, then this must be understood as wilful ignorance. While the Greeks viewed such ignorance as the inevitable consequence of the human condition, biblical faith sees it as willing self-deception. Behind ignorance is "hardness of heart" (Eph. 4:18).

In the biblical perspective the seat of evil, instead of being in the world of nature, is to be found in the spirit of man. Evil is not to be traced to the "backward pull of an outgrown good" (Shailer Mathews) nor to the "zoo level" within us (Alan Hunter). Its locus is not in the beastly strain inherited from Neanderthal man (Case) nor in the resistance of our lower nature to God-consciousness (Schleiermacher). Meister Eckhart was nearer to the truth when he said that the body of man was given to purify the soul.

The seat of evil is in man himself — in his heart, the center of his personality. In the words of Jeremiah: "The heart is deceitful above all things, and desperately corrupt; who can understand it?" (Jer. 17:9). Evil consists in the struggle of the soul against God, not in the dichotomy between soul and body. Evil comes from "following the desires of body and mind" (Eph. 2:3). St. Paul constantly contrasts the spirit and the flesh, but by the flesh he almost always means the old man, not the body of man. Also by the spirit he means the new man in Christ, not the mind of man. On those occasions where he equates flesh and body, he makes clear that we should not hate our own flesh but rather nourish and cherish it (Eph. 5:29).

The antithesis, as the Bible understands it, is not between spirit and nature, nor is it between knowledge and ignorance; instead it is between the holy God and man the sinner. The conflict lies in will against will, not force against matter. The core of evil is the lust for power rather than mere concupiscence. Evil is to be associated not with the realization of finite nature but with its distortion.

We must not be beguiled by the subterfuge devised by some of the schoolmen that evil may occur although it does not

[20]Hans Küng, *Justification*, trans. Thomas Collins, Edmund Tolk and David Granskou (N. Y.: Nelson, 1964), p. 175.

exist. We affirm that evil has a frightfully real existence while recognizing that it is temporal, not eternal. It is fallacious to argue that there is only good and the absence of good. Evil is not part of man's essential nature, but it is surely a part of the human condition.[21]

For evangelical theology the ultimate reason for evil remains a mystery. We can understand some things about this mystery, but we cannot fathom it. Gustaf Aulén maintains that there is no rational explanation of evil. In coping with this problem, he says, we must seek to avoid the pitfalls of both an idealistic monism and a metaphysical dualism.

Yet theology insists that some light on the nature of evil is given in revelation. The Scriptures tell us that the source of evil lies in a personal rebellion of the creature against the Creator, but the full explanation of this revolt is not given to us. Man was created in the image of God, but he has marred this image by his defiance and arrogance. Moreover, we are told that an angelic rebellion preceded and prepared the way for the rupture in man's relationship with God. This is to say that there was sin before man; in Genesis this is symbolized by the serpent. We must also insist against Hellenic philosophy that spiritual sin is prior to the chaos or the darkness: indeed the latter grows out of the former. To phrase it another way, moral evil precedes and makes possible physical evil.

The reality of a demonic adversary of God is acknowledged by all theology that claims to be biblical and evangelical. Yet the devil is not a principle of explanation for the existence of evil. Why God permitted the angels to fall and why man yields to their enticements cannot be comprehended by reason. The devil, we are told in the Bible, is an instrument in the hands of God. He is a power who was decisively defeated at the cross of Calvary and who will finally be destroyed. But this is a real objective and dynamic power, not a negative reality shorn of power (as in Barth). The devil still has real power in the world even after the cross; he can even cast Christians into prison (Rev. 2:10; cf. 11:7; 13:7). He is not an empty negation but a "positive negation" (Brunner). Against Edwin Lewis we maintain that he signifies a mixture

[21]It can also be said that evil is part of man's existential nature in that his innate disposition, his inherent tendencies are now turned in the direction of evil.

of creativity and discreativity. Perhaps it is still better to say that the devil embodies misdirected creativity.

Our adversary is not an irrational chaos but an evil spiritual power with purpose and direction. The devil's strategy, to be sure, has an irrational character, since in his inveterate pride he has open contempt for the canons of reason.[22] Yet he is highly endowed with intelligence, and he seeks to use it to further his boundless ambition.

The devil should be understood not as nonbeing but as a spiritual anti-divine being. He is not a negative principle but "perverse and powerful affirmation" (Tillich). He is the personification and embodiment of radical evil. In opposition to Barth we contend that the devil is God's adversary as well as man's. We are not to treat the devil lightly but always to be on watch for him (cf. I Pet. 5:8, 9).

Yet the devil has no ultimate ontological status. He is certainly not co-eternal with God; he is rather a heavenly creature greater than man but much less than God (Mt. 4:1-11; Eph. 6:12). The struggle between God and the devil is not one between equals; indeed, God rules through the devil even against the will of the latter. The devil is not a second god but a fallen angel (cf. Is. 14:12-20; Lk. 10:18; Jude 6; Rev. 12:7-12). Moreover, he is powerless before Jesus Christ, who gives victory to all who call upon His name. As Luther phrased it in his *A Mighty Fortress*, "One little word shall fell him."

Demonic sin is different from human sin in that the latter is always a mixture of weakness and rebellion (Brunner). Demonic sin is sheer rebellion, and this is why it merits total damnation.

Sin, like the devil, cannot be regarded as a rational explanation for evil. It illuminates the problem but does not explain it satisfactorily. The one who sins is required not to explain his sin but to confess it. Bonhoeffer has said that sin is inexcusable and therefore cannot be explained. Whenever we proffer reasons for it, these reasons become excuses, rationalizations that hide the fact that we are personally responsible, that we are guilty.

[22]Among the various meanings of "irrational" are not being endowed with reason or understanding and not being open to reason. The Platonic chaos is irrational in both senses; the demonic strategy in biblical religion is irrational only in the second sense. The devil does not lack the ability to reason, but there is a perversity in his reasoning: his judgments are warped by the lust for power.

Sin is a perversion of our nature, but it is not a product of our nature. It is not human but inhuman, not rational but irrational. The opposite of sin is not virtue but faith. The essence of sin is unbelief, hardness of heart. The prime manifestations of sin are prideful pretension and base sensuality, but the core of sin is a distrustful or perverse will.

The mystery of sin is cogently described by Augustine:

> What was the efficient cause of their evil will? There is none. For what is it which makes the will bad, when it is the will itself which makes the action bad? And consequently the bad will is the cause of the bad action, but nothing is the efficient cause of the bad will.[23]

Some thinkers mistakenly point to original sin as the key that unlocks the mystery of evil. Original sin must be affirmed, but it does not rationally explain evil in man. We cannot blame Adam for our sin, since we ourselves voluntarily assent to temptation. The federal theory in theology, in which the sin of Adam is imputed to members of the human race, patently contradicts Scripture. Man is always personally responsible even though he may be inwardly propelled in a downward direction.

Man has been created not with the freedom to sin but only with the freedom for obedience. There is nothing in man's created nature that makes him peculiarly vulnerable to sin. Sin is not one way besides others but an abyss which lies beyond the possibilities opened to us by God (Barth). This is why Barth calls it "an ontological impossibility." It signifies a misuse rather than a responsible use of our freedom.

Sin at its core is irrational and arbitrary, although man constructs an elaborate rationalization to hide his transgression. Sin has its source in the perversion of the will, not in a lack of rational capability or understanding. Bavinck describes sin as lawlessness and formlessness, but we need also to recognize that it can just as well appear in the guise of "law and order."

The irrational and disruptive character of sin must not be taken to mean that it is devoid of purpose and direction. On the contrary, it frequently entails rational deliberation but

[23] Augustine, *The City of God*, Bk. 12, Ch. 6, in *Basic Writings of Saint Augustine*, ed. Whitney J. Oates (N. Y.: Random, 1948), Vol. II, p. 183.

The Problem of Evil 123

one that lacks a solid rational basis. Sinful reasoning is characterized more by blindness than by wisdom, more by scheming than by disinterested inquiry, but nevertheless it is still reasoning. We must not suppose that sin resides in the passions instead of in reason, for the driving power of sin engulfs the whole man including his rational faculties. Sin is irrational in that it turns reason from its divinely ordained end, the knowledge and service of God. It signifies the perversion and misuse of reason, but not the abandonment of reason. Man's understanding becomes darkened by sin, but it now is exercised in the service of evil (Eph. 4:18, 19). Sin does not have a rational basis, but it assumes a rational veneer.

The predisposition towards sin comes before the act of sin. But man is still responsible for his sin because he wilfully submits to this perverse inclination. The question is not whether he could choose another way but whether he voluntarily assents to the evil way.

The ultimate origin of evil is shrouded in mystery. The secret lies in the heart of God Himself. Yet we must not say that sin itself lies in the heart of God. Sin is what God does not will and what He excludes from His kingdom. God does not create evil, but He uses evil. He is present in evil in order to alleviate and counteract it. He allows it a certain kind of existence in order to overthrow it. The prophet Hosea affirms that God "has torn, that he may heal us; he has stricken, and he will bind us up" (Hos. 6:1).

We must not contend as do some Calvinist scholastics that God causes or decrees sin. Man, not God, is the author of sin. God's deeds are always gracious (Ps. 145:13). Not every action is directly willed by God, though it is surely included in His plan. Not everything that happens is God's intentional will, though nothing happens apart from His will. God has chosen to realize His plan through the prayers and struggles of His children; the final outcome is not in doubt, but the ways by which His purposes will triumph are not absolutely determined. One thing is certain: sin, evil and earthly suffering will finally be destroyed.

In the Bible the blame for evil is placed upon man. He is personally responsible for his predicament, even though the devil provides the occasion for sin. God, on the other hand, is given the credit for overcoming evil. He has done this in the person of Jesus Christ, who by His resurrection from the grave broke man's bondage to the powers of darkness. Man is now free by virtue of the cross of Christ and the gift of the Spirit to fight against evil and to overcome it.

The final solution to the problem of evil from the Christian perspective is practical rather than theoretical. As Langdon Gilkey has put it: "Christian faith deals with the evils of life not so much through an intellectual understanding of their origins as with the hope of their actual resolution and of their ultimate redemption."[24] And in the words of Dr. Forsyth: "The final theodicy is in no discovered system, no revealed plan, but in an effectual redemption. It is not in the grasp of ideas, nor in the adjustment of events, but in the destruction of guilt and the taking away of the sin of the world."[25] He goes on to affirm: "It is not really an answer to a riddle but a victory in a battle. . . . We do not see the answer; we trust the Answerer, and measure by Him."[26]

Christianity offers no all-encompassing explanation of evil. But it does point to the sure and final answer — Jesus Christ. Faith in Christ brings man the freedom to battle against evil. The Christian cannot say, as did the Epicurean Lucretius in his *De rerum natura*, that "only knowledge of nature's forms" dispels the "dread and darkness of the mind." What overcomes our dread and guilt is none other than knowledge of what God has done for us in past history, in the person of Jesus Christ, a knowledge that not only informs but transforms. The solution to the problem of evil lies in the substitutionary atonement, the message that "God was in Christ reconciling the world to himself" (II Cor. 5:19). Evil is not outgrown by evolution but is overthrown by the cross and resurrection of Christ.

While the natural man is continually haunted by the question, "How can God permit evil in the world?", the Christian is captivated by another question: "How can God have such love for a sinner like me?" The love of God is both more significant and more inexplicable than the horror of evil. It is also more powerful, for evil is expelled by love. It is not natural human love that overcomes evil, but the conquering love of God which was victorious in the sacrificial life and death of Jesus Christ. This love is also at work in the lives

[24]Langdon Gilkey, *Maker of Heaven and Earth* (Garden City, N. Y.: Doubleday Anchor, 1965), p. 240.
[25]P. T. Forsyth, *The Justification of God* (London: Independent, 1948), p. 53.
[26]*Ibid.*, pp. 211, 220, 221.

of His followers, enabling them to give of themselves beyond the call of duty. The good news that the Christian faith proclaims is that the light of God's love shines in the darkness of our sinful world, and the darkness cannot overcome it (Jn. 1:5).

SEVEN:

THE MEANING OF TRUTH

TWO APPROACHES TOWARDS TRUTH

In the history of Western thought two general approaches towards truth can be discerned, the theological and the philosophical. Sometimes a static philosophical understanding of truth has penetrated Christian thinking, and the dynamic biblical conception of truth has been obscured.

In biblical theology truth is a liberating word with power given in a divine-human encounter; it is not an idea or principle that can be discovered or conceived. Truth is God in action, God revealing His will and purpose to mankind.

In the Old Testament truth *(emeth, emunah)* basically signifies the faithfulness and resoluteness of God. His truth is closely associated with His steadfast love *(chesed)*, the love that never fails. God's word and His works are also true in the sense of being reliable and trustworthy. The Psalmist declares: "The sum of thy word is truth; and every one of thy righteous ordinances endures for ever" (Ps. 119:160). Moreover, God calls men to enter into the truth, i.e., to keep His commandments, to conform to His will.

The New Testament term for truth, *alētheia,* has a more cognitive connotation, probably under Greek influence, but the ethical and mystical dimensions are also very much present. Truth has an ontological aspect as well, particularly when the references are to divinity.

Truth in the New Testament sense essentially means personal encounter and participation. In order to be in the truth, one must do the truth. In order to have the truth one must receive the truth. Truth cannot be found in abstract speculation and detachment; rather it entails personal participation and surrender.

In classical Greek philosophy *alētheia* means the immutable essence of being behind or within the changing appearances, an essence that is accessible to human reason. This essence is "always and everywhere present and approachable in the depths of things."[1] To speak in the manner of the Fourth Gospel of the "becoming of the truth" understood as a divine act in history goes counter to the Hellenistic mind, for truth is conceived of as the unchangeable order of reality or as eternal being.

Even the pre-Socratic Heraclitus, who envisioned everything in flux, held that the essence of the world is the invisible harmony in which opposites are held together in unity. In addition to being the law for human thinking, the *logos* was seen as the law of nature, the order underlying the rhythm of events, and not a living, personal word from God.

It should be noted that the biblical concept of truth that enters into history and becomes incarnate in human personality is as far removed from the philosophical notions of dynamism and becoming as it is from the philosophical concept of eternal being. Truth in the New Testament is identified not with the most universal (whether this be process or being) but with the historical fact Jesus Christ.

In biblical thought truth is understood as a divine word or act by which men are inwardly changed. It is well to note that the Hebrew word *dabar* signifies God's word as well as His act. The prophets and apostles did not herald a timeless truth, an eternal idea, but the living Word of God, a divine message directed to a concrete human situation. Truth is not an unveiling of a primal Being, as Heidegger contends, but the self-revelation of a living God in a particular person and in a decisive series of events in history.[2]

For the biblical theologian the truth of faith cannot be known apart from decision and commitment: therefore it can be said to be more existential than theoretical. This truth must be received by the whole man and not merely his mind. And yet the reason of man is included; but reason here can only bow before the mystery of this truth; it cannot grasp or possess it. The truth of faith can be known, but it cannot be comprehended.

The deepest meaning of truth in the biblical sense is where

[1] Paul Tillich, *The Protestant Era*, trans. James L. Adams (Chicago: University of Chicago, 1948), p. 30.

[2] Heidegger's position is partly a return to and partly a correction of the Greek philosophical meaning of truth. See Martin Heidegger, *Existence and Being*, Introduction by Werner Brock (Chicago: Regnery, 1949), pp. 117-167; 292-324. See also Laszlo Versényi, *Heidegger, Being, and Truth* (New Haven: Yale, 1966). Heidegger's affinities seem to be with mysticism.

it is conceived of as a Person. Indeed, both Jesus Christ and the Holy Spirit are referred to as the truth (Jn. 14:6; I Jn. 5:7). It was said of Jesus that he was "full of grace and truth" (Jn. 1:14; cf. Eph. 4:21). In Christ the truth was embodied in flesh.

The Word of God signifies both person and act; indeed, it can be equated with God in action. We should also point out that it includes the meaning of this act; indeed, revelation entails God speaking as well as God acting. God not only discloses Himself but also His will and purpose for the world, but this meaning can be apprehended only in the act of personal surrender.

How very different is the traditional philosophical understanding of truth. Instead of truth as a person, truth is envisioned as idea — *veritas* (the virtual Latin equivalent of the Greek philosophical meaning). Philosophers have in mind discursive, propositional truth arrived at by analysis and experimentation. Truth is either right conception or right perception. It is an idea that either corresponds with the object-world or mirrors the whole of reality.

Whereas the knowledge of God in Christian theology is the knowledge of personal acquaintance, such knowledge in the mainstream of philosophy "is a scientific knowledge, a knowledge of conclusions which are derived from self-evident principles and factual experience."[3] While philosophy generally understands God as an extension of man's reason or experience, the God of theology always stands over against the world of man's experience.

The theological approach does not exclude propositional truth, but it places it in the service of personal truth. Secular or philosophical meanings of truth can sometimes be appropriated by the church, but they will be transformed in the process. We shall try to show how this transformation takes place in the succeeding sections. The theories that will be discussed do not exhaust the philosophical options, but these are the salient types that have recurred ever again in the history of philosophy.

THE CORRESPONDENCE THEORY

In philosophy the correspondence theory of truth signifies the correspondence of an idea and its object. Truth is said

---

[3] Henri Renard, S. J., in the foreword to M. R. Holloway, *An Introduction to Natural Theology* (N. Y.: Appleton-Century-Crofts, 1959), p. ix.

to lie in a correlation or agreement between concept and thing. This type of approach is most often associated with empiricism and modern realism. In the words of one contemporary empiricist: "Truth is the correct designation and description of features of the world."[4]

The correspondence theory generally presupposes a dualistic view of reality; there is the world of ideas or universals and that of things or particulars. In the more idealistic type of philosophy correspondence means the conformation of appearance to reality.

Christian theologians can also speak of correspondence, but they have in mind the correspondence of our thinking and the meaning of the Gospel. But the Gospel is not an object at our disposal but rather a personal message addressed not simply to the mind but to the heart of man, that is, the very center of his personality. It presupposes participation and commitment. In the moment of decision not only our mind but our whole being is taken up into the Gospel.

For biblical faith correspondence means not simply an agreement between our ideas and the Gospel but a conforming of our total life-orientation to the demands of the Gospel. This, of course, includes our thought-world. Yet reason must not be viewed as a correlative of revelation but instead as a servant of revelation. Moreover, our reasoning is brought into conformity with the Gospel by the power of the Gospel itself and not merely by an act of the will.

Truth for the Christian is not so much the factual as the eventful. Yet truth is not simply that which makes an impression upon the mind of man but that which effects his total conversion to the living God. Truth gives man not only a new horizon but a new nature, a new being. Truth is not external history as such but God in history, history seen through the eyes of God, history seen in the perspective of divine revelation. Truth is more than a momentous occasion: it is the divine significance of this occasion as it bears upon the destiny of man.

Some modern philosophers, in order to get away from the dualism of thought and thing associated with the correspondence theory, have proposed new terms in place of correspondence. G. T. W. Patrick suggests "fidelity": for him truth is "fidelity to objective reality." John Wisdom prefers the

[4]Henry Nelson Wieman, *The Wrestle of Religion with Truth* (N. Y.: Macmillan, 1927), p. 213.

term "accordance"; thus we can say that "our judging accords with reality." The theologian can certainly speak of "fidelity" in this connection, but he will mean fidelity to the living God in whose light we see the objective world correctly. As the Psalmist affirms: "In thy light do we see light" (Ps. 36:9). Again, when our minds are brought into accordance with the mind of Christ, then our judging indeed accords with reality.

The correspondence theory may also have a place in the Christian doctrine of God. In the Bible, and this is particularly evident in the Old Testament, God always corresponds to Himself, He is true to Himself. This means that He is also faithful to His Word and to His covenant. God's children are expected to be faithful to the covenant because He is faithful. Correspondence in this context means devotion and fidelity to the ordinances of God.

THE COHERENCE THEORY

According to the coherence theory in philosophy, the meaning of the part can only be understood through the meaning of the whole. The measure of truth is the illumination and integration of our total experience in the light of an overarching idea or principle. A proposition is said to be true if it fits into an all-encompassing logical system. As Whitehead has put it, "there is a truth relation when two composite facts participate in the same pattern."[5] Truth is here understood as a self-sustaining system of inner relations. There is a virtual identification between our ideas and their empirical references.

Those philosophies that have leaned upon the coherence theory of truth have usually tended towards monism, which holds that thought and reality are one and the same. Absolute idealism is perhaps the most consistent type of monism, but all idealism has monistic tendencies and generally rests its case upon rational coherence. The criterion in idealistic, monistic philosophy is "the systematic coherence of the All" or "experience as a whole." The idealistic system is implicative: each phase of the argument is shown to imply all the rest. The organized whole includes and determines the parts; in-

[5] Alfred North Whitehead, *Adventures of Ideas* (N. Y.: Macmillan, 1933), p. 310. Whitehead's theory incorporates idealistic as well as naturalistic motifs. It should be noted that his God is both static and dynamic. His affinities to Plato can be seen in his epistemology and ontology.

deed, it can be said that the whole is more than the parts.

Theologians may also speak of the illumination and integration of our total experience, but they will go on to emphasize that our experience stands in need of transformation as well. The criterion for the integration of our experience, moreover, is not some overarching metaphysical principle or idea but rather God's reconciling deed in biblical history. Only God's self-disclosure in Jesus Christ can make sense of our experience and give our lives meaning and direction.

The theologian will warn that we cannot perfectly resolve the antinomies and contradictions of life in any system of meaning; there are some mysteries that simply cannot be comprehended and that must be accepted on faith alone. The absolute synoptic perspective lies outside our grasp, although we can show that the suprarational affirmations of faith give meaning to the seeming contradictions that run through life and history.

Theology also insists that the meaning of the part can be understood only through the meaning of the Word, which is not identical with the whole of the reality that is generally experienced but which enters our reality from the beyond. By the Word we do not mean the universal Logos that resides in all things but rather the Word become flesh, the event of God becoming man in Jesus Christ. It is not simply the Word as an idea but the Word as personal address which gives meaning to our lives and throws light upon the perennial questions of man.

In contrast to speculative philosophy, theology recognizes that there are things and events that are absolutely unique and therefore cannot be coordinated into any rational system. The event of God becoming man in Jesus Christ is one such event; it is incomparable and unrepeatable and thereby eludes rational comprehension. But once it is accepted, it then makes more sense of the human predicament than do purely philosophical perspectives. The Christian theologian can only affirm with Forsyth that though "we do not see the answer," we must "trust the Answerer and measure by Him."[6] We do not have the final answer to all of life's riddles, but we know the One who is the Answer and in His light we are able to find our way in this present darkness.

[6] P. T. Forsyth, *The Justification of God*, pp. 220, 221.

The idealist begins with universal principles and then proceeds by the method of deduction to logical conclusions. The theologian, on the other hand, seeks to glean meanings from the written and oral testimony to a particular historical revelation. Whereas idealistic philosophy follows "the logic of deduced conclusions," the Christian faith adheres to "the logic of adduced meanings" (Arthur Holmes), inasmuch as it deals with unique events and persons.

While the system of an idealistic philosophy is implicative, that of the Christian faith is open-ended and paradoxical. Seemingly contradictory affirmations are held together in creative tension rather than resolved into a higher synthesis. Faith deflects logic from drawing conclusions that might very well be implied in the guiding principles of faith but which are nevertheless unwarranted in the light of the total biblical witness. Faith, for example, affirms the predestination of all believers to eternal life, but it is unbiblical to infer from this double predestination, the view that certain people are foreordained to hell even before they have had the opportunity to believe. Strict logic supports the decree of double predestination, but the mystery of predestination, like all the other mysteries of faith, is not amenable to syllogistic reasoning or what Brunner calls "straight-line" inference.

THE PRAGMATIC THEORY

The pragmatic theory as this is understood in philosophy says that truth is a matter of fulfilling genuinely human needs and solving the perplexing problems in life. According to the pragmatist that which works to satisfy our deepest needs and integrate our experience is true. In other words, the truth is that which serves to give one meaning and purpose. One will know the truth by its effects upon him. The method of discovering truth is "trial and error"; the key word is "satisfaction." An idea is true if it gives guidance to desired and satisfying consequences. It must be tested and validated as we apply it in daily life. William James put it this way: "True ideas are those that we can assimilate, validate, corroborate and verify. False ideas are those that we can not."[7]

The principal question that is asked by the pragmatist is not "What does it mean?" but rather "What is it supposed to do?" The meaning of an idea indeed lies in its purpose or in

[7]William James, *Pragmatism* (London: Longmans, Green, 1914), p. 201.

the way it works to fulfill its purpose. Pragmatism as a philosophy is empirical in that it does not appeal to any reality that transcends experience; it is contextual in that it tries to see every problem in its concrete social and behavioral setting; it is existential in that it holds that truth is discovered not by detached observation but by total human involvement.

Pragmatism is probably the dominant philosophy in contemporary American culture. Not timeless truth but workable truth is the concern of most Americans. It is not the problem of the One and the Many but the problem of a better life for myself and my neighbor that occupies our attention. The criterion for truth is whether it serves the human enterprise, whether it has beneficial effects upon the human community.

Theologians can also be pragmatists — up to a point. The need that Christianity speaks about, however, is liberation, not integration or satisfaction. Man's greatest need is to be born again rather than to realize his natural potential. Instead of saying "that which works," the theologian will point to "He who works," for truth is a Person. Jesus Himself laid down a pragmatic criterion when He said: "You will know them by their fruits" (Mt. 7:16; cf. Lk. 6:43-44). Yet Jesus was speaking not about ideas that are true but about people who are in the truth. Moreover, the fruits that He had in mind were works of love, and the hallmark of love is self-denial, not self-fulfillment or self-satisfaction (Mt. 16:25, 26). Paul becomes somewhat of a pragmatist when he points to the lives of the Corinthian Christians as his "letters of recommendation" (II Cor. 3:1-3), but like Jesus he regards such fruits as a confirmation or, still better, an illumination of the truth of the Gospel rather than the basis of this truth.

Pragmatic philosophy still retains the classical Greek notion of ideas that are true, though it seeks to relate these to the work-a-day world in which men find themselves. Christian theology, on the other hand, understands truth primarily in terms of the person of Jesus Christ and His self-revelation. Granted that we might have true ideas about a person, we cannot actually know him until he addresses us and thereby reveals himself to us.

THE MYSTICAL THEORY

Still another theory of truth in the history of philosophy is the mystical theory, sometimes also called the intuition theory, although the latter term is more inclusive. Here the locus of truth is an identification with essential being or the whole of reality. Truth consists in participation in the underlying unity that lies behind the world of appearances. This ultimate reality or primal unity has been called by various names in the history of philosophy: the World Soul, the One, the ground of being, Being, Being-itself, the Absolute Spirit, the Comprehensive, the Eternal Rest, the Godhead and the undifferentiated unity. The criterion of truth is immediacy; the experience of truth is self-verifying in character. In the experience of identity the subject-object relationship is transcended. One is now no longer related to an objective world, but he has been taken up into the encompassing fullness of the deity.

For mysticism truth is discovered in the depths of one's soul rather than in a historical event or an external authority. The mystic, even the Christian mystic, looks not to a divine revelation in history but to the inner light. Meister Eckhart attached much more importance to the birth of the Son in the soul than to the historical incarnation of Christ.

Theologians can also speak of identification, although they seek to distinguish it from "identity," a term that is in common use in mysticism. But biblical faith does not seek identification with the Godhead or being in itself but with the New Being, Jesus Christ.

The term "participation" is also used in Christian theology, but here again the meaning is slightly changed. The Christian is said to participate in the passion and victory of Christ, not in the essence of God. In faith there is no absorption into the being of God but instead a union with the will of God. We enter into the fellowship of the sufferings of Christ, but we do not lose our identity in union with Christ.

Christian theology also affirms a transcending of the subject-object cleavage in faith. But instead of an identity with some primal reality behind the dualism of subject and object, Christian faith envisions a subject-Subject relationship. We now enter into relations with another Subject, a divine Thou, and through this relationship we are enabled to treat other persons also as subjects rather than objects. The subject-object antithesis is replaced by personal fellowship.

In contrast to mysticism biblical faith speaks of a union not with the deepest within but with the Christ within, who is other than ourselves. According to Tillich self-discovery is

God-discovery. We contend that when one has discovered God, he has discovered someone other than himself.

Like the mystical experience the experience of faith is self-authenticating, but this experience is occasioned by the hearing of the Word of God. Although we have a direct experience of God in faith, this experience is always tied to a knowledge of what God has done for us in Jesus Christ, witnessed to in the Bible and the sermon. Again, we experience not God in Himself but God as He relates Himself to man in Jesus Christ. Man through his sin is not able to come before the holy God and stands in need of someone who will intercede for him. Biblical faith, unlike mysticism, points to the necessity for a mediator through whom we can gain access to God.

Whereas Christian theology views the knowledge of God as something given in revelation, mysticism tends to see truth hidden in the depths of the soul and waiting only to be discovered. As Brunner affirms: "In the idealist-mystic teaching, knowledge is neither revelation nor decision, but a perception of something that was always 'there,' ready to be perceived."[8]

THE THEOLOGICAL UNDERSTANDING OF TRUTH

It can be seen that the correspondence and pragmatic theories of truth have an affinity with the cosmological philosophy of religion, and the coherence and mystic theories are more closely associated with the ontological approach.[9] In the cosmological approach knowledge of God is attained by looking at the outside world and inferring the existence of God from His effects in nature. In the ontological approach ultimate reality or God is to be found by looking within the soul and discovering there an awareness of the unconditional or an idea of perfection. The correspondence and pragmatic theories gain a hearing in the circles of empiricism and naturalism whereas the coherence and mystical theories find their natural home in idealism and mysticism.

The theological approach must not be confused with either the cosmological or ontological approaches. For the theologian God is to be found first of all neither within the self nor

[8] Emil Brunner, *Truth as Encounter* (Philadelphia: Westminster, 1964), p. 90.
[9] For the differences between the cosmological and ontological approaches see Paul Tillich, "The Two Types of Philosophy of Religion," *Union Seminary Quarterly Review*, I (May, 1946), 3-13.

in the world but in His Word, which then throws light upon His activity in nature.

Moreover, for the theologian truth is to be identified neither with the most universal nor with the relatively singular. Rather we find truth in the absolutely singular, the person of Jesus Christ. Theology is oriented about the God-Man, not an abstract idea of God. This is why Barth has called the theological approach "unionistic" as over against idealistic or materialistic, since it is based upon the Word becoming flesh (Jn. 1:14).

Tillich grounds his theology in the biblical picture of Christ, but this is still an idea and not a divine deed or personage in history. In my opinion, Tillich has not overcome his dependence upon idealistic philosophy and thereby fails to give an authentically biblical understanding of Christ.

The truth about God and man cannot be discovered nor conceived; it must be revealed. Truth is not "something effected by man, a successful adjustment between his purposes and the world," as the pragmatist contends;[10] rather it is a word spoken by God which contravenes and judges the purposes of man. The validation of truth comes in its being disclosed, accepted and obeyed. The subject is elected and grasped by the truth. Moreover, he is established in the truth by daily communion with the One who is the truth.

Truth is not to be found in a venture that entails absolute uncertainty (as in existentialism) nor in a feeling of absolute dependence (as in the mysticism of Schleiermacher); instead it is to be found in an absolute receptivity towards its Object, the living Christ. Truth is not procured by man through speculation, but it is received by man in a moment of total surrender. It consists not so much in a rational conclusion as in a life and death decision.

The truth of the Gospel cannot simply be handed over to another person; the truth itself must seize the person and turn him in an altogether new direction. Truth possesses the man and not vice versa. Truth must not be allowed to petrify into dogma, even though dogma can express and convey truth. Küng rightly observes that "truth is not like stone," but it is "a thing of the spirit" which is lost if it is permitted to harden into a dogmatic formula.[11]

[10]William Kelly Wright, *A History of Modern Philosophy* (N. Y.: Macmillan, 1960), p. 520.
[11]Hans Küng, *The Church* (N. Y.: Sheed and Ward, 1967), p. 290.

Theology recognizes that not only events but also ideas can be true insofar as they point beyond themselves to the One who is the Truth. St. John boldly affirms that he has given a true testimony (Jn. 21:24; III Jn. 12). Our ideas in order to be true must be anchored in and informed by the Word of God who embodies the fullness of truth. They can be said to be true in a derivative or relative sense inasmuch as they are dependent for their validity on Jesus Christ and His revelation. Moreover, there is never an identity between our ideas and God's ideas, as some idealists maintain, but at the most a correspondence or analogical relation. Our ideas cannot encompass the truth, but they can reflect it and be open to it and thereby be a channel by which the truth is conveyed.

Truth in the biblical sense does not simply give man new knowledge, but a new life characterized by freedom, purpose and vision. As our Lord declared: "'If you continue in my word, you are truly my disciples, and you will know the truth, and the truth will make you free'" (Jn. 8:31, 32). To know the truth means to be awakened spiritually, to be brought into a new relationship with God. It means that one is now free from the terror of sin and at peace with God, who is both just and loving. Knowing the truth is not so much an intellectual matter as a matter of personal salvation. Some philosophers also speak in this way, but the salvation that they envision is not justification before a holy God but a transcending of the limitations of the self.

While theological and philosophical systems are constantly open to revision, truth itself is unshakable and irrevocable, though not as a timeless idea that exists in its own right but as a divine plan or purpose that cannot be annulled. The ways by which God deals with men are amenable to alteration, but His ultimate purposes are fixed. The prophet affirms: "The Lord of hosts has sworn: 'As I have planned, so shall it be, and as I have purposed, so shall it stand'" (Is. 14:24). And again: "The grass withers, the flower fades; but the word of our God will stand forever" (Is. 40:8).

Truth is both ontological and personal, and therefore its appropriation means an alteration in our being as well as in our personal attitudes. When we are in the truth, we then begin to reflect our new being in Christ. To receive the truth means to be given a new spirit and a new heart (Ps. 51:10).

Truth also has both objective and subjective aspects. Its

basis or ground is objective, but its appropriation is subjective. When Kierkegaard proclaimed that "Truth is subjectivity," his intention was not to deny that truth is rooted in objective reality but that truth can be apprehended in a purely intellectual or objective manner. In his view: "Christianity exists before any Christian exists, it must exist in order that one may become a Christian, it contains the determinant by which one may test whether one has become a Christian, it maintains its objective subsistence apart from all believers, while at the same time it is the inwardness of the believer."[12] How different is this perspective from that of the secular existentialists of our time who reject the validity of any truth outside the thinking and acting self.[13]

The theologian could not say with William James: "I believe in God, not because I have experienced his presence, but because I need it so that it must be true." Still less could he concur in the judgment of Karl Jaspers: "I do not even know whether I believe; however, such faith . . . strikes me as meaningful."[14] It is not vital anguish or human need that drives man towards the Gospel but divine grace. True faith in God begins only when the Word of God personally addresses man, convicts him of his sin and grants him the assurance of forgiveness. Faith is not a leap in the dark but heartfelt confidence and trust in the mercy and love of God. We believe in Christ not because He might be the truth but because we know from the depths of our being that He is the truth. We make the venture of faith not *as if* Christ were the Son of God but because we *know* that He is God's Son, for we have experienced His love in our hearts. As the apostle affirmed: "But I am not ashamed, for I *know* whom I have believed, and I am sure that he is able to guard until that Day what has been entrusted to me" (II Tim. 1:12, *italics mine*).

The theologian also asserts that outside of revelation man exists in untruth. The man without faith is bound to what Luther called the *cor curvum in se* (the heart turned in upon itself). In Bonhoeffer's words:

[12] Søren Kierkegaard, *On Authority and Revelation*, trans. Walter Lowrie (Princeton: Princeton University, 1955), p. 168.
[13] See J. Rodman Williams, *Contemporary Existentialism and Christian Faith* (Englewood Cliffs, N. J.: Prentice-Hall, 1965), pp. 1-23.
[14] Karl Jaspers, *Way to Wisdom*, trans. Ralph Manheim (New Haven: Yale, 1951), p. 95.

> Godless thought — however ethical — remains self-enclosed. Even a critical philosophy is powerless to place the philosopher in truth, because its criticism issues from itself. . . . Revelation is its own donor, without preconditions, and alone has the power to place in reality. From God to reality, not from reality to God, goes the path of theology.[15]

This is not to deny that secular philosophy may incidentally reflect the truth of God which is imbedded in the creation, but its overall orientation is nevertheless incurably anthropocentric. We also affirm that the relative truth within philosophy, and indeed within the realm of common sense as well, has its validity only because it rests upon the absolute truth revealed in Jesus Christ. This is to say the truth that theology proclaims is the ground of the truth that the philosopher may occasionally stumble upon in his reflection. Though the wise of the world may discover segments of the truth, the truth itself is hidden from them. Moreover, the truth that they have is always placed in the service of untruth because man and not God is the center of attention.

In the Book of Revelation Jesus Christ is pictured as saying: "Behold, I stand at the door and knock; if any one hears my voice and opens the door, I will come in to him and eat with him, and he with me" (3:20). Christ is knocking at the door of every soul, but sin prevents man from hearing Him. It is only when our spiritual ears are opened by the regenerating work of the Spirit that we can hear our Lord and invite Him into our abodes. Both faith and the condition to receive it come from the holy God. This is why liberating, saving truth is not a live option or one possibility among others; it must be given to man by God Himself.

---

[15]Dietrich Bonhoeffer, *Act and Being*, trans. Bernard Noble (N. Y.: Harper, 1956), p. 89.

EIGHT:
FAITH AND MYSTICISM

FAITH VS. MYSTICAL RELIGION

Evangelical theologians have always sought to distinguish faith from mystical religion. Even where the mystical element in Christian spirituality is acknowledged, they have taken pains to point out that Christianity is not mysticism. John Wesley wrote that "all the other enemies of Christianity are triflers: The Mystics are the most dangerous of its enemies. They stab it in the vitals."[1] In the words of Benjamin Warfield: "We may be mystics, or we may be Christians. We cannot be both. And the pretension of being both usually merely veils defection from Christianity."[2] Among other evangelically oriented scholars who have taken a forthright stand against mysticism are Karl Barth, Anders Nygren, Reinhold Niebuhr, Emil Brunner and Friedrich Heiler.

Roman Catholic theology has been more open to mysticism, and yet warnings can also be heard from this side. Hans Küng maintains that whereas the God of mysticism is basically passive, the God of the Bible is ever active, calling men to obedience.[3] Baron von Huegel, a noted Catholic devotional writer, declares: "The fact is that Pure Mysticism is but Pantheism; and that Pantheism is, on principle and incurably, a non-moral, a supra-moral and a non-personalist position, within which there is really no place for a distinct and definite God, for Sin, for Contrition, for the sense of our being creatures, and for Adoration."[4]

That there are tensions between what might be called "faith piety" (Heiler) and mystical spirituality is incontestable.

[1] John Wesley, *The Journal of John Wesley*, Standard Edition, ed. Nehemiah Curnock (London: Epworth, 1938), Vol. I, p. 420.
[2] Benjamin Warfield, *Studies in Tehology* (N. Y.: Oxford, 1932), p. 666.
[3] Hans Küng, *Freedom Today*, trans. Cecily Hastings (N. Y.: Sheed and Ward, 1966), pp. 136, 137.
[4] Baron Friedrich von Huegel, *The Life of Prayer* (London: Dent, 1960), p. 43.

Whether there is a clear-cut contradiction between these two types of religion remains to be seen.

Mysticism is derived from the Greek *mystikos,* which simply means "hidden" or "secret." The Greek word *mueō* means to shut one's eyes and mouth. Mysticism has consequently come to signify a direct experience or awareness of the divine presence, an experience that bypasses the senses. It is a type of experience in which the subject-object antithesis is transcended. Some mystics have described it as the experience of "identity" or "identification" in which man becomes united with the ground of being (which is at the same time the ground of the self).

Faith is derived from the Greek *pistis,* meaning heartfelt trust and confidence in a living Savior. Faith is not an intuitive knowledge, nor a knowledge of identity, but a personal relationship, one that entails inner conviction, trust and obedience. In this chapter faith shall always be understood as personal commitment to the incarnate God, trust in Jesus Christ as Savior and Lord.

Mysticism might be described in two different ways. It first refers to an immediate experience of the presence of God. But it has also come to mean a system of thought, a philosophy of life, a type of religion. In this sense mysticism is an ideology that competes with the Christian faith. According to Köberle it can be defined as a "form of piety that finds its highest satisfaction in the *immediate* union of the soul's essence with the divine essence."[5]

German scholars have distinguished the two aspects of mysticism by the terms *Mystik* and *Mystizismus.* The former refers to a type of experience; the latter connotes a type of religion or piety or philosophy. As a type of religion mysticism is oriented about the mystic way, the stages that lead to the vision of God — purgation, illumination, union and ecstasy. Mysticism here is seen as a pathway to salvation; in this connection it entails asceticism, spiritual exercises that enable one to mount the ladder to perfection. Much of the terminology in mystical literature is derived from Platonism and Neo-Platonism. Another dominant influence has been the religions of the East, Hinduism and Buddhism. Heiler even maintains that mysticism in the West has Indian sources. Christian mysticism is a result of the fusion of evangelical biblical faith

[5]Adolf Köberle, *The Quest for Holiness,* trans. John Mattes (Minneapolis: Augsburg, 1938), p. 9.

with Platonic and Neo-Platonic (and perhaps also Oriental) philosophy.

Christian faith opposes *Mystizismus,* mysticism understood as an ism or ideology or philosophy of life. Mysticism in this respect is "the perennial philosophy," the ever present temptation to transcend the bonds of the flesh, to overcome the restrictions of finitude, and to lose oneself in the Absolute.

It is well to note some differences between faith in the biblical sense and mysticism as a type of religion. First the foundation of faith is an objective historical revelation, the revelation that took place in the life and death of Jesus Christ. The foundational criterion in mysticism is religious experience. As Spencer observes: "For the mystic, whatever his professed creed, final authority lies in his own experience."[6]

Again, faith is a gift of God whereas mystical rapture is to some degree a work of man. To be sure, the final union with God is regarded as a divine gift, at least in the circles of Christian mysticism, but it is held that one can prepare oneself for this union by spiritual exercises.

Faith is a response to Agape, the outgoing love that God has for man, whereas mystical religion is centered in Eros, the self-regarding love that prompts man to seek union with the divine. Faith speaks of the descent of God to man, while the concern in mysticism is man rising to God.

Faith is rational as well as experiential. It involves an assent to the truth about Christ as well as a personal acquaintance with Him. Mystical experience, on the other hand, is ineffable or inexplicable. While the message that faith assents to is in itself rational (although it can only be known brokenly by human reason), the mystical experience is basically non-rational. One interpreter of mysticism contends that "it entirely transcends our sensory-intellectual consciousness."[7] This experience does contain a noetic quality, however, but the knowledge that it brings is self-knowledge, not a knowledge of the will and purpose of God.

Faith is based on an exclusive message; mystical religion, on the other hand, is almost always syncretistic. The mystic appeals to a universal experience present in all religions. The Christian mystic contends that the union with God is most

[6]Sidney Spencer, *Mysticism in World Religion* (Baltimore: Penguin, 1963), p. 337.
[7]Walter T. Stace, *The Teaching of the Mystics* (N. Y.: Mentor, 1960), p. 15.

manifest in the person of Jesus, but all men can enter into this union to some degree.

Whereas faith is dualistic and personalistic, mystical religion is monistic and pantheistic. Schleiermacher described the mystical experience as "immediate self-consciousness." The lines between God and the self are obscured in mysticism, while faith holds that the holy God stands over against man the sinner.

Mysticism can also take the form of panentheism, in which God and the world are depicted as mutually dependent rather than identical. God is in the world, and the world is in God, but neither is to be equated with the other. John Robinson contends that mysticism seeks to break through the impasse between subject and object "to a non-duality, to a *coincidence* of opposites, to a higher all-embracing unity."[8] In panentheist terminology the mystic goal is "identification without identity," "a 'coinherence' of the divine Spirit with the human."[9]

Whereas the mystic way leads from purgation to illumination and finally to union, the way of faith consists in daily repentance under the cross on the basis of a prior union with Christ through His Spirit. Faith upholds not a spiritual ascent to the Godhead but a constant humbling of oneself before the high and holy God. It is not self-fulfillment or self-realization but self-denial that characterizes the way of faith. Mystics also speak of self-denial, but only as a means to self-realization. They may well engage in rigorous practices of mortification but for the ultimate benefit of the self.

The soul of faith is supplication, heartfelt petition to a personal God. Mystical prayer, on the other hand, consists in meditation and contemplation upon the being of God. Mystics generally denigrate petitionary prayer as unworthy of the spiritual man. Eckhart could say that the "pure in heart" do not pray in the sense of asking anything from God; they seek "only to be uniform" with Him.[10] For the mystic the aim is to be wholly conformed to God's will and empty of all natural desire; the man of faith, on the contrary, seeks to change what seems to be God's immediate will so that His final will might more readily be accomplished. Prayer for the latter is not a passive resignation to God's will but a

---

[8] J. A. T. Robinson, *Exploration into God* (Stanford, Calif.: Stanford University, 1967), p. 154.

[9] *Ibid.*, p. 128.

[10] Raymond B. Blakney, trans. and ed., *Meister Eckhart* (N. Y.: Harper, 1941), pp. 88, 89.

wrestling with God so that one might discover the best way in which His will can be fulfilled. In biblical religion God's ultimate will is unchangeable, but the method by which He implements His purposes in the world can be altered by the prayers of the faithful.

FAITH AS EXPERIENCE

Faith is not based upon experience but upon the Word of God; yet faith is realized in experience. Faith is a commitment that entails decision, trust and obedience, but it also includes experience. Indeed, it is a commitment made possible by experience. Decision and trust comprise one dimension of faith; experience signifies the other dimension.

The experience of faith has a certain similarity to the mystical experience. Indeed, faith entails not only personal encounter but also ecstatic rapture (although the latter is not integral to faith). It is not only an experience of conversion but also one of union. In faith we are engrafted into the body of Christ; we become branches of the living vine (Jn. 15:1-6).

It should be recognized that faith is a direct experience of God as well. The Reformed theologian Francis Turretin contends that the Spirit in effectual calling not only acts mediately through the Word but He also acts immediately with the Word on the soul so that conversion is necessarily effected.[11] The Lutheran scholar Gustaf Aulén also holds that God works immediately upon man, although always in connection with external means.[12] There is no direct perception of God, but there is an immediate experience of God through His Spirit. One basic difference between the "evangelical experience" and the mystical experience (as understood in classical mysticism) is that in the former the encounter with God is seen to be a work of His Spirit both within and without. Again, we are said to encounter not God in Himself but God in His Son, God revealed in Jesus Christ. Also for the man of faith the Word of God (both written and proclaimed) is the occasion or means by which we are confronted by the divine presence.

[11]Francis Turretin, *Institutio*, XV, iv, 23. Cf. Heinrich Heppe, *Reformed Dogmatics*, ed. Ernst Bizer (London: Allen and Unwin, 1950), p. 521.
[12]Gustaf Aulén, *The Faith of the Christian Church*, trans. Eric Wahlstrom and G. Everett Arden (Philadelphia: Muhlenberg, 1948), pp. 45, 46.

Faith and Mysticism

In the experience of faith we are brought into relationship with the divine Thou, but He is enveloped in mystery. There is meaning within this mystery, but this meaning is not accessible to the senses; it must be given directly by God.

It might be said that the experience of faith is a transfigured or personalized mystical experience. Or still better it is a transmystical experience in that it goes beyond the universal mystical awareness of the presence of God. In one sense it may be considered the only authentic mystical experience because we encounter not simply the void or the nothingness but the living God.

In order to make our comparison of faith and mysticism more specific, we shall proceed to examine the four basic elements in mysticism and then ascertain whether they are also present in faith. First there is in all mysticism an immediate awareness of a higher power. Second, there is an encounter with mystery, thereby attesting to the ineffability of this experience. Again, mysticism is characterized by a sense of union or identity with this higher power or spiritual presence. Finally, mysticism is associated with a feeling of beatitude or inner peace; mystics call this "ineffable peace."

Faith too is a direct experience of God in that it bypasses the senses. As Luther put it: "Faith in Christ . . . is being rapt and translated from all things of sense, within and without, namely into the invisible, most high and incomprehensible God."[13] Yet although the faith experience transcends the senses, it does not occur apart from the senses but always in conjunction with the preached Word of God. Again, this experience is not direct if we mean by it an experience of God in Himself. We encounter not the *deus nudus* but God in Christ, not the Godhead but the Mediator. Therefore the evangelical Christian can be said to uphold a Savior-mysticism, but certainly not a mysticism of being.

In faith we veritably meet the risen, living Christ, but He is always hidden in the veil, sign and work of His redemption. We truly experience His presence, but we hear His Word indirectly. We experience God not in His primary but only in His secondary objectivity, in the biblical events and testimony. Therefore our knowledge of God can be said to be mediate and indirect, even though we are confronted directly by His Spirit.

[13] *D. Martin Luther's Werke* (Weimar: Böhlaus, 1939), 57, 144, 10.

Although a few mystics speak of an immediate perception of God, this idea is foreign to the mainstream of Christian mysticism. Garrigou-Lagrange contends that for both John of the Cross and Thomas Aquinas "faith and immediate positive perception are mutually exclusive: the act of vision cannot be an act of faith." He is willing to allow only for "an obscure, negative intuition" which "shows us better and better what God is not, that He surpasses all conception; it is to this quasi-unknown God that infused love unites us."[14] For the mystics we can know God by love but not by thought.

In contradistinction to the general tendency in Christian mysticism we contend that although we have no direct perception of the being of God, we do truly know God because He reveals Himself to us in Jesus Christ. Apart from faith God is indeed unknown, but in faith we are given a basic understanding of His will and purpose. We do not know Him exhaustively, but it can be said that we know Him intimately and assuredly. Faith is not to be understood primarily as a venture in the darkness (a common mystical notion) but as walking in the light of Jesus Christ (Jn. 12:35; I Jn. 1:7). It is not "a blind groping for the naked being of God"[15] but, in Calvin's words, "a firm and certain knowledge of God's benevolence toward us, founded upon the truth of the freely given promise in Christ."[16] Luther described faith as "a living, daring confidence in God's grace. It is so sure and certain that a man could stake his life on it a thousand times." The note of assurance and confidence in the merciful love of God shown forth in Christ remains with faith even where it is divested of experiential support.

This brings us to the second main component of mysticism, the fact of mystery in the experience of God. To be sure, the man of faith does encounter mystery, but this is the mystery of God's saving work in Christ, and this means that it is no longer wholly mystery. The element of mystery in the experience of faith is well attested by Luther: "No understanding can fathom nor tongue can express, no writing can record, but

---

[14]Reginald Garrigou-Lagrange, *Christian Perfection and Contemplation*, trans. Sister M. Timothea Doyle (St. Louis: B. Herder, 1958), p. 270.

[15]Clifton Wolters, ed. and trans., *The Cloud of Unknowing* (Baltimore: Penguin, 1967), p. 64.

[16]John Calvin, *Institutes of the Christian Religion*, ed. John T. McNeill, trans. Ford Lewis Battles (Philadelphia: Westminster, 1960), Bk. III, Ch. II, Sec. 7, p. 551.

only the inward feeling can grasp, what is involved in the suffering of Christ."[17]

Karl Barth also points to the mystery in Christian faith:

> It is not God who stands before us if He does not stand before us in such a way that He is and remains a mystery to us. Mystery means that He is and remains the One whom we know only because He gives Himself to be known. He is and remains the light visible and seen only in His own light.[18]

We encounter Christ as the Absolute Paradox, but this does not mean that He is wholly inexplicable. We not only encounter the mystery of the incarnation, but we also apprehend in faith the significance of this event. The incarnate Christ is mystery to be sure, but He also gives meaning to our lives.

Just as mysticism places the accent upon union with God, so faith speaks of the necessity for union with the crucified and risen Christ. But this is not identity but a union of will, a voluntaristic union. Faith entails an identification with the passion of Christ but not an absorption into His nature. The mystical union that evangelical theology envisions is one that involves profound intimacy but yet a distinction in persons. Our Lord described it this way: "In that day you will know that I am in my Father, and you in me, and I in you" (Jn. 14:20). Luther pictured it as follows: "Just as iron becomes red like fire through its union with the fire, so does the soul become like the word through its union with the word."[19] Brunner maintains that faith should eventuate in fellowship rather than in union as in mysticism. Yet as Bonhoeffer reminds us, faith is more than an I-Thou encounter; it is at the same time a mystical union whereby Christ no longer confronts the believer as Thou "but 'enters into' him as I."[20] While it is not permissible to speak of a mixing of divinity and humanity, we can surely affirm that there is interaction or communion at the deepest level.

[17]*Luther's Meditations on the Gospels*, ed. Roland Bainton (Philadelphia: Westminster, 1962), p. 137.
[18]Karl Barth, *Church Dogmatics* (Edinburgh: Clark, 1957), II, 1, p. 41.
[19]Martin Luther, *The Freedom of a Christian*, in Bertram Lee Woolf, ed., *Reformation Writings of Martin Luther* (London: Lutterworth, 1952), Vol. I, p. 362.
[20]Dietrich Bonhoeffer, *Sanctorum Communio*, trans. R. Gregor Smith (London: Collins, 1963), p. 37.

Faith, like mystical ecstasy, gives rise to peace and joy; yet this peace does not result from self-transcendence but from reconciliation. It consists in the gladness at knowing that one's sins are forgiven and that Christ is even now interceding for us at the right hand of God. The peace of God is not nirvana but a comforted despair based on the certain knowledge that our sins are covered by the righteousness of Christ. This peace is not the absence of conflict (as in pure mysticism) but the presence of God. It is not the eradication of tension but a stability amid tension.

In the experience of faith the subject-object cleavage is transcended, and in this respect we are again close to mysticism. Yet although the cleavage or antithesis is surmounted, the distinction between God and man still remains. The difference is that God is no longer an object but another Subject. Moreover, He is a Subject with whom we not only have external relations but also internal relations through His Spirit.

In faith we are united not only with the historical Christ but with the mystical Christ, the ever present Christ, the One who makes our hearts His dwelling place. Yet the mystical Christ is not immediately accessible to us because He is concealed or hidden in conscience. The uncreated light (also called the inner light) is refracted and blurred by the flickering created light of a conscience seared by human sin.

That there is a mystical dimension in faith is incontrovertible in the light of what has been said. The truth of faith is received in a spiritual experience that has definite mystical overtones. Yet this truth is not derived from the experience but mediated through it.

The term "Christian mysticism" is not a misnomer, but it is open to misunderstanding when applied to the religion or spirituality upheld in the Bible. It would be better to speak of faith-piety or an experiential faith; it is only a source of confusion to refer in this context to mystical faith or to faith-mysticism. Faith begins in an experience of the heart, but it does not arise out of this experience but rather out of the Word of God.

The truth of faith is received in a spiritual experience, but it is not received by an autonomous or independent reason. Philosophy enters into the interpretation of faith but always as an alien element. What faith seeks to combat is an exclusively mystical interpretation of this experience which undercuts or obscures its historical foundations. Mystical categories derived from secular philosophy must be baptized or given new meaning if they are to be of use in evangelical theology.

The experience of faith may possibly be denominated a mystical experience but with several qualifications: it is personal rather than impersonal; it is anchored in the historical rather than the metaphysical; it is a gift of divine grace rather than a fruit of ascetic endeavor. Because this experience focuses upon the cross and resurrection of Jesus Christ, it can be termed an evangelical experience. Because it involves the self-disclosure of God in the person of His Son, it can be considered a revelatory experience. It should also be seen as a crisis experience in which we are turned in an altogether new direction. It entails the renunciation not of the ego (as in radical mysticism) but of the sinful way of life.

The tension between faith and mysticism commences when the mystical experience is interpreted in the light of autonomous reason. It is then explained as an experience not of the Spirit of God but of the sum total of things or of the undifferentiated unity. Mysticism as a system of thought or even as a type of religion stands in contradiction to faith. But mysticism as an experience of the living Christ is an integral part of faith itself.

THE NORMS OF FAITH

It is well to bear in mind that the Christian faith has several norms. The Bible is the objective historical norm. It also might be considered the confessional norm. It is both the definitive witness to the revelation of Christ and the medium of this revelation.

The church is also an authority for evangelical Christians. It can be regarded as the steward of the revelation of Christ; it is also the means by which this revelation is proclaimed to the world. The church is both the institutional norm and the norm of tradition. Insofar as the church is built upon the means of grace, the Word and sacraments, it is also to be seen as the sacramental norm.

Despite the strictures of neo-orthodoxy upon experiential theology, we must insist that religious experience is likewise a norm for faith. This has also been called the norm of conscience and the inner light. It basically refers to the inner illumination of the Spirit. Just as Scripture and church tradition are objective norms, so the experience of faith is the subjective or mystical norm.

Over all of these is the transcendent norm, the living Word of God, Jesus Christ. He alone can be considered the absolute or dogmatic norm for faith. He alone is the indefeasible criterion, the foundational authority for the Christian. He meets us, however, only in the relative or derivative norms of the Bible, the proclamation of the church and religious experience.

The Christian faith is opposed to mysticism as a type of religion. We should take care not to absolutize the subjective norm but to relate it to the historical norm and the transhistorical norm, Jesus Christ. We should seek to place the mystical norm in the context of the sacred history of Scripture. The Christian indeed not only looks inward to the indwelling Christ but also backward to the historical Christ, to the cross and resurrection. He also looks forward to the triumphant Christ who is coming in glory, and upward to the heavenly Christ who intercedes for men at the right hand of God.

The mystical dimension in faith must not be ignored or obscured. But it is not to be isolated from the historical and superhistorical dimensions of the Gospel. The Christian mystic places the accent upon subjective experience and thereby is in danger of losing sight of the historical basis of faith.

Pascal is one of the few Christian thinkers in history who have for the most part succeeded in holding in balance mystical and evangelical spirituality. He declared: "The Stoics say, 'Retire within yourselves; it is there you will find your rest.' And that is not true. . . . Happiness is neither without us nor within us. It is in God, both without us and within us."[21] For Pascal the knowledge of God and self-knowledge are mediated by the knowledge of Christ.

Faith has a mystical pole, but it is not based upon mystical experience. Rather its foundation is the Word of God who confronts man in and through this experience. Faith consists not only in mystical communion but also in personal confidence in Christ. Moreover, faith leaves experience behind and proceeds on the basis of the promises of God. In the higher stages of the spiritual life faith is divested of experiential support and consequently takes the form of absolute trust.

[21]Blaise Pascal, *Pensées and the Provincial Letters*, trans. W. F. Trotter and Thomas M'Crie (N. Y.: Random, Modern Library, 1941), p. 154.

Faith and Mysticism

Christian faith should be regarded as transmystical rather than mystical in the narrow sense. The reason is that the higher levels of faith are characterized more by naked trust than by a felt presence of God. The God of Christian faith cannot be grasped by mystical experience, but He may descend into this experience. He cannot be reached by spiritual exercises, but He may come to man in these exercises or even despite them. The mystical or religious experience is the garment of faith. It both conceals and preserves the truth of faith; but it may also distort this truth.

The mystical or experiential element in faith is present even in the dark night of the soul, when God seems to withdraw Himself from the believer. The mystical communion is still maintained, but it is hidden even from the eyes of faith. But we must not absolutize this element and try to interpret the Christian life in terms of it alone. The Christian faith is not mysticism, but it has a mystical dimension. We seek not a mystical faith as such but an evangelical, catholic faith that includes the mystical element.

The church is grounded in and illuminated by the Bible. Both church and Bible are judged and expounded by Jesus Christ, who is the uncreated light within every believer, the concrete content of the Bible, and the Lord and Head of the church.

TENSIONS BETWEEN EVANGELICALISM AND MYSTICISM

There will always be tensions between evangelical, biblical religion and mystical religion.[22] Yet the genuinely Christian elements in the mystical tradition should be incorporated by biblical faith if it is not to become a barren confessionalism.

Whereas evangelicalism is oriented about the historical events recorded in the Bible, mysticism fixes its gaze upon eternity. In that strand of mysticism which is more ostensibly Christian, Jesus Christ is generally treated as a symbol of a universal principle or as a revelation or mirror of divine

---

[22]Friedrich Heiler has called these two types of religion the prophetic and the mystical. We have preferred the term evangelical to prophetic, since the former refers to the center of biblical faith, the message of salvation; prophetic religion as Heiler understands it is more inclusive than biblical faith. See Friedrich Heiler, *Prayer*, trans. and ed. Samuel McComb (N. Y.: Oxford, 1958), pp. 135ff.

Being rather than the Messiah of Israel in whom God was acting decisively for our salvation. It is the biblical picture of Christ or the Spirit of Christ rather than the atoning work of God in the man Jesus that is regarded as most important. The historical Jesus is seen to be the means or occasion by which we come to know the Eternal God. Augustine reflects the thinking of most Christian mystics in his axiom "through the man Christ you reach the God Christ."

The evangelical focuses his attention upon personal fellowship with God; the genuine mystic seeks to transcend the personal and become one with God. Tillich, for example, upholds the God who transcends the divine-human encounter; like many others who stand in the mystical tradition he understands faith more in terms of participation in God than of personal fellowship with Him.

The doctrine of the justification of the ungodly, which formed the core of the message of the Protestant Reformation, also constitutes a barrier between faith and mysticism. For the man of faith (in the biblical sense) God loves us while we are yet sinners (Rom. 5:8). The mystic, on the other hand, sees God's love as conditional on personal worth. As one mystical writer has expressed it: "For it is not what you are or have been that God looks at with his merciful eyes, but what you would be."[23] For Christian mystics justification is understood not as a forensic imputation of righteousness but as inner transformation. This is true even of such mystics as Johann Tauler and the author of the *Theologia Germanica,* both of whom emphasized the gracious initiative of God. The essence of salvation is not forgiveness by a righteous and loving God (as in the evangelical view) but rather reunion with the ground of being.

The hallmark of the evangelical experience is the conviction of sin and repentance. For the mystic the experience of God is marked by rapture and ecstasy. Evangelical (or faith) piety is penitential; it is oriented about the sin and helplessness of man rather than his perfectibility. The theology that is informed by faith-piety is essentially a *theologia crucis* (theology of the cross) rather than a *theologia gloriae* (theology of glory).

The evangelical seeks to witness primarily by upholding the message about Christ in his words and life. The mystic,

---

[23] Wolters, *The Cloud of Unknowing,* p. 144.

Faith and Mysticism

on the other hand, witnesses by embodying in his life the spirit of Christ. For the evangelical, Christianity is primarily a way *to* life, a promise of salvation that can be laid hold of only by faith. The mystic generally understands Christianity as basically a way *of* life, walking in the steps of the Master and becoming holy as He is. What is most important in evangelical spirituality is the proclamation of Christ; the necessary component in Christian mysticism is the imitation of Christ *(imitatio Christi)*.

We must ask, however, whether there is not a place for both strands of devotion in a faith that is at the same time catholic and evangelical. Evangelical piety is grounded in the personal knowledge of God's forgiveness effected in an unrepeatable vicarious sacrifice in history. The accent in Christian mysticism is on spiritual communion with the Word of God within the soul. Did not Christ not only die for us but also make His dwelling place within us? Apart from the inner communion with Christ our faith in His redemptive work could not long maintain itself.

Again it should be recognized that the ascent to holiness, so prominent in the writings of the mystics, is also spoken of in the Bible. To be sure we can only ascend to God on the basis of His descent to our level in Jesus Christ, but faith entails walking in holiness as well as repentance and trust. The Epistle to the Hebrews declares: "Strive . . . for the holiness without which no one will see the Lord" (12:14). Perhaps one major difference between faith-piety and mysticism is that in the former holiness is not so much a desire for separation from the sinful world as a vicarious identification with the sinner. Again it is seen primarily as active obedience to the Holy rather than participation in the Holy (although the latter is not discounted).

H. Richard Niebuhr in his book on the kingdom of God contrasts the two types of religion in terms of their understanding of man's relationship to God.[24] When the vision of God is made the ultimate principle, he maintains, then the emphasis is placed upon contemplation. Such a view, which sees God as basically passive, pervades Roman Catholicism, although it is ultimately derived from Plato, Plotinus and Aristotle. Evangelical Protestantism, on the other hand, has

---
[24] H. Richard Niebuhr, *The Kingdom of God in America* (N. Y.: Willett, Clark, 1937), pp. 20ff.

made the sovereignty of God the primary principle, and the accent is thereby placed upon ethical obedience. In this view the initiative lies with God, whereas in the mystical view the initiative lies with the one who seeks to see. The goal of life in Evangelical Protestantism is to advance the kingdom of God in the world; the goal in Catholic mysticism is the beatific vision which transcends this world. Niebuhr acknowledges that in the classical Catholic view activity is both the fruit of and the preparation for contemplation, but contemplation is nevertheless regarded as superior to action.

While basically agreeing with Niebuhr's incisive analysis, we nevertheless contend that the great saints in both traditions sought to hold contemplation and action in balance. Can there be obedient activity that does not spring from contemplation, understood as prayerful communion with God? And can contemplation be fruitful unless it issues in ethical obedience? Roger Schutz, prior of the community of Taizé, astutely perceives the mutual relation of the two sides of the Christian life: "Contemplation moves us to bold action and rules out the possibility of lukewarmness."

A statement by the prophet Isaiah is very germane to our discussion: "For thus says the high and lofty One who inhabits eternity, whose name is Holy: 'I dwell in the high and holy place, and also with him who is of a contrite and humble spirit, to revive the spirit of the humble and to revive the heart of the contrite'" (57:15). Here we are told that God is not only transcendent, but He is also present with those who are contrite and humble. God not only dwells in heaven but also in the hearts of those who cast themselves upon His mercy. This indeed is the mystical dimension of faith, and apart from this kind of mysticism faith would be impossible.

In the New Testament too it is said that God's Spirit, who is also Christ's Spirit, dwells within the hearts of believers (I Cor. 3:16; II Cor. 13:5; Eph. 3:17). The New Testament not only upholds Christ for us *(Christus pro nobis)* but also Christ in us *(Christus in nobis)*. Paul proclaimed: "Christ in you, the hope of glory" (Col. 1:27). He also affirmed that we are built into the temple of the Lord "for a dwelling place of God in the Spirit" (Eph. 2:22). The Holy Spirit is not only the inner life of God and Christ but also the inner life of the Christian.

Surely the Reformers perceived the mystical dimension in

genuine Christian faith. This is particularly evident in the early Luther, who could write that "faith has the incomparable grace of uniting the soul to Christ as bride to husband, so that the soul possesses whatever Christ himself possesses." And this statement of Calvin definitely has mystical overtones:

> Christ is not outside us but dwells within us. Not only does he cleave to us by an invisible bond of fellowship, but with a wonderful communion, day by day, he grows more and more into one body with us, until he becomes completely one with us.[25]

Evangelicalism and mysticism are the two notes in the Christian symphony. Mysticism that is not integrally related to evangelicalism becomes spiritualism. Evangelicalism that is divorced from mysticism deteriorates into a rationalistic biblicism. Faith indeed includes both mystical participation and personal encounter. It entails solitary communion as well as fellowship in community. What is important to remember is that faith in all its dimensions is a product of the initiative of God: our salvation is a work of free grace.

This is not to imply that we favor a synthesis between evangelical Christianity and the mystical tradition. Simply to combine aspects of biblical personalism with the perennial philosophy of mysticism would be a dangerous compromise. What we advocate is that evangelicalism rediscover the mystical elements in its own piety and tradition, elements very much apparent in the Scriptures and also in the writings of the Reformers. The immediate experience of the crucified and risen Christ needs to be given due recognition if evangelicalism is to be solidly biblical as well as truly catholic.

---

[25]Calvin, *Institutes* (McNeill, Battles), Bk. III, Ch. II, Sec. 24, pp. 570, 571. For a contemporary reappraisal of the mystical dimension in Calvin's thought see Lewis B. Smedes, *All Things Made New* (Eerdmans, 1970), pp. 48ff., 171ff.

NINE:
PHILOSOPHY, MYTH AND CULTURE-RELIGION

PHILOSOPHY AND RELIGION

Whereas philosophy might be defined as the search for wisdom, religion is the state of being grasped by an ultimate concern. The two principal types of religion might be considered to be the revelational and the cultural or natural. In the former the primary vision is grounded in a divine revelation in history; in culture-religion the fundamental orientation is largely determined by cultural and economic forces. It can be said that philosophy is basically a reflection either of culture-religion or irreligion. At its best it is the intellectual fruit of natural religion; it may also be the fruit of irreligion, meaning here relativism, cynicism or nihilism. This is to say that the creative thinking of the natural man has its source either in a spurious faith or in a lack of faith. Christianity can be viewed as the only authentic revelational religion, but because its cultus and institutions are thoroughly historical it also contains elements of culture-religion and ipso facto philosophy.

Cornford in his *From Religion to Philosophy* adduces convincing evidence that philosophy has its roots in some faith or religion which has been more or less accepted without question. He contends: "Philosophy is the immediate successor of theology, and the conceptions held by philosophers of the relation between the ultimate reality and the manifold sense-world are governed by older religious conceptions of the relation between God and the human group or Nature."[1] In this same vein he continues: "Almost all philosophic arguments are invented afterwards, to recommend, or defend from attack, conclusions which the philosopher was from the outset bent upon believing, before he could think of any arguments at all."[2] Cornford's study is mainly of ancient Greek philos-

---
[1] F. M. Cornford, *From Religion to Philosophy* (N. Y.: Harper, 1957), p. 135.
[2] *Ibid.*, p. 138.

ophy, but what he says appears to hold true for all philosophy.

The philosopher Nietzsche, despite his attacks upon the Christian religion, perceived the integral relation between philosophic thinking and personal faith. He declared: "Modern philosophy . . . is covertly or overtly, *anti-Christian* — although . . . by no means anti-religious."³ And again: "Gradually it has become clear to me what every great philosophy so far has been: namely, the personal confession of its author and a kind of involuntary and unconscious memoir; also that the moral (or immoral) intentions in every philosophy constituted the real germ of life from which the whole plant had grown."⁴

In the light of the above reflections philosophy might be considered the rationalization of a spurious or unauthentic faith. Philosophical systems are sacrifices offered to the gods (Shestov). Philosophy will often rise above and expose the popular religion and mythology of the time, but it will do so in the name of a covert faith or faith-principle. As Freeman observes: "Philosophical *theoria* which began its history as a new autonomous religion in ancient Greece must be recognized to have still in its unacknowledged heart, presuppositions which are religious."⁵ Some philosophers do not hide their faith-presuppositions; John Dewey openly acknowledges his fidelity to what he calls "the common faith,"⁶ and Jaspers resolutely upholds the "liberal faith." Philosophers such as these are guided not by a covert but by an overt faith. Philosophy in this sense can be seen as secularized theology.

Paul Tillich is one contemporary theologian who acutely discerns the religious roots of philosophy. Every philosophy, he contends, presupposes some ultimate concern. "Every creative philosopher is a hidden theologian (sometimes even a declared theologian). He is a theologian in the degree to which his existential situation and his ultimate concern shape

³Friedrich Nietzsche, *Beyond Good and Evil*, trans. and ed. Walter Kaufman (N. Y.: Vintage, 1966), p. 66.
⁴*Ibid.*, p. 13.
⁵David Freeman, *Recent Studies in Philosophy and Theology* (Grand Rapids: Baker, 1962), p. 150.
⁶Dewey has averred: "Faith in the continued disclosing of truth through directed cooperative human endeavor is more religious in quality than is any faith in a completed revelation." *A Common Faith* (New Haven: Yale, 1955), p. 26.

his philosophical vision."[7] From our perspective it is better to say that the philosopher works as a pseudo-theologian rather than a bona fide theologian.

The relation between philosophy and ideology should also be given attention. Ideology can be defined as a system of thought that reflects the vested interests of a particular class in society. In Marxist theory ideology signifies a rationalization of the privileged status of the ruling class. We can say that there is also a proletarian ideology which masks the struggle for power on the part of the dispossessed. Every philosophy is largely ideological in that the philosopher cannot wholly disengage himself from the biases of his society. Even though its revelatory criterion grounds it in the unconditional, theology too is a fully human enterprise and thereby bears the marks of cultural relativity. This is why the truly authentic or perfect theology is an ideal type, a goal rather than a present possession.

Consideration should also be given to the relation of philosophy and myth. Myth in its fundamental meaning is an imaginative symbolic description of a germinal idea or principle that gives purpose and direction to life. It is a vision or intuitive perception of what is thought to be an abiding or eternal truth; such a vision or truth provides for the subject the ground of meaning in life. Myth springs from a deep-seated conviction about life and the world. It can be said to signify the crystallization of religious faith; it is the primary way men seek to understand their faith in relation to the world about them. It can also be seen as the pictorial cloak or vessel of religion. Tillich defines myths as "symbols of faith combined in stories about divine-human encounters."[8] And in the words of Bernard Meland: "The myth of a culture is a symbolic utterance of long standing, attesting to a persistent outreach in man toward what is ultimate in that which is other than man."[9]

Myth must not be misunderstood as a fanciful expression of faith. One authority concludes that myths "are products of imagination, but they are not mere fantasy . . . true myth presents its images and its imaginary actors, not with the

[7] Paul Tillich, *Systematic Theology* (Chicago: University of Chicago, 1951), Vol. I, p. 25.
[8] Paul Tillich, *Dynamics of Faith* (N. Y.: Harper, 1957), p. 49.
[9] Bernard Meland, *Faith and Culture* (N. Y.: Oxford, 1953), p. 87.

playfulness of fantasy, but with a compelling authority."[10] According to Tucker myth arises when a drama of the inner life is felt to be taking place in the outer world. Cassirer holds that myth is a picture or vision that inspires to action. "Here thought does not confront its data in an attitude of free contemplation . . . but is simply captivated by a total impression."[11]

Myth can be viewed as a "life-symbol" (Susanne Langer) and signifies the first stage of metaphysical thinking. The transition from myth to philosophy is the transition from poetic to discursive thinking. While myth tells a story and expresses intuitive insights, philosophy deals with universal concepts (Jaspers). Yet it can be shown that behind the abstract theory of philosophy lie seminal intuitions of a religious or mystical nature.

Mythos originally signified the story of nature gods and goddesses. Yet as Barth reminds us, natural phenomena comprised the real content of myth:

> The customary definition that myth is the story of the gods is only superficial. In myth both the gods and the story are not the real point at issue, but only point to it. The real object and content of myth are the essential principles of the general realities and the relationships of the natural and spiritual cosmos which, in distinction from concrete history, are not confined to definite times and places.[12]

Barth is quite insistent that authentic myth is ahistorical, and this is why it stands in contradiction to biblical religion. "Genuine myth never means a genuinely pre-historical emergence, a beginning of the reality of man and his cosmos in encounter with distinct divine reality."[13] For this reason Barth prefers the term "saga" to myth in order to describe the biblical accounts of the creation, fall and flood. Saga is a kind of legend which has a historical reference and yet which refers to realities that are inaccessible to historical science.

[10]Henri and H. A. Frankfort, "Myth and Reality" in H. and H. A. Frankfort, *et al.*, *The Intellectual Adventure of Ancient Man* (Chicago: University of Chicago, 1957), p. 7.
[11]Ernst Cassirer, *Language and Myth*, trans. Susanne K. Langer (N. Y.: Harper, 1946), p. 57.
[12]Karl Barth, *Church Dogmatics* (Edinburgh: Clark, 1958), III, 1, p. 84.
[13]*Ibid.*, p. 85.

C. S. Lewis, on the other hand, maintains that the essential characteristic of myth is not that it is nonhistorical but rather nondescribable. Perhaps it is well to distinguish myth from mythology, since the latter definitely deals with the phenomena of nature. Some modern myths may be said to be partly historical in orientation, but this is perhaps due to Christian influence.

Reinhold Niebuhr differentiates between primitive and permanent myth, maintaining that the latter contains suprascientific rather than pre-scientific truth.[14] Primitive myth in his view appears to be mythology whereas permanent myth expresses an abiding insight into the mystery of human existence. According to Niebuhr the biblical myth has permanent validity, since it accurately describes the predicament and salvation of man; it must be taken seriously but not literally. Niebuhr acknowledges primitive elements in the biblical myth, but these pertain more to its form than to its content.

It is the consensus of a growing number of scholars (including Langer and Jaspers) that myth is the elemental seed of philosophy. Philosophy might be regarded as the conceptual expression of myth. In Barth's words, "Myth is the preform of speculation, and speculation is the essence of myth coming to light."[15] Although primitive mythology is abandoned by philosophers, they usually retain a mythic vision that gives direction and meaning to their thought. Tillich in this connection speaks of "broken myth" in which myth and critical thinking co-exist.

In a rationalistic or autonomous culture myth finally breaks down either in the direction of metaphysics or poetry. "The rational dynamic forms take possession of the holy symbols, now more in an aesthetic form, now more in a logical form."[16] When metaphysical systems collapse, however, there is "often a movement toward a modern mythical consciousness."[17] The tendency today in avant-garde theological circles is to replace a metaphysical with a historical orientation, but history itself

---

[14] See Reinhold Niebuhr, "The Truth in Myths" in Julius Bixler, ed., *The Nature of Religious Experience* (N. Y.: Harper, 1937), pp. 117-135.
[15] Karl Barth, *Church Dogmatics*, III, 1, p. 84.
[16] James Luther Adams, *Paul Tillich's Philosophy of Culture, Science, and Religion* (N. Y.: Harper, 1965), p. 245.
[17] Gordon D. Kaufman, *Systematic Theology: A Historicist Perspective* (N. Y.: Scribner's, 1968), p. 273.

"may function as myth or as symbol when men use it . . . for understanding their present and their future."[18]

For purposes of clarification I think it is best to differentiate between two principal kinds of myth. The first, which might be called the ideological myth, is a symbolic description of what man imagines or hopes to be true. It is generally oriented about a universal truth, but this truth may have pronounced historical implications. Cultural bias plays a determinative role in the forming of this kind of myth.

The second type of myth, the revelational, is a symbolic description of what God declares to be true. This myth is more noticeably historical, since what God declares true He makes true. Indeed, an analysis of the Hebrew *dabar* (word) shows that it signifies God's act as well as His word. Revelational myth is oriented about God's redemptive action in history. It is not a product of wishful thinking but is solidly grounded in empirical reality. It represents not the fulfillment of man's dreams but a searing judgment upon them. Between the myth of biblical revelation and that of cultural imagination there is a supreme qualitative difference.

Because myth has a double meaning in theological discourse, it might be better to follow Karl Barth in calling the biblical myth "sacred saga," since it has a historical reference even though it might at the same time have universal significance. Some of the biblical myths or sagas are more ostensibly centered in history than are others. Some theologians prefer to speak of the biblical myth as occurring in sacred history or superhistory rather than history as such, since the acts that are described did not arise out of history but signify a divine incursion into history.

It is interesting to note that the New Testament sharply distinguishes the Gospel from myth (cf. I Tim. 1:4; 4:7; II Tim. 4:4; Titus 1:14; II Pt. 1:16). Myths are said to promote speculation rather than divine training (I Tim. 1:4). Moreover, they leave out the work of God (I Tim. 4:7) whereas the Gospel gives glory to God. Myths are cleverly devised by man (II Pt. 1:16) while the Gospel comes from God (Gal. 1:12).

[18]H. Richard Niebuhr, *The Responsible Self* (N. Y.: Harper, 1963), p. 156. In this connection also see W. Taylor Stevenson, *History as Myth* (N. Y.: Seabury, 1969).

The question can be raised as to whether there are not myths in the pagan sense present in the Bible. It is to be admitted that the Old Testament in particular borrowed much mythical imagery from pagan cultures, and yet it sought to give this myth new meaning. According to Cullmann the Bible already demythologizes, for it tries to see everything in a historical context.[19] The biblical writers can be said to historicize the myths, so that the content of the myth is drastically changed even though the form remains. The story of the creation is a good example of how the biblical writers give new meaning to pagan myth. According to Avery Dulles, "The creation account in Genesis, far from falling in the same category as the Babylonian cosmogonies, may be viewed as a polemic against them."[20] Dulles, following Barth, goes on to affirm that the Genesis story "asserts precisely what myth cannot grasp, namely, the transcendent and creative act whereby God gave the universe an absolute beginning."[21]

The biblical doctrine of God is not mythological but analogical. Moreover, the analogies are drawn not so much from universal human experiences as from the incarnation of God in Jesus Christ. The biblical doctrine is constructed on the basis of the *analogia Christi* rather than the *analogia entis* (analogy of being), which forms the criterion of the classical philosophical tradition.

If biblical faith is based on revelation rather than a purely cultural myth, why should Christians acquaint themselves with this kind of myth? We contend that it is important for us to know the religion or irreligion or ideology of the culture which is competing against Christianity. The Christian must be exposed to the alternatives confronting modern man so that he can better present the one alternative that alone brings salvation. Modern man is not tempted to embrace the old mythology; but new pagan myths, often of an insidious character, are arising that seek to fill the spiritual vacuum of Western culture, and these present a serious challenge to the Christian faith.

[19]Oscar Cullmann, *Salvation in History* (N. Y.: Harper, 1965), pp. 93ff., 136ff.
[20]Avery Dulles, "Symbol, Myth and the Biblical Revelation" in *New Theology No. 4*, eds. Martin E. Marty and Dean Peerman (N. Y.: Macmillan, 1967), p. 56.
[21]*Ibid.*

MYTH IN THE HISTORY OF PHILOSOPHY

Mythical elements have persisted in various philosophical systems through the ages. Since myth is the basic content of culture-religion, it is important to discern the integral relation between philosophy and the popular religion of the time.

Plato wrote against the background of Greek polytheism, and his philosophy signifies an attempt to transcend popular religion. Yet although he attacked mythology, he continued to affirm a pluralistic divinity, namely, the Idea of the Good, the World Soul and the Demiurge. His essays were often cast in mythical form, thereby pointing to the symbolic character of his metaphysical scheme. Myth was not just a literary device for him but rather an abiding element in his conception of ultimate reality. Cornford contends:

> The mythical form of this whole cosmology is not a poetical dress, in which Plato arbitrarily chooses to clothe a perfectly definite and rational scheme, such as modern students set themselves to discover in it. If Plato could have stated it as a *logos*, he would have done so, only too gladly; but he cannot. It is not rational, but mystical — a *mythos* in substance as well as form, and drawn from mythical, mystical sources.[22]

Among the myths that Plato affirmed were the perfection of beginnings, the eternal return of things, the primeval chaos, the exiled soul, the heavenly city and the nether world. These were present in varying degrees in the polytheistic culture of his time, but he gave them a more sophisticated interpretation. Within and behind his conceptual embellishment the old myths lingered on, though in a new form. Plato criticized crude popular mythology, but he was not able to transcend an essentially mythical world view. One critic maintains that Plato's thought is essentially dependent upon the Orphic myth of the soul in exile and salvation through knowledge *(gnōsis)*.[23]

Just as Plato often made use of mythical imagery to express an abiding truth, so Jesus employed parables; neither were merely literary devices. The principal difference is that Jesus heralded the living God who enters history and encounters man personally in the depths of his being. In general Plato's

[22]Cornford, *From Religion to Philosophy*, pp. 260, 261.
[23]Paul Ricoeur, *The Symbolism of Evil*, trans. Emerson Buchanan (Boston: Beacon, 1967), pp. 279ff.

gods are elements of nature and the principles of motion in things. Plato's myths point to universal principles and to the mystical ground of being; Jesus' parables witness to God's redemptive acts.

Aristotle much more than Plato sought to transcend myth in metaphysical theory. Yet one must raise the question whether his God, the Unmoved Mover, is a myth or a purely theoretical concept. God is equated with pure thought, but does this mean that He is only an abstract principle or a self-conscious Spirit? Aristotle speaks of a "beholding" of pure thought as the highest knowledge and fullest bliss. He contends that Pure Actuality (i.e., God) moves the world "even as the beloved moves the lover, unmoved itself" *(Met.* XII, 1072b). Gilson reminds us that Aristotle was the first of the philosophers to unite the metaphysical first principle and the idea of God.

The fact that Aristotle opens the door to the worship of the Unmoved Mover shows that the latter is in some sense a mystical vision. In the twelfth book of his *Metaphysics* he dedicated a moving hymn to the One who moves all things through love. Although this God does not demand worship, he does compel our wonder. Cassirer maintains that it is characteristic of the mythic consciousness that "the entire self is given up to a single impression, is 'possessed' by it."[24] Whether Aristotle was possessed by the vision of an Unmoved Mover in a mystical way is a matter of conjecture.

It is interesting to note that Aristotle held to many gods in his later speculation. He posited fifty-five divine intellects corresponding to astronomical spheres. Moreover, each sphere must be in love with a different beloved. Is not this a secularized mythology?

Just as their metaphysical speculation reflected the polytheistic mythology of their time, so Plato and Aristotle proved to be children of their time in their political thought. The ideal of the ordered society, which they both upheld, mirrored the Greek city-state with which they were so familiar.

While both philosophers sought to move beyond intuitive insight to rational theory, Aristotle was probably more successful, since he identified his god with pure thought. Yet, as has been shown, remnants of mythology persist even in his very abstract speculation.

[24]Cassirer, *Language and Myth,* p. 33.

Stoicism, which sought to overcome the dualism of Plato and Aristotle in a cosmic pantheism, signified a still further divergence from Graeco-Roman mythology. Even so the Stoics saw the symbolic value of the old mythology and utilized the names of the gods to symbolize different aspects and processes of the universe. The real god of Stoicism was Destiny, also called the Ether and the Everlasting Fire. It seems that this god was not only a metaphysical first principle but at the same time a mythical vision.[25] The fact that the Stoics sought to cultivate piety and conformity to the divine reason of the universe reflects a religious attitude that is not to be found in a purely theoretical philosophy (at least overtly). The myth of a Golden Age also found its way into Stoicism; this idyllic state in the past, characterized by equality and freedom, was believed to have disappeared forever. The rise of Stoic philosophy signaled a failure of nerve in Graeco-Roman culture, since the aim in life was now simply the courage to be rather than the conquest of evil.

In the thought of Plotinus (third century A.D.), the philosopher of Neo-Platonism, the mythical consciousness appeared to make a comeback. Plotinus envisioned the idea of the Good as beyond the forms and therefore also beyond the intellect. This ultimate reality, which is also called the One, can be apprehended only in mystical experience. It is not a rational concept but a mytho-poetic vision. Among the myths which seemed to form the thought of Plotinus were those of light proceeding into darkness, the exile of the soul, the reincarnation of the soul and the eternal return. Like Plato he was heavily influenced by the Orphic doctrine of the imprisonment of the soul in an earthly body.

It has been said that with the dawning of the Age of Reason man has become emancipated from the spell of mythology. But as Gilson remarks: "Just like the world of Thales and of Plato, our own modern world is 'full of gods'. There are blind Evolution, clearsighted Orthogenesis, benevolent Progress and others which it is more advisable not to name."[26] Luther stated that when God is gone, "the fairy tales arrive,"

[25]One of the recurring myths in the ancient world was that of fate or destiny. See John Dunn, *The City of the Gods* (N. Y.: Macmillan, 1965), pp. 5-6, 12, 13, 27, 112.
[26]Etienne Gilson, *God and Philosophy* (New Haven: Yale, 1941), p. 136.

and the modern world has witnessed a host of new myths and gods that truly rival those of ancient Greece and Rome.

The Enlightenment of the eighteenth century spurned mythology and myth, but it succeeded only in camouflaging its myths.[27] In the Age of Reason there arose a secularized version of the myth of the three stages: instead of the coming Age of the Spirit as heralded by certain Christian mystics, the rationalists such as Lessing envisioned the triumph of human reason through education.[28] Kant's "Ethical Commonwealth" and Hegel's German state also reflect what is sometimes called the myth of the third age. Closely associated with the preceding was the myth of the inherent perfectibility of man. Other mythical notions present in the Age of Reason were the perfection of beginnings (Rousseau) and the reincarnation of the soul (Lessing).

The French Revolution, which climaxed the Enlightenment, saw the enthronement of reason in which statues of saints were replaced by busts of philosophers. On one occasion an actress from the opera attired as the goddess of Reason received homage from her worshippers in the Cathedral of Notre Dame. When men of reason suddenly become religious fanatics, it can be seen that they have been motivated not by a dispassionate pursuit of truth but by some religio-mythical vision.

Leibniz envisaged the world as comprised of monads, with God being the supreme monad (or mental force). Monads are indestructible, absolutely simple and immortal. They are closed to one another but open to the supreme monad, God. Is the monadology of Leibniz mythology, or are we dealing with a theoretical construct? In my estimation the monad is a concept and a mytho-poetic symbol at the same time. It corresponds to the image of the self-sufficient individual, the ideal of the newly arising bourgeois culture. The myth of universal Progress can also be detected in Leibniz's thought, since in his *On the Ultimate Origin of Things* he speaks of a free progress of the universe, advancing always to a still greater improvement. Behind his metaphysical speculation

[27] See Carl Becker, *The Heavenly City of the Eighteenth-Century Philosophers* (New Haven: Yale, 1952).
[28] The myth of the three stages is generally traced back to the medieval mystic Joachim of Floris, but according to Eliade it reflects the archaic myth of universal regeneration. See Mircea Eliade, *Myth and Reality*, trans. Willard Trask (N. Y.: Harper, 1963), p. 180.

was present a religious faith that can be considered more humanistic and deistic than evangelical and catholic.

In the philosophy of Kant, who both fulfilled and conquered the Enlightenment, we find the mythical vision of the *Ding-an-sich* (the thing in itself or the unconditional). He frankly acknowledges that this is not a concept because it is outside the bounds of knowledge. We have access to the unconditional or noumenal realm not by speculative reason but by practical reason (i.e., moral intuition). The ideology or myth of perpetual Progress can also be found in Kant. In his *Critique of Practical Reason* he declared: "For a rational but finite being, the only thing possible is an endless progress from the lower to the higher degrees of moral perfection."[29] His delimitation of speculative reason reflected the caution of the new age.[30] His vision of the free soul and his stress on practical reason mirrored the image of the independent individual upheld by bourgeois culture.

Hegel, whose philosophy partly reflected the concerns of the Enlightenment, acknowledged that myth is the precursor to metaphysics, but he failed to see that his own metaphysics did not transcend myth. His vision of the Absolute Spirit *(Geist)* realizing itself in history and finally culminating in the German state is at least partly mythical. He utilizes what Tillich calls "broken myth" in that myth is conjoined with critical thought. When Hegel avers that the state is the supreme or most perfect reality, that it is "the divine idea as it exists on earth," he is giving utterance to a vision that is basically mythical and religious.[31]

Nietzsche, although heralding the death of God, nevertheless could not escape the bonds of myth and religion. The myth of the superman was his substitute for the doctrine of

[29] Immanuel Kant, *Kant's Critique of Practical Reason and Other Works on the Theory of Ethics*, trans. Thomas Kingsmill Abbott (London: Longmans, Green, 1948), p. 219.

[30] Despite his curb on the rationalistic *hubris* of the Enlightenment, Kant could nevertheless affirm with something akin to religious passion: "The system of the *Critique* rests on a fully secured foundation, established forever; it will be indispensable too for the noblest ends of mankind in all future ages." *Kant: Philosophical Correspondence 1759-1799* (Chicago: University of Chicago, 1967), p. 254.

[31] The integral connection between Hegel's political thought and the modern myth of the state is ably delineated by Cassirer in his *The Myth of the State* (New Haven: Yale, 1946), pp. 246ff.

God. For the Christian doctrine of immortality he substituted the myth of eternal recurrence. It has been said that his real god was a secularized version of Dionysus, the god of vitalistic intoxication. The mythical vision that impelled him was the will to power best exemplified in the mythical figure Zarathustra.

In Auguste Comte, the French positivist (d. 1857), can be seen a modern version of the myth of the three stages: instead of the ages of the Father, Son and Spirit he spoke of the theological, metaphysical and positivistic periods. In his view the salvation of the world depends on its being reorganized on a scientific basis. We are now on the threshold of the third age in which the scientific method will replace metaphysical speculation, and industrial, technical civilization will dominate everywhere. The new age will be characterized by a high degree of social harmony and world peace. Positivism, for Comte, was not only a philosophy but also a religion, since he sought to substitute the worship of Mankind or Humanity for the worship of the Christian God. He even perceived the need for outward symbols and rituals if this new faith was to triumph. Here we can discern how a philosophy, having repudiated the traditional religion of a culture in the name of science, becomes itself a religion, a secular faith for a new age.

In order to explain the malaise within civilization Sigmund Freud posited a primal horde that was ruthlessly dominated by a primal father who by seeking to monopolize the woman curbed the gratification of the instinctual needs of his sons. Eventually the sons killed their father, thereby gaining their independence and right to pleasure, but they were compelled to reassert the principle of authority and repression in an effort to assuage their guilt feelings and also to protect their own privileges. This conflict between the pleasure principle and reality principle is, according to Freud, rooted in the biological constitution of both the individual and race and accounts for the progress as well as the repressiveness of civilization. Only through curbing the pleasure principle can an effective labor force come into being which makes civilization possible; yet the price of civilization is that man's will to pleasure is constantly thwarted. What is important to recognize is that Freud's theory has no anthropological or scientific verification. It is a myth concocted by a discern-

Philosophy, Myth and Culture-Religion 169

ing but misguided thinker, a phantasy that has exerted a wide but deleterious influence upon the modern world.[32]

Karl Marx, while espousing scientific materialism, nevertheless constructed a system that is in large part mythical. The mythical vision that inspired him was a classless society being ushered in by a worldwide revolution of the dispossessed. It is possible to see here a reflection of the etiological myth of the Golden Age which, according to various traditions, lies both at the beginning and end of history. We can also detect in his thought a secularized version of the myth of the three stages: history was seen to be progressing by means of an immanental dialectic from feudalism to capitalism to communism. Together with the vision of a class struggle, the prognosis of a proletarian utopia inaugurated by revolution comprised the dynamic basis of Marxist speculation. That these are prophetic-artistic creations and not verifiable realities has been shown by various scholars. It is well to note that Marx calls the collective capital-personality by such ironic names as "Monsieur Capital" and "My Lord Capital." The collective labor-personality is called the "Collective Worker." These are not theoretical concepts but mythical symbols. Tucker says concerning Marx's depiction of the warfare of labor and capital: "It is through and through a moralistic myth, a tale of good and evil, a story of struggle between constructive and destructive forces for possession of the world."[33] Marx and Communist theoreticians in general disclaim any mythical remnants in their philosophy. But according to Tucker: "One of the characteristics of true mythic thinking is that the thinker is not aware of it as mythical. For him it is a revelation of what empirically *is*."[34]

National Socialism has also proved to be mythical as well as metaphysical in orientation. Eliade maintains that the ancient myth of recurrent creations and destructions was reborn in Nazism. The institution of the German "Third Reich" is

---

[32] For the influence of this myth on three contemporary thinkers see Paul Robinson, *The Sexual Radicals* (London: Temple Smith, 1970). For a sympathetic presentation and appraisal of the Freudian myth see Herbert Marcuse, *Eros and Civilization* (Boston: Beacon, 1969). Unlike Freud Marcuse deems it possible to reconcile the will to pleasure with the demands of civilization.

[33] Robert C. Tucker, *Philosophy and Myth in Karl Marx* (Cambridge, England: Cambridge, 1961), p. 222.

[34] *Ibid.*, p. 224.

intelligible only when it is seen in relation to the myth of the third stage. Another myth that spurred the Nazis to creative endeavor was that of the master race. Although a great effort was made to show that this idea was firmly grounded in science, it is thoroughly mythical and therefore in this context fanciful. It is significant that Alfred Rosenberg, the chief philosopher of National Socialism, named his book *The Myth of the Twentieth Century*. National Socialism was not only a political philosophy but a culture-religion, a new mystique born out of the frustrations and racist inclinations of a considerable segment of the German people. The Führer was invested with the godlike qualities of omnipotence and infallibility; the racial-national consciousness was also virtually enthroned.

Process philosophy mirrors the naturalistic mysticism, the often shallow optimism and the relativism that are rampant in the upper middle and upper classes of Anglo-American society.[35] Emergence, organism and evolution are key concepts in its interpretation of the world. For the omnipotent God of biblical faith process philosophers and theologians have substituted the finite god of "Creative Good," "the Creative Process," or "the Principle of Concretion" who is caught up in the striving of his creation for fulfillment. Process philosophy with its emphasis on interrelatedness and community also reflects the longing for togetherness in a culture plagued by loneliness and inner emptiness. This kind of philosophy might be regarded in general as a secularized version of the ancient archetypal myth of perpetual growth.[36]

Whitehead, probably the foremost representative of process philosophy, had basically a mythic view of nature. It is a matter of debate whether his first principle "Creativity" is myth or abstraction; Hartshorne maintains that it is the latter. It cannot be denied, however, that Whitehead's concepts of the "Creative Urge" and "Creative Advance" are at least partly mythical. When he speaks of God as "the fellow-sufferer who understands," this is figurative rather than univocal language. Surely this depiction of God is essentially

[35] Relativism is somewhat checked in Whitehead's philosophy, since he posits a world of "eternal objects" or eternal ideas in the mind of God. For him God changes in His concrete but not in His abstract nature.

[36] J. Dunn also calls this the myth of perpetual life or perpetual vitality. See his *The City of the Gods*, pp. 4-5, 13, 27, 112.

mythical: "He does not create the world, he saves it: or, more accurately, he is the poet of the world, with tender patience leading it by his vision of truth, beauty, and goodness."[37] With Bernard Meland we hold that Whitehead sought to build upon the Platonic myth rather than the biblical Hebraic vision, and his philosophy cannot be adequately understood apart from this mythical background.[38]

Existentialist philosophy with its stress upon the leap of faith and the courage to create one's own meaning expresses the mood of pessimism and despair in modern culture, particularly European culture. It also mirrors the relativism that has been so widely pervasive following the breakdown of idealistic philosophy. One of the myths that informs existentialism is the "encounter with Nothingness," which is much more mystical than theoretical.

In Martin Heidegger's thought the concept of Nothingness is related to the Platonic myth of primal being. Nothingness for Heidegger is not simply the void but the "veil of Being." When we are confronted by the Nothingness we are at the same time confronted by the Holy and possibly also the gods. Nothingness can be grasped only by poetic insight, not by speculative reason. According to Barth Heidegger's doctrine is really a "mythological theogony."[39] Jonas contends that in this philosophy Nothingness signifies the concealment of "the gods." When Heidegger says that "Being reveals itself" or when he calls language "the house of Being" and describes man as the "shepherd of Being," he is employing mytho-poetic language. John Macquarrie holds that Heidegger's thought has affinities to Gnosticism. Heidegger seeks to penetrate behind appearance to Being or ultimate reality. His concept of "Being" is not only theoretical but religious; indeed, it can be said that "Being" is his substitute for God. Unlike many other philosophers he does not seek to replace myth with a metaphysical construct. Rather his aim is to penetrate behind the tree of philosophy and the root of metaphysics to the ground in which the tree grows. This ground is the light or truth of Being and can be apprehended only in a flash of insight.

[37]Alfred N. Whitehead, *Process and Reality* (N. Y.: Macmillan, 1929), p. 526.
[38]Bernard Meland, "How Is Culture a Source for Theology?" in *Criterion*, Vol. III, No. 3 (Summer, 1964), p. 12.
[39]Karl Barth, *Church Dogmatics*, III, 3, p. 343.

Unlike most mystics, however, Heidegger maintains that the encounter with the Nothing or Being is mediated by language, but this is a quasi-mystical or poetic language.

Karl Jaspers, another existentialist luminary, candidly acknowledges the necessity of myth to grasp the meaning of "the Comprehensive" or "Transcendence." He maintains that Transcendence is not itself a cipher or symbol but something we relate to in cipher language. The reality of Transcendence is only present to us in the language of code or cipher. Jaspers' conceptualizing betrays his adherence to the myth of the God above God, the mystical primal unity of all things. He admits that the primary reality is an existential concept and is intuited more than conceived. It appears that he holds to the mystical "ascent from God to the Godhead." He acknowledges that his philosophy is rooted in a religious faith, which he calls both the "liberal faith" and the "philosophical faith." In his words: "Preaching in church and conjuring Transcendence in philosophy refer to the same thing. The difference is that conjuration is a free, critical movement in ciphers, while a sermon is bound to proclaim the revelation."[40] Jaspers like most philosophers seeks to transcend ciphers and categories because they are "delimiting," but what he ends in is not a pure philosophy but a mixture of rational conceptualization and broken myth. He acknowledges that *mythos* is the vessel of *logos,* but he does not see that myth can also obscure truth, particularly if it is the product of man's vain imagination.

In the philosophy of D. H. Lawrence can be discerned the repristination of the ancient sex and fertility gods. Such mythological deities as Eros and Venus are by no means dead. The primeval myth of the Earth Mother is very much apparent in the speculation of Lawrence. His philosophy can be described as a sophisticated expression of the pagan culture-religion of sex mysticism. Lawrence has confessed: "My great religion is a belief in the blood, the flesh, as being wiser than the intellect. We can go wrong with our minds, but what our blood feels and believes and says is always true. . . . The real way of living is to answer one's wants."[41] This is not

[40]Karl Jaspers, *Philosophical Faith and Revelation,* trans. E. B. Ashton (N. Y.: Harper, 1967), p. 357.

[41]Quoted in Arnold Lunn and Garth Lean, *The New Morality* (London: Blandford, 1964), p. 80.

a detached philosopher speaking but a devotee of a new and at the same time old religion.[42]

THE SPIRITUAL SITUATION TODAY

Western culture presently finds itself in a metaphysical vacuum. Emil Brunner has wisely observed that the mind of man must always have a metaphysical content, for it cannot remain empty.

A spurious faith, i.e., one that has its seat in man's imagination, is not lasting. Historical and social pressures can break the foundations of this kind of faith. Only the Word of God can fill and satisfy the longings and emptiness of man. Cultural myths must be replaced by divine truth. As the apostle proclaimed: "For we did not follow cleverly devised myths when we made known to you the power and coming of our Lord Jesus Christ, but we were eyewitnesses of his majesty" (II Pt. 1:16).

Even revelational myth must be replaced by truth in the moment of revelation. But the Spirit of God does this replacing; it is not our task to separate the wheat from the chaff in the Bible. There can be no permanent setting aside of the biblical imagery or myth, since the truth of revelation is incarnated in the myth. Paul reminds us that we have the heavenly treasure in earthen vessels (II Cor. 4:7).

The biblical myth or saga is necessary to the expression of faith, since the human word and the divine content cannot be severed. This myth might be regarded as the poetic garment in which the truth of faith is encased. We must, of course, seek to interpret the myth and even express it in new language, but in our proclamation we must ever again return to what Barth calls "the language of Canaan." What is needed is not the superseding of the myth of the Bible but the appropriating of the truth within and behind this myth.

The observations of Hans Jonas, a critic of those who seek to demythologize the biblical myth, should be taken seriously. He reminds us that myth taken literally is "crudest objectification." Myth that is taken allegorically can be regarded as "sophisticated objectification." When myth is treated sym-

[42]For the role of myth in Lawrence's thought see Philip Rieff, "A Modern Mythmaker" in Henry Murray, ed., *Myth and Mythmaking* (Boston: Beacon, 1968), pp. 240-275.

bolically, on the other hand, it is "the glass through which we darkly see."[43] It should be borne in mind, however, that only that myth directs us to the truth that has been made by God a medium of His self-revelation.

The emerging philosophies on the horizon both reveal and veil the new gods, the new myths that are lurking in the shadows, waiting for their *kairos* or time of fulfillment. These new deities are, of course, idols, and this is why Christians must be forever on their guard. Shestov has made this acute observation:

> The mortal sin of the philosophers is not the pursuit of the absolute. Their great offense is that, as soon as they realize that they have not found the absolute, they are willing to recognize as absolute one of the products of human activity, such as science, the state, morality, religion, etc.[44]

The alternative facing man today is either a new idolatry or the worship of the true God. The church is under a heavy obligation to explode the false absolutes of our time and turn people towards the living God of the Bible. The biblical vision of God's reconciling work in the history of Israel culminating in the cross of Christ is to be forever contrasted with the mythical vision of man's self-salvation, the essential vision of culture-religion.

The task of theology today is to demythologize not the biblical myth or saga, which is the divinely chosen vessel of the Word of God, but the secular myths of our time. We are also called to deideologize the cultural dogmatisms of the contemporary world, whether these be racism, nationalism, social determinism, naturalistic hedonism, humanism or scientism. Surely it is also incumbent upon Christian theologians to dereligionize an idolatrous culture, to expose and seek to overthrow the modern Molochs that beguile man in the secular city.

Sometimes the new myths of any particular era masquerade under the name of science, whether this be physics, psychology, biology, political science, sociology, education, etc. This is not to deny that there is verifiable truth in each of these

---

[43] Hans Jonas, "Heidegger and Theology" in *The Review of Metaphysics*, Vol. XVIII, No. 2 (Dec., 1964), pp. 232, 233.
[44] Lev Shestov, *Athens and Jerusalem*, p. 385.

disciplines, but it is to recognize that secular dogmas have arisen within and in the name of these disciplines. We are then confronted with the phenomenon known as scientism, and this is a perpetual temptation in the modern technicalized world.[45] Among the mythical notions that have been spawned by a spurious science are the infinity of space and time, cosmic Evolution, the Oedipus Complex, the collective unconscious and the Open Universe. Secular mythical visions of a more political coloration are the inevitable perfectibility of man, the sovereignty of the general will, the fundamental goodness of man, the inherent infinite worth of personality, the world come of age, the universal equality of man and white supremacy. It is well to note that with the exception of the last all these mythic political concepts in some form or guise have had a noticeable influence upon modern secular Democracy, and several have also had an impact upon Marxist Socialism.

Emile Cailliet has remarked that Christianity in its inception presented a radical challenge to the society of its day, since it set out to demythologize the naturalism and humanism that were all-pervasive.[46] We too live in a society dominated by a naturalistic world view. May we too seek to unmask the hidden and not so hidden pagan myths of our time and remind our contemporaries of that ultimate reality, the living God, who infinitely transcends both the visible world of our senses and the thought-world of our minds.

[45]See David Horrobin, *Science Is God* (London: Chiltern, 1969); Anthony Standen, *Science Is a Sacred Cow* (N. Y.: Dutton, 1950); and Rousas J. Rushdoony, *The Mythology of Science* (Nutley, N. J.: Craig, 1968). The latter book is slightly marred by a too rigid biblical literalism.
[46]Emile Cailliet, *Journey into Light* (Grand Rapids: Zondervan, 1968).

TEN:

FAITH AND REASON

Theologians have ever been divided concerning the relationship between faith and reason. Some have understood faith as a wholly rational act made on the basis of rational evidence. In the view of Jeffrey Hart, contemporary Catholic lay theologian, faith "is to affirm propositions which the reason has ratified."[1] Other Christians have defined faith in a radically different way — as trust and confidence in a living Savior. Thus we find this definition from Charles Spurgeon: "True faith in its very essence rests in this — a leaning upon Christ."[2] In general it can be said that the tradition of scholastic orthodoxy (both Catholic and Protestant) sees reason as playing a creative and significant role in man's coming to faith; the Protestant Reformation and the traditions of Pietism and Puritanism take a dimmer view of the power of reason to apprehend the truth of faith. The emphasis in both scholastic orthodoxy and liberalism has been to make the faith credible and plausible to the world; the concern in the tradition of original evangelicalism was to herald the faith.

Ernst Wilhelm Hengstenberg, German Lutheran theologian in the nineteenth century, illustrates the danger of making our schema too rigid. Although he was an avowed defender of confessional orthodoxy, he had one foot in evangelical Pietism, and this perhaps partly accounts for his antipathy towards rationalistic theology. In his view there is no philosophical road that leads to the knowledge of God. He also argued that revelation is contrary to reason and therefore cannot be buttressed by an appeal to universal truths. Hengstenberg's position on this matter is at marked variance with both the older scholastic theologians and many modern fundamentalists.

[1]In *The National Catholic Reporter*, Vol. V, No. 18 (Feb. 26, 1969), p. 9.
[2]Charles Spurgeon, *The Treasury of Charles H. Spurgeon* (Westwood, N. J.: Revell, 1955), p. 160.

THE HISTORICAL DEBATE

Augustine is one who seeks to relate faith and reason very closely but yet who sees faith as being the more decisive. His motto was "I believe in order to understand." Before one can come to a right understanding of God he must first believe in God's revelation in Jesus Christ. Yet Augustine also held that before one believes it is necessary to determine what one believes. Reason therefore also a role prior to faith. Yet he contended that reason apart from faith cannot bring us valid knowledge of God. "When I thought of You it was not as of something firm and solid. For my God was not yet You but the error and vain fantasy I held."[3] Faith is more than mere feeling; it also involves intellectual assent. "No one indeed believes anything, unless he has first thought that it is to be believed."[4] Yet faith does not bring us perfect knowledge: it only sets us on the way. A sure faith, he said, is the foundation of knowledge, but a sure knowledge will not be perfected until life after death.

Augustine held that faith is given by the Spirit through the preaching of the Gospel, but it must at the same time be rationally appropriated or accepted by man. Once it is so appropriated it then illumines man's life and world. "For faith is understanding's step, and understanding is faith's reward."[5]

In the thought of Thomas Aquinas reason has a creative role prior to faith, but it is also very necessary after faith. Natural reason can discern the law of nature and the effects of God in nature. It appears that in his theology this natural knowledge of God is the condition or presupposition of faith. He also holds that reason can to some degree prepare the way for faith, although the primary cause of faith is "God moving man inwardly by grace."[6]

Nature and grace do not permeate each other as in Augustine; rather they complement one another as do natural and revealed theology. In his view revelation enriches and

[3]Augustine, *Confessions*, IV, c. VII, n. 12.
[4]Erich Przywara, *An Augustine Synthesis*, 4th ed. (N. Y.: Sheed and Ward, 1945), p. 61.
[5]*Ibid.*, p. 52.
[6]Thomas Aquinas, *Summa Theologica*, II-II, p. 6, Art. 1. In A. C. Pegis, ed., *The Basic Writings of Thomas Aquinas* (N. Y.: Random, 1945), Vol. II, p. 1116.

completes reason rather than contradicts it. Reason deals with what can be demonstrated whereas faith concerns that which is taken on authority. Thomas held that we cannot prove the God of revelation, but we can show that it is not unreasonable to posit the existence of a supreme power as the Author of nature. The Christian recognizes this power to be the living compassionate God who revealed Himself in Jesus Christ, but this truth is hidden from the natural man.

For Thomas faith is not yet knowledge; it stands between knowledge and opinion. It falls short of knowledge because it does not yet have vision. The highest knowledge that we can have of God in this life is to know that He is above all that we can think of Him. Thomas could readily concur with Augustine's dictum: "That which thou understandest is not God."[7]

Thomas perceived the rightful place of philosophy, which in his view is the wisdom of the natural order, that which reason can attain on its own. He was not, however, sufficiently aware that this wisdom is both severely limited and distorted. Neither Thomas nor Augustine saw clearly enough that autonomous reason is essentially imperious, grasping and defiant. The former in particular did not fully consider that revelation not only transcends but also in some sense contradicts the claims of reason.

St. Thomas acknowledged that theology, being the science of revealed mysteries, can alone deal with saving truth, the truth that is effectual for salvation. Philosophy can know the divine truth implanted in the natural order but not that of the supernatural order. He believed that it is possible for the Christian to convince an adversary of the validity of the first kind of divine truth by demonstrative arguments. Yet the only way to convince an outsider of the truth of divine revelation, i.e., the truth of Christianity, is to appeal to the authority of Scripture.

Martin Luther, who illustrates the position of evangelical fideism, saw faith as standing in contradiction to reason. At one place he called reason "the monster without whose killing man cannot live." It can be said that he sought to exchange "the light of reason" for "the darkness of faith." Reason is incapable of discerning the things of faith because,

[7]Augustine, *Serm.* (de Script. N. J.), LII, vi, 16.

first, it is exceedingly limited in its vision and, second, it is enslaved by man's sinful will.

Yet Luther made a distinction between natural reason and a reason enlightened by faith. Reason by itself can know nothing about the plan of salvation, but faithful reasoning can tell us much about these matters. "Before faith and the knowledge of God, reason is mere darkness; but in the hands of those who believe, 'tis an excellent instrument'. All faculties and gifts are pernicious, exercised by the impious; but most salutary when possessed by godly persons."[8] In a similar manner Luther held that the works of the law avail nothing for our salvation but faithful doing is very necessary in the Christian life.

At the same time Luther contended that even an enlightened reason cannot comprehend the articles of faith. It can understand to some extent the law of God and the religion of the Jews, but articles like the Trinity and the incarnation of Christ "do not tally with reason." These are divine mysteries that can only be grasped by faith.

Faith, for Luther, is heartfelt confidence and trust in the mercy of God. It is *fiducia* (trust) much more than *assensus* (mental assent), although it also entails the latter. In his words, "There is a faith which believes what is said of God is true; there is a faith which throws itself on God." Only the latter is effectual for salvation.

Pascal might be considered a representative of fideism in the Catholic Church, although he did not deny the validity of reason in certain areas. Pascal, unlike Luther, did not see faith as contrary to reason; rather faith goes beyond reason. Faith is above our senses but does not contradict them. "If we submit everything to reason," he declared, "our religion will have no mysterious and supernatural element. If we offend the principles of reason, our religion will be absurd and ridiculous."[9] Reason cannot prove the existence of God, but it can show us our inability to believe. It cannot induce faith, but it can remove certain obstacles to faith.

Faith alone, according to Pascal, can lay hold of the self-revelation of God in Christ. Faith is an experience of the

[8]Thomas Kepler, ed., *The Table Talk of Martin Luther* (Cleveland: World, 1952), p. 49.
[9]Pascal, *Pascal's Pensées and the Provincial Letters* (N. Y.: Random, Modern Library, 1941), p. 94.

heart, which is the unitive center of personality. "This, then, is faith: God felt by the heart, not by the reason."[10] He also said that the heart has its reasons which reason does not know.

It should be borne in mind that when Pascal contrasts faith and reason he is thinking primarily of discursive or technical reason. Discursive reason proceeds syllogistically, and God is not the conclusion at the end of a syllogism. Faith is inward, spiritual and intuitive while reason is external, objective and geometric. Yet Pascal is not an irrationalist, for he acknowledges that reason is very capable in spheres other than religion. The scientific method works quite well in the world of nature, but not in religion. Heart-knowledge, on the other hand, pertains only to God and His mercy.

Pascal addressed his famous wager to the skeptics of his time: if one would but venture to believe, he would gain everything if God really exists and would lose nothing if He does not exist. Yet he acknowledged that rational argument is persuasive only to those who earnestly bewail their doubt and seek God, not to those who do not even seek God. Those who have a "real desire to meet with truth" may be convinced of the proofs of the Christian faith. By the proofs of the faith Pascal was thinking mainly of the biblical signs and miracles. Miracles might have some value to those who seek for salvation, but it is the cross of Christ alone that makes one believe, not wisdom or signs. Proofs are not necessary, but they may be helpful where faith or a yearning for faith is already present.

For Pascal the only real proof of the Christian faith is the experience of the crucified Christ, the conviction of sin and the assurance of salvation. This is both a mystical and an evangelical experience in that it is a direct experience of God but mediated by the knowledge of Jesus Christ.

For Immanuel Kant faith comes after reason, but it lacks rational certainty and clarity. While classical Christian theology has always held that faith gives real knowledge, Kant contended that faith is less than cognitive or noncognitive. He defined it as follows: "Faith is the moral attitude of reason as to the belief in that which is unattainable by theoretical cognition."[11] It is a postulate which concerns that which is

[10] *Ibid.*, p. 95.
[11] Immanuel Kant, *Kant's Kritik of Judgment*, trans. J. H. Bernard (London: Macmillan, 1892), p. 409.

Faith and Reason

subjectively certain and objectively uncertain. It is less than knowledge, for it cannot determine a metaphysical system. Faith is applicable only in the realms of willing and feeling, not knowing. The object of faith is the immanent moral law and/or the Lawgiver, but not the living God of the Bible who acts in history.

In line with his Lutheran background Kant affirmed that the empirical ego is transcended in the experience of faith. But in contradistinction to Lutheran thought he held that faith has its roots in self-effort; it is not a gift of God. Also faith is an affirmation of the categorical imperative within rather than trust and confidence in a personal Savior.

Kant had said that he limited the rights of reason in order to make room for faith. Not surprisingly some Christians have been led to regard Kant as a defender of the faith. We concur with Shestov who contends that "Kant's faith is a faith within the limits of reason; it is reason itself but under another name."[12]

Søren Kierkegaard, in contrast to Kant, envisioned the object of faith as a person, not a principle or idea. Faith, moreover, entails decision and commitment rather than rational assent. It is existential more than intellectual. Faith alone can perceive the existence of God in Jesus Christ, since thought cannot comprehend existence. For reason the revelation of God in Christ is an absolute paradox, and even faith cannot fully penetrate this mystery. He declared:

> When the believer has faith, the absurd is not the absurd — faith transforms it, but in every weak moment it is again more or less absurd to him. The passion of faith is the only thing which masters the absurd — if not, then faith is not faith in the strictest sense, but a kind of knowledge.[13]

According to Kierkegaard we can use our reason to expose man's limited horizon. Reason can point to its own limits by raising without answering the question of faith implied in the actual situation of the existing individual. Reason both precedes and follows faith. After faith we can use our reason to show that we cannot understand fully.

[12]Lev Shestov, *Athens and Jerusalem*, p. 164.
[13]Søren Kierkegaard, *Søren Kierkegaard's Journals and Papers*, ed. and trans. Howard V. Hong and Edna H. Hong (Bloomington, Ind.: Indiana University, 1967), Vol. I, p. 7.

Charles Hodge, professor of theology at Princeton Theological Seminary (d. 1878), typifies a quite different approach to the problem of faith and reason. Whereas Kierkegaard and Pascal had little confidence in the power of reason to apprehend the things of God, Hodge sought to bring reason to the aid of faith. He thought in pre-Kantian rationalistic terms. With the later Enlightenment he defended induction over deduction. Despite the criticisms of Hume and Kant, he stoutly affirmed that our sensory perceptions are a reliable index to truth; he apparently held that they have an exact correspondence to reality.

Hodge saw reason as preparing the way for faith, just as apologetics prepares the way for dogmatics. He had a deep confidence in both man's senses and mental faculties, and he believed this to be a prerequisite to confidence in God. Although definitely skeptical of the ontological argument for the existence of God, he was very sympathetic to the cosmological and teleological arguments.

Like many Christian rationalists before him, he affirmed a definite continuity between reason and revelation. Reason, he maintained, is even able to judge the credibility of revelation. How does reason proceed in this matter? First of all the impossible cannot be believed: that is impossible which either involves a logical contradiction or requires God to do what is morally wrong. Reason must also judge the evidence by which revelation is supported.

Hodge saw a similarity and difference between theology and philosophy. Their objects are the same, but their methods differ. Theology utilizes the inductive method, not the speculative method of rationalistic philosophy in which one starts out from principles and proceeds to facts. According to Hodge principles are to be derived from facts. The theological method is simply the inductive or scientific method applied to Scripture. Like the scientist the theologian observes, arranges and systematizes without participating in his experiment.

Hodge affirmed a general revelation in nature and a general knowledge of God, but he contended that such knowledge does not suffice for salvation. The special revelation given to man in Scripture alone can bring man the knowledge that effects his salvation.

Faith for Hodge has a decidedly intellectual character. It is "an intelligent reception of the truth on adequate grounds."[14] Scripture never demands faith "except on the ground of adequate evidence."[15] The object of faith is the divinely revealed truth contained in Scripture. Faith involves an assent to the facts in Scripture and to their Scriptural interpretation.

Gordon Clark also stands in the tradition of rationalistic idealism and orthodox Calvinism. In stark contrast to Hodge, however, he disdains all empiricism and thereby reflects the Age of Reason in its earlier phases. Clark is an avowed opponent of "neo-orthodox irrationalism" and Pietism.

Clark, like Augustine, takes his stand on faith *and* reason and even more consistently than Augustine understands faith as assent to propositional truth. Revelation for Clark is an axiom of reason, a datum accessible to reason. He acknowledges, however, that the will must be turned or converted by the Holy Spirit before our reason is free to appropriate the truth of revelation.

He regards the Bible as a verbal revelation from God: it represents the very mind or thought of God. The Bible is significant because here we find a communication of the thought of God to the mind of man. We do not gain knowledge of God by an empirical encounter with the Bible as a historical record. What the Bible gives is not so much a history of God's dealings with man as information about God.

Clark holds that we know the world not by means of our senses but instead by innate ideas which are to be found not simply in man's mind but in God's mind in which we "live and move and have our being." He asserts that "our existence in the mind of God puts us in contact with the ideas in the mind of God."[16] Knowledge of God, he insists, is prior to knowledge of the facts; indeed, we know the facts of the world only through God. With many philosophical rationalists Clark contends that universal and necessary truths cannot be justified on empirical grounds.

Accepting the term "rationalistic Calvinist," Clark has constructed a deductive axiomatic system. In his view our logic

---

[14]Charles Hodge, *Systematic Theology* (Grand Rapids: Eerdmans, 1940), Vol. I, p. 53.
[15]*Ibid.*
[16]Ronald H. Nash, ed., *The Philosophy of Gordon H. Clark* (Philadelphia: Presbyterian and Reformed, 1968), p. 406.

and knowledge are identical with that of God, though this
does not mean that we have as much knowledge as God. Our
ideas participate in the very ideas of God. We can have not
merely analogical but univocal knowledge of God. Clark holds
that the image of God is logic or reason. The logical structure
of reason is not affected by sin, although sin has noetic
implications.

Clark has a deep affinity to both rationalistic philosophy
and the older scholastic theology. One can discern in his
thinking the influence of Descartes and Leibniz as well as
Plato and Aristotle. He asserts that Aristotle's definition of
God as "thought-thinking-thought" can be accepted if the
world is included within this thought-that-thinks-thought. His
marked philosophical orientation can be seen when he affirms,
"God and logic are one and the same first principle."[17] Again,
paraphrasing John 1:4 he declares: "In logic was life and the
life was the light of man."[18]

With Thomas Aquinas he sees a harmony between faith
and reason, but while Thomas held that there is only an
ontological harmony, Clark sees in addition a psychological
harmony. Thomas said that we cannot believe what we
know; Clark contends that what we believe we know, since
faith is a rational act.

Either Luther or Kierkegaard would undoubtedly criticize
Clark for not taking seriously the infinite qualitative gulf
between God and man. When Clark makes logic or reason
the point of contact between God and man, he does not seem
to recognize that reason has both finite limitations and a sinful bias. Neo-orthodox theologians might justifiably censure
Clark for not taking history seriously, for viewing revelation
as the communication of ideas rather than personal encounter.
He also does not see that the demands of faith sometimes run
counter to the demands of logic, that faith must sometimes prevent logic from seeing through a problem to its harsh conclusion. For example, on the basis of an abstract concept of the
sovereignty of God he is compelled to affirm that God is the
ultimate cause of evil.

To the credit of both Hodge and Clark, they remind us that
faith is not only a volitional but also an intellectual act.
Revelation entails both personal confrontation and the com-

---

[17]*Ibid.*, p. 68.
[18]*Ibid.*, p. 67.

munication of truth. Yet one cannot deny that their basic approach to the problem of faith and reason stands at marked variance with that of the Protestant Reformers whose faith they share.

This historical survey would not be complete without including Karl Barth, who makes a noteworthy and fresh contribution to the subject. Barth stands in the tradition of Anselm and accepts the Anselmian formula "faith seeking understanding." He also leans heavily upon the Reformers, Luther and Calvin. But he has appropriated insights from modern movements as well, including Kant and the Enlightenment. That Barth has a marked preference for Mozart over Bach shows that one should be hesitant in regarding him as a neo-Reformation theologian.

Barth understands faith primarily as knowledge of what God has done for us in Jesus Christ. It is an awakening to the truth concerning our deliverance through the cross of Christ, an awakening that is brought about by the action of the Holy Spirit. Faith is also an act of the will, and this means that it is an acknowledgment of Jesus Christ as well as a knowledge of Him.

Faith is prior to human reasoning, but in itself it is rational, not suprarational. Barth recognizes the element of mystery in faith, but his emphasis is on its cognitive dimension. The object of faith is a divine message which has a rationally determinative content. The truth of faith can be received by reason, even though reason must first be illumined by the Spirit of God before it perceives this truth. Barth holds that we can have objective or conceptual knowledge of God, but only as we are known by Him. The truth of revelation is not an object at our disposal, but it becomes an object for our knowledge on those occasions when man is encountered by the Spirit of God. With Anselm Barth holds that reason can demonstrate the existence of God to faith; at the same time he insists that it cannot prove God's existence to the unbeliever.

Like Thomas Aquinas he holds that our knowledge of God is analogical rather than univocal, but insists that this is based on the *analogia fidei* (analogy of faith), not the *analogia entis* (analogy of being). This is to say, we should begin with the revelation of God rather than the being of man and derive characteristics of man from God as He discloses Himself in Jesus Christ.

With Kant and the Enlightenment Barth upholds the courage to use one's own reason, but in contradistinction to the Enlightenment he begins not with an independent reason but with a reason enlightened by faith. His antipathy to mysticism, his view that all men are children of God, his understanding of redemption as a fulfillment of creation, his this-worldly optimism, his anti-sacramentalism, and his monistic tendency also ally him with the Enlightenment. His understanding of man as being basically good also bears the marks of the modern mythos; orthodox theology has always affirmed that man was originally good but is now depraved both in spirit and nature.

Barth sometimes speaks of revelation as the demonstration of an eternal truth, namely, that God has overcome sin in Himself from all eternity, and here he again tends to reflect Enlightenment motifs. Yet at other times he seems to regard revelation as an event that actually changes the situation regarding man's salvation, and this would place him in the camp of biblical, Reformation theology. It should also be noted that Barth's optimism concerning the course of this world is based on the grace of God and not the ingenuity or moral excellence of man. Whether his view of the errancy of Scripture is traceable to the Enlightenment is a matter of conjecture, since he tries to ground this particular notion in the witness of Scripture itself. The traditional Reformed position is that the Bible is wholly reliable and trustworthy in all of its teaching. Where Barth definitely stands with the Reformation against the Enlightenment is in his acknowledgment of mystery in faith, his denial of natural theology, his understanding of Christ as primarily Reconciler and Mediator rather than moral exemplar, and his conviction that salvation is a product of the free grace of God.

In contrast to the older Protestant orthodoxy, Barth has eschewed the temptation to treat the knowledge of God as being of the same order as other kinds of knowledge. Yet he has not fallen into the error of modern religious existentialism, which denies the possibility of objective knowledge of God. Barth admits that man cannot objectify God, but he holds that God in His freedom can make Himself an object for our knowledge. We can truly know God and yet we cannot possess or control God. Moreover, our knowledge of God is indirect in the sense that "it is never identical with our theological perceptions and conceptions as such."[19] Barth admittedly underplays the mystical dimension of faith in which we have a direct communion with God by His indwelling Spirit. At the same time his thought in this area has certainly proved to be an invaluable contribution to the theological discussion.

THE MEANING OF FAITH

My position is much closer to fideism than to rationalism in that I see faith as determining reason and not vice versa. I stand in that tradition which includes Forsyth, Kierkegaard, Pascal, Edwards, Luther, Calvin, Irenaeus and also Paul the Apostle. Some Christian mystics (Bernard of Clairvaux and John of the Cross), as well as luminaries of neo-orthodoxy like Emil Brunner and Karl Barth, evangelical Calvinists such as Martyn Lloyd-Jones, and neo-Lutherans like Helmut Thielicke and Gustaf Wingren, also belong to some degree to this general tradition. As with many of those mentioned I uphold not a mere fideism but a trinitarian fideism, one that has its source not in the leap of faith but in divine revelation. Faith should be understood in this context not as a venture in the darkness but as an intelligible response to the gift of Jesus Christ. In contradistinction to radical fideists we do not see a divorce between faith and reason but the conversion of reason by faith. The position presented here is not an existentialist subjectivism but rather a biblical evangelicalism that seeks to hold in balance objective revelation and subjective decision.

Faith has its origins in that divine light which does not arise out of experience but which is given in experience. This light is both the foundation and the core of faith. It not only gives man illumination but also empowers him for service to God. This divine light is the grace of God, and it becomes the light of faith when it leads man into an act of commitment. The light of faith and the act of faith might be considered the two dimensions of faith. Some persons who have been exposed to the divine light do not yet have faith because they have not appropriated this light.

[19]Arthur Cochrane, *The Existentialists and God* (Philadelphia: Westminster, 1956), p. 47.

In Catholic thought the objective basis for the possibility of faith resides in divine revelation, but the subjective basis for this possibility resides in us. In my view the subjective basis resides not in us but in the Holy Spirit. The presupposition of faith is not the light of nature but the Spirit of God.

Faith is experiential as well as cognitive and volitional. It entails an experience of the divine presence as well as trust in this presence. Bultmann is not quite correct when he says, "We can believe in God only in spite of experience." Faith contradicts sight, but it itself is an experience of that which transcends the senses.

Faith is given by the Holy Spirit, but with the Reformers we hold that the Spirit makes use of external means, namely, the written and proclaimed Word of God. Paul declared: "So faith comes from what is heard, and what is heard comes by the preaching of Christ" (Rom. 10:17). And again: "For since . . . the world did not know God through wisdom, it pleased God through the folly of what we preach to save those who believe" (I Cor. 1:21). That the preaching of the Gospel is the primary external means by which we receive faith (the Spirit being the internal means) is affirmed not only by the Reformers but by such noted Roman Catholic theologians as Augustine and Thomas Aquinas. We wholeheartedly subscribe to the view expressed by Thomas in a sacramental hymn:

> *Sight, feeling, taste delude themselves about thee.*
> *By hearing alone is sure faith given.*
> *Only what God's Son has said do I believe.*
> *The Word is truth, and what can be more true?*[20]

Faith is given to man directly from God, but it does not operate independently of reason and the senses. It can be said to convert or redirect our reason. Faith does not overthrow reason but places it on a new foundation. We believe against our reason but not without our reason. When man's will is turned in a new direction, he is then enabled to reason in the light of faith.

The truth of faith is not amenable to rational appropriation. It can be known but not possessed by reason. Faith alone

---

[20]Quoted in Karl Barth, *Theology and Church*, trans. Louise Pettibone Smith (N. Y.: Harper, 1962), p. 317.

lays hold of God's Word apart from human power and aid. Luther put it this way: "Human reason can't grasp it by speculation. With our thoughts we can't get beyond the visible and physical."[21] And again: "For one cannot seize the word of God; it must be received from God as he commits it to one and sends him to preach it."[22]

If it is said that man can by his own power apprehend the Word of God, then this would mean that man could control this Word. Apprehending means encompassing, and we are spiritually masters of what we can encompass (Karl Barth). But in the act of faith man is possessed by the object of faith and not vice versa.

The central mysteries of the faith can be described but not fully explained. They can be known but not comprehended. We can truly know them through the mind of Christ. God can be known as He gives Himself to be known, but He is not an object immediately accessible to our perception and therefore at our disposal. Reason must finally bow before the mystery of divine truth. As Bernard of Clairvaux has expressed it: "I believe though I do not comprehend, and I hold by faith what I cannot grasp with the mind."

Idealistic philosophy has always pictured God as an object of man's thought; Leibniz described God as the "immediate object of our perceptions." For Luther, on the other hand, it is not reason or sight but faith that lays hold of God. Faith, moreover, is "being rapt and translated from all things of sense, within and without, into those things beyond sense within and without, namely into the invisible, most high and incomprehensible God."[23]

Roman Catholic theology is often accused by evangelical Protestants of substituting rational certainty for the certainty of faith in an attempt to come to terms with classical philosophy. Yet Catholics too have warned against transforming the living God into an object of man's thought. In the words of Maurice Blondel: "Is not the metaphysician involved in some sort of idolatry when he pretends to have encapsulated in his thought the infinite object of his pursuit or when in his

[21]Martin Luther, *Luther's Works*, ed. and trans. Theodore Tappert (Philadelphia: Fortress, 1967), Vol. LIV, p. 326.
[22]Wilhelm Pauck, ed., *Luther: Lectures on Romans* (Philadelphia: Westminster, 1961), p. 299n.
[23]*D. Martin Luther's Werke* (Weimar: Böhlaus, 1939), 57, 144, 10.

conceptions, precepts, systems and natural religion he imagines that he is going to lay his hand on the transcendental Being in order to conquer and master Him?"[24]

It should be recognized that we are drawing a distinction between knowing and understanding. We can know God through faith, but we cannot comprehend Him by our reason. This is acknowledged also by Charles Hodge, who at this point reflects his Calvinistic heritage: "A child knows what the words 'God is a spirit' mean. No created being can comprehend the Almighty unto perfection."[25] Once we have faith then we are moved to seek an ever deeper understanding of our faith, but we cannot attain a full or comprehensive understanding in this life.

The question can be raised whether philosophers too have not acknowledged the limitations of man's reason concerning the things of God. Not all philosophers are absolute idealists who tend to make reason omniscient. We grant that philosophy is also capable of discerning the fallibility and deficiency of man's reason, but it does not see the real basis of this fallibility. Kierkegaard had some wise words on this point: "The philosopher can also acknowledge his deficiency in comprehension, but the question remains whether he shall then acknowledge the basis of it to be in his limitation . . . or . . . assume that it is rooted in man himself and his sinfulness."[26]

Reason is not the foundation of faith, but it can be an exceedingly useful instrument of faith. We cannot share Leibniz's view that "faith must be grounded in reason," but we should certainly acknowledge that reason can serve faith. Natural reason is stone-blind in matters of faith, but faithful reasoning can bring much light to bear upon such matters.

It can be said that we reason *in* faith but not *to* faith. We do not arrive at faith by reason, but we can explicate faith by reason. It is not permissible to postulate a "Christian reason" (in the sense of a reason that is inherently Christian), but we can speak of a Christian exercise of reason.

Faith is not a substitute for knowledge (as in medieval scholasticism) but the ground and source of knowledge. In

---

[24]Quoted in Henri Bouillard, *The Knowledge of God* (N. Y.: Herder and Herder, 1968), pp. 22, 23.

[25]Charles Hodge, *Systematic Theology*, Vol. I, p. 50.

[26]*Søren Kierkegaard's Journals and Papers*, trans. H. V. and E. H. Hong, p. 13.

faith we are united with the ground of all meaning and thereby are enabled to see the meaning in all things. Through the knowledge of God which faith brings, we come to know ourselves and the world about us.

It has been said that faith is more a "being known" than a knowing (Luther). We do not so much apprehend Christ as we are apprehended by Him. Yet the complementary truth must also be affirmed, that in and through Christ we are enabled to apprehend Him. Faith is not less than knowledge, as Kant said, but a special kind of knowledge, one that contains the key to all other knowledge. The knowledge of faith is now only partly confirmed in our experience, but it will someday be verified in the full sense of this word (Kuitert).

Faith is both an awakening and a commitment; the latter might be said to include the former. It is a commitment to the living Christ, one that entails knowledge, trust and obedience. The Reformers stressed the note of trust and confidence in faith *(fiducia)*, but faith is also obedience to God's commands and perseverance amid trial and tribulation.

Need it be said that philosophers view faith quite differently from theologians? When the former speak of faith they usually mean a belief on the basis of evidence that is lacking. Christian theology, on the other hand, understands faith as trust on the basis of evidence that faith itself provides, namely, the assurance of forgiveness and the joy of salvation. Classical philosophy has always taught the wisdom of moderating our beliefs as well as our desires. But theology views faith as passionate commitment, the kind of commitment that often entails the sacrifice of our dearest dreams and desires. Philosophers are inclined to view such faith as nothing but fanaticism. Forsyth points to the wide chasm between these two views:

> It is the triumph of Hellenic and philosophical wisdom to think that "it is as wise to moderate our beliefs as our desires". But with Christian wisdom it is not so. We cannot love God too much, nor believe too much in His love, nor reckon it too holy. A due faith in Him is immoderate, absolute trust, and it has a creed to correspond.[27]

Faith is the sole means by which one perceives revelation.

[27] P. T. Forsyth, *The Justification of God*, p. 126.

We concur with John of the Cross: "Faith is . . . the only means whereby God manifests himself to the soul in his divine light, which surpasses all understanding."[28] It should be recognized that faith is an inward seeing, an inward hearing. The experience of faith transcends the senses, although it occurs only in conjunction with the outward hearing of the word of the Bible.

Emil Brunner has said that it is the duty of reason to "answer" the call of revelation. But this must be understood as a reason illumined by the light of divine grace; in other words it is faithful and not natural reason. To hold that man has within himself some power or capacity to lay hold of divine revelation is to fall into the heresy of synergism and to compromise the evangelical principle that our salvation is a work of free grace. There can be no preparation for revelation from our side. God must grant both the revelation and the condition to receive it. But after it is received, it then can make sense of all our experience.

Revelation is mediated through the world of nature, but it does not arise out of this world. Romano Guardini also expresses our sentiments:

> It is the hallmark of a genuine revelation that it cannot be deduced from any forms or potentialities of this world, but rather is utterly independent of them and, indeed, disrupts them. Revealed truth can only be recognized if we cease to approach it with earthly standards and are prepared to accept it on its own terms. . . . And though, indeed, revelation must be accepted without justification by earthly standards, once accepted, it forthwith throws light upon this very world, encourages it to ask questions of essential importance to it, and gives answers far exceeding natural wisdom.[29]

Revelation both renews and redirects reason, just as grace revitalizes and at the same time alters the course of nature. It is somewhat misleading to say that revelation supplements or adds to reason, for what we have here is not so much a quantitative addition as a qualitative change, not a building upon the old but a conversion to the new. Man's perspective is not simply broadened but also drastically revised so that

---

[28] John of the Cross, *Ascent of Mount Carmel*, II, 9.
[29] Romano Guardini, *The Last Things*, trans. Charlotte Forsyth and Grace Branham (Notre Dame, Ind.: University of Notre Dame, 1954), p. 58.

in fact he has a radically new perspective, a wholly new vision. He at the same time is given a new nature, new desires, new hopes: the heart of stone is replaced by a "heart of flesh" (Ezek. 11:19; 36:26; cf. II Cor. 5:17; Eph. 4:22-24).

It is fashionable today to affirm that the new man is man restored in the image of God; yet he is at the same time man reborn into the body of Christ. The divine-human encounter not only renews our original human nature but also enables us to partake in the divine nature (II Pt. 1:4). Grace not only restores us to essential manhood but also raises us to Godmanhood (II Cor. 3:18). In opposition to some strands of neo-Protestant theology, I hold that grace is both personal and ontological: in addition to divine favor it communicates the new Being.

Without affirming a general revelation that can serve as a bridge to special revelation, we acknowledge a general presence of God, a universal working of the Spirit of God. This is not to be confused with the doctrine of prevenient grace, however, since the Spirit of God works in the world not to save men but to restrain their rapacity and to help them maintain a measure of rationality, thereby enabling them to survive. The Holy Spirit accomplishes our salvation only in conjunction with the Word as this is proclaimed by the church. In line with the older Reformed theology we affirm not a universal prevenient grace but common grace. Common grace creates a yearning for Christ's salvation, but it does not result in a positive seeking for this salvation, because sin still reigns in the world outside the community of faith.

Because he is related to God in his innermost being and because of the working of God's Spirit in the world, man can be said to have a general awareness of God. But this natural knowledge or awareness of God is sufficient only to condemn, not to save man (cf. Rom. 1:20, 21, 32). It certainly cannot serve as a foundation for a natural theology, which has indeed no legitimate role in Christian thinking. Because of original sin every natural theology gives a distorted rather than a true picture of God. Instead of being viewed as a stepping stone to faith, it should be considered a "misunderstanding" (Brunner) and a "blind alley" (Colin Brown). This is not to deny, however, that the believer can discern the working of God in nature, but in this context one should speak of a theology of creation, not of natural theology.

REASONS FOR FAITH

Are there reasons for our faith in Jesus Christ? I would reply in the affirmative, but these are reasons which faith itself gives, namely, the witness of the Scriptures, the resurrection of Christ and the assurance of salvation. These are reasons given in revelation itself: they comprise part of the truth of revelation. Such reasons for the faith are not arrived at independently of revelation; they are the evidence which faith itself provides.

In addition to reasons that are implied or given in revelation itself, there are reasons which illumine the faith but do not prove or prepare the way for it. We are thinking here of reasons which help us to understand the faith and to make sense of our experience once we have faith. We also see the need for reasons for holding to particular interpretations of the faith.

Yet we insist that faith does not need reasons for validation or confirmation. This is because faith rests upon divine revelation, not human reason. The conviction of faith, as Kuyper rightly says, "is *not* the outcome of observation or demonstration."[30] Faith brings to nought the vanity of reason, but at the same time it seeks to utilize reason in the service of the glory of God.

We agree with Hugo of St. Victor who contended that although faith is not really supported by any reason "because reason does not comprehend what faith believes," yet it is possible for reason "to honor the faith which it still does not perfectly succeed in grasping."[31] Reasons cannot prove that faith is true in the light of external standards, but they can point to the inherent truth of faith. They cannot bring light upon the Light of the World, but they can reflect this Light. Reason is not the springboard of revelation, but it can become the servant of revelation.

Can reasons play a role in overcoming doubt? Our answer is that reasons are not effective in this area, for behind doubt is hardness of heart, which can be dealt with only by grace.

[30] Abraham Kuyper, *Principles of Sacred Theology* (Grand Rapids: Eerdmans, 1954), p. 131.
[31] Hugo of St. Victor, *De Sacramentis*, I, 3, XXX. Note that Hugo believed that faith is not given aid by reason only in those things "which are above reason."

Doubt has its source in man's sinful will; there is no doubt in faith itself. An enlightened reason can, however, clear up misunderstandings or deficiencies in understanding concerning the articles of faith. Its role is not to dispel doubt but to clarify faith and sharpen understanding.

It should be recognized that there are two types of doubt, Christian and sinful doubt. Christian doubt is doubt of ourselves, of our own wisdom and capabilities; this is a fruit of faith. Sinful doubt, on the other hand, is doubt of faith or of God's Word. This kind of doubt is the intellectual form of sin. Reasons cannot help us here; only prayer can avail.

The person who walks by faith alone is characterized not by uncritical reasoning but by a reasoning that is searching and discriminating. It has rightly been said that the person who does not stand for something will fall for anything. One can also argue that only he whose life is informed by an overarching vision or faith can be truly discriminating in his judgments. The reasoning that faith employs is one that is disciplined and critical. To walk in faith makes one not more blind but more perceptive. Faith is not a leap in the dark but a walking in the light (Jn. 12:35).

We affirm not reason seeking faith but faith seeking understanding. The place of reason is not in the quest for truth but in the search for theological integrity. Reason in the context of faith also seeks for a deeper understanding of the mysteries of divine revelation.

The question can be raised whether faith has a metaphysical dimension. Does faith entail a particular understanding of the world and history? Our position is that faith is not metaphysics, but it has far-reaching metaphysical implications. We cannot go along with Ritschl in calling for the expulsion of all metaphysics from theology. The Christ-event throws light upon ultimate reality as well as the meaning of human existence. Casserley rightly reminds us that although "faith must seek to understand itself . . . it is equally . . . true that it must go on to understand everything else by interpreting reality in terms of its own vision and from its own standpoint."[32]

It is possible to speak of a fundamental Christian orientation towards life and the world, but this must not be confused

---

[32] J. V. Langmead Casserley, *The Christian in Philosophy* (New York: Scribner's, 1955), p. 252.

with any specific philosophical or scientific world picture, which is very much a product of the culture. Faith involves a definite perspective on life and history, but the description of the precise nature of the world is more a matter of empirical investigation; moreover, the transcendent overall view of the universe is outside its grasp.

While not bound to any particular metaphysical construct, faith is tied to the basic biblical vision of the world as temporal, having a definite beginning and end. Faith is free to utilize various kinds of metaphysics, but it does not draw from them its fundamental insights. H. R. Mackintosh has rightly declared:

> Faith must always be metaphysical, for it rests upon convictions which, if true, must profoundly affect our whole view of the universe and the conduct befitting us within it. In this important sense, a metaphysical import belongs to every judgment concerning Ultimate Reality. Yet the belief or judgment in question need not have been reached by way of metaphysical argument, and in point of fact no essential Christian belief has ever been so reached, although metaphysical argument may later have been employed to defend it.[33]

Although the Christian faith entails a world outlook, its main thrust is to uphold Jesus Christ as the invader of world history and the conqueror of the kingdoms of this world. Only in the light of this divine incursion into the historical panorama do we begin to see a purpose and direction in history and in the whole of creation.

Christianity is rational but not rationalistic. It is surely not irrational, for it is centered in a message that can be received by reason, although its import cannot be fully grasped. The Christian faith, moreover, calls one not to an arbitrary decision but to a decision based upon evidence that faith itself provides. Sin, not faith, is irrational.

Yet the Christian faith is anti-ideological. It opposes the pretension and vanity of reason. It judges and calls into question all attempts at rationalization and dissimulation. Faith contradicts the arrogance of reason but not the basic structure of reason.

[33]H. R. Mackintosh, *Types of Modern Theology* (London: Nisbet, 1949), p. 142.

Faith is not only rational but also suprarational. This is to say, it concerns itself with mysteries that elude rational comprehension (cf. I Cor. 2:9, 10). It should be recognized that these mysteries stand above human but not divine reason. The incarnation is a paradox to the human mind, but it is not a paradox to God, and this means that it is ultimately rational.

Christianity is certainly not nonrational, as it is sometimes described in mystical writings. Once the Gospel is accepted, it gives meaning and direction to human life. Faith does not signify the wholesale abdication of reason but its liberation. It can even be said that in one sense faith has a rational foundation, but this is the Word of God and not human philosophy.

Because the full meaning of God's reconciling deed in Christ is too vast to be comprehended by any human mind, theology itself must always remain incomplete and deficient. In this life one cannot arrive at any absolute or final system. In the words of James Orr, one of the fathers of the new evangelical theology:

> Existing systems are not final; as works of human understanding they are necessarily imperfect. . . . I do not question, therefore, that there are still sides and aspects of divine truth to which full justice has not yet been accorded; improvements that can be made in our conception and formulation of all the doctrines, and in their correlation with each other.[34]

The question can now be posed as to whether reason has any role at all prior to faith. We are not thinking here of faithful reason but of natural reason. There are some Christian thinkers who contend that the reasoning of the natural man ends only in confusion and despair but by this very fact it can make man open to the Gospel. Yet we contend that only a despair over one's sins makes one ripe for the Gospel, not a despair of the world. Natural knowledge leads to condemnation, not to salvation. For Barth natural reason is severely limited and partially blind. We might ask whether it is not also perverse. Man by his own reasoning is driven into ever deeper despair and anguish, but this does not make him more ready or willing to hear the Gospel. The natural man is in flight from God, not in quest of God, and this is

[34] James Orr, *The Progress of Dogma* (London: Hodder and Stoughton, 1901), pp. 30, 31.

why he can be reached only by the miracle of divine grace.

This now brings us to the question whether there is an apologetic side to the Christian faith. Is a reborn reason capable of leading people outside the church to faith in Jesus Christ? Apologetics has traditionally been understood as the defense of the faith before the man of the world on the basis of a mutually acknowledged criterion for the purpose of convincing him of the truth of the faith. I hold that to appeal to common ground with non-Christian thought is suspect. Apologetics in the traditional sense cannot penetrate the heart of the unbeliever because he is bound to powers and forces beyond his control. If we take seriously the biblical and Reformation doctrine of the bondage of the will, then we must conclude that the outsider or unbeliever could not believe in Jesus Christ even if this were his intention. Christians have much in common with the children of darkness because they share a common humanity and a common sinfulness. But the Christian revelation stands in diametrical opposition to the thought-world of the natural man and this is why the Christian, although he can cooperate with unbelievers in many areas (e.g., social welfare), cannot by rational argument persuade them of the credibility of his faith.

This is not to imply that there is no place whatever for an apologetic task in Christian theology. The Christian is obliged to answer attacks upon the faith in order to remove misunderstandings of the faith that obstruct both believers and nonbelievers. An intelligible defense of the faith can silence the criticisms of our opponents, although it cannot induce nor even facilitate the decision of faith. It can remove false stumbling blocks, but it cannot make the man of the world more receptive or open to the truth of the Gospel. For those who are earnestly seeking salvation, that is, those whose consciences have been pricked by the Spirit of God, apologetics can be of some help in holding doubt in check; but even here it has only a negative role.

An apologetic wrestling with the questions of unbelief is of much more value to the Christian himself, since it can strengthen him in his faith. Apologetics should ideally be seen not as a prolegomenon to dogmatics but as that branch of dogmatics which concerns itself with the encounter between faith and unfaith. It should be reinterpreted as a supplementation rather than an introduction to the sermon. We concur

Faith and Reason

with the judgment of P. T. Forsyth: "Apologetic is not so valuable to convert the world as to confirm the Church which does convert . . . and to unify its knowledge of the Son of God."[35]

Where so much traditional apologetics has gone astray is in its tendency to view intellectual doubt as the main barrier to belief. Kierkegaard has some strong words on this matter:

> It is claimed that arguments against Christianity arise out of doubt. This is a total misunderstanding. The arguments against Christianity arise out of insubordination, reluctance to obey, mutiny against all authority. Therefore, until now the battle against objections has been shadow-boxing, because it has been intellectual combat with doubt instead of being ethical combat against mutiny.[36]

Christian faith is not characterized by intellectualism nor by anti-intellectualism but by an obedient intellectualism. The intellect must neither be elevated nor denigrated but rather subordinated to the Word of God. The ambassador of Christ is called to make the faith intelligible and understandable, and this means translating it into language familiar to his hearers. But he cannot make the faith credible or palatable. It is incumbent upon him to proclaim a logically coherent message, but he cannot make this message acceptable to the modern mind. He should try to explain God's reconciling deed in Christ to the best of his ability, but he cannot make Christ real to people. Only the Holy Spirit can penetrate the hearts of those who are bound to the power of sin, and He has chosen to act wherever God's Word is faithfully proclaimed and obeyed (Jn. 16:8; I Cor. 1:21; 12:3; Gal. 3:2, 5; Eph. 1:13).

APPENDIX TO CHAPTER X

Some light is thrown on the relation between faith and world views by an examination of the German words *Weltbild* and *Weltanschauung*. *Weltbild* signifies an ordered picture of the empirical world, one that is open to scientific investigation.

---

[35] P. T. Forsyth, *The Principle of Authority*, p. 33.
[36] *Søren Kierkegaard's Journals and Papers*, trans. H. V. and E. H. Hong, p. 359.

It primarily concerns the structure of the world rather than its metaphysical significance. *Weltanschauung* refers to a comprehensive outlook upon life and the universe. It is to be regarded more as an interpretation of the meaning of life and the world than a construct of the way in which the world appears to man. *Weltanschauung* is sometimes distinguished from philosophy as a basic outlook upon the world is distinguished from its systematic articulation, but for all practical purposes it can be viewed as an all-embracing philosophy of life, a metaphysical world-perspective.

Christianity should never be tied to any *Weltbild*, since the empirical description of the world is the task of natural science, and the scientific picture of the world changes from generation to generation. But we also affirm that the Christian faith should never be united with any *Weltanschauung* that characterizes a particular age, for both the ground and object of faith differ considerably from that of cultural philosophy. Christianity is not so much a view of the world as a report of the saving deeds of God (Arthur Cochrane).

At the same time the Christian faith does throw light upon God's will for man and His plan for the world. Biblical religion can be said to offer an interpretation of history, an abiding insight into the unique role of man and his final destiny, as well as that of the whole creation. Yet it seeks to understand man and his world not as they are in themselves but only in their relation to the living God and His revelation in Jesus Christ. Its view of the world is derived from its conviction concerning the character and purpose of God, which are disclosed in the Bible and especially in the person of Christ; in most philosophy, on the other hand, one's conception of God is subordinated to one's view of reality. Moreover, biblical faith resists an over-arching conceptual synthesis — the perennial temptation of all philosophies and ideologies. In contrast to metaphysical philosophy, its understanding of life and the world is determined more by divine revelation than human speculation. Again, its affirmations concerning the meaning of life are basically religious rather than metaphysical, even though they contain metaphysical import. This is to say that the primary concern in Christianity is redemption and reconciliation and not metaphysical knowledge.

Christianity, to be sure, brings not simply a new relationship with God but a new horizon regarding the world. Yet only in a very limited sense can we call this a "world view," since it is based on an objective revelation rather than a subjective interpretation. Moreover, it does not involve a comprehensive understanding but rather a metaphysical vision. Faith provides enough knowledge for salvation but insufficient knowledge for a rationally coherent system. It should also be recognized that the Christian conception, unlike every ideological position, invariably goes counter to the *Zeitgeist* (spirit of the times).

It is permissible to speak of a biblical perspective on life and the world so long as this is not confused with any particular scientific theory or philosophical world view. In contrast to most philosophers the biblical prophets and apostles refer to God in an analogical fashion, thereby confessing their inability to grasp the essence of the Divine. They also utilize graphic imagery, not categorical concepts to describe the significant events of sacred history, including the beginning and end of the world. The Bible offers a mytho-poetic vision rather than a theoretical construct of the world, an intuition into the meaning of the world rather than a speculative description of the world.

Biblical religion is concerned not so much with man's interpretation of himself and his world as with the opening of his eyes to the divine interpretation, which cannot be comprehended but can only be believed. This interpretation, which is given in Scripture, should be translated into the language of today, but it cannot be subsumed under modern categories of thought. Our formulation by itself cannot convey the inner meaning of the divine Word; ours is at the most a sign and witness of this Word. Only God Himself can communicate His Word, and He does this by His Spirit who works in and through our broken proclamation.

In contradistinction to the general tendency in neo-orthodoxy, we contend that the Christian faith entails a metaphysical perspective of its own which indeed conflicts with every *Weltanschauung* and philosophy of life. But in opposition to Protestant scholastic orthodoxy we insist that this perspective cannot be systematized into an all-encompassing world view. It is an incomplete metaphysical perspective, but in the eschatological future it shall be consummated and fulfilled in perfect knowledge. Now we know in part, but then we shall understand fully even as we are understood (I Cor. 13:12).

The two dangers that one must guard against are subordinating the biblical vision to a metaphysical construct, and emptying this vision of any metaphysical import. Christian faith is more than a matter of feeling and personal trust; it entails a definite conviction concerning the meaning and purpose of human existence and indeed of all creation. Its statements of God and the world are statements of knowledge although they still await their final verification. Granted that the underlying convictions of the faith point in a metaphysical direction, they must not become assimilated into any metaphysical or ideological system, even one that goes under the name of "Christian." A fully articulated world view can be informed and inspired by the Christian faith, but it must always be recognized as a human and therefore fallible interpretation. The all-encompassing perspective belongs to God alone, although by faith we can now share in it partially.

It is always important to differentiate between the basic intuition of faith, which is given in revelation, and the systematic interpretation, which is several steps removed from revelation. A metaphysical and even a theological construct must never be equated with the truth of faith itself. Barth contends that Christianity is free from all world views, and while this affirmation appears to contain much truth we must insist that Christian faith does entail a definite perspective of its own on life and the world. Christianity is free, however, from all cultural or philosophical world views. It would be more accurate to affirm that the Christian faith is neither derived from nor based on a world view. At the same time world views should be bound as much as possible to the Christian revelation. A fresh formulation of the biblical witness concerning life and the world is needed in our time, but such a formulation must always be regarded as incomplete and tentative and therefore open to correction and revision in the light of the Word of God.

Within the context of the phenomenology of religion or the history of religions it is permissible to refer to a Christian or biblical point of view that may rightly be compared with others. But speaking as theologians we must go on to contend that the biblical position on life and the world differs qualitatively from philosophical and ideological positions. The Bible gives not so much a synoptic view of the world as a witness to God's redemptive actions in the world. It also does not engage in a discourse upon the idea of God as a metaphysical theme, but it proclaims the entrance of God into world history. Although this proclamation is fraught with metaphysical significance, it is not in itself a metaphysical construct. For biblical theology the truth of faith should be seen not simply as another world view but as the divine judgment upon all world views.

Theology, of course, must seek to systematize the biblical witness and therefore is compelled to utilize theoretical concepts. It must declare the truth about God, man and the world and differentiate this truth from the misunderstandings endemic to cultural philosophy. At the same time it recognizes that its formulations are provisional and deficient, that the overall metaphysical system is hidden with Christ in God. The theologian acknowledges himself as a stranger in the world of philosophy, for he constantly seeks to bring thought into obedience to faith. The ideological temptation is to bring faith into accordance with thought, and this accounts for the compromises that often go under the name of "philosophical theology." The theologian may feel called upon to present a biblically informed view of life and the world, but he will always recognize the gulf between his own feeble constructions and the truth of faith itself. He will see that his own world view as it stands by itself is also to some degree philosophical or cultural, and therefore he should always seek to relate it to the revelation of Jesus Christ so that it becomes not so much a view of the world as a testimony concerning the salvation of the world through the cross of Christ.

INDEX OF SUBJECTS

Agape 34, 96, 142
Age of Reason 87, 166, 183
agnosticism 46, 66
Albigenses 109
alcoholism 117
analogia Christi 162
analogia entis 100, 162, 185
analogia fidei 100, 185
analytic philosophy 55, 56, 83, 84
apologetics 26, 28, 29, 30, 36, 40, 42, 43, 46, 63, 198, 199
assurance 68, 146, 194
atonement 96, 124
authority 35, 59, 71, 72, 73, 83, 87, 159
autosoterism 94

beatific vision 32, 154
behaviorism 66
Bible, the Holy
  authority of 74
  infallibility of 72, 74, 186
  inspiration of 13, 18
biblical-classical synthesis 15, 30f., 35, 36
biblicism 155
Buddhism 21, 94, 95, 106, 141

Calvinism 112, 123, 183, 187, 190
Cathari 109
Christian democracy 65
Christian education 20
Christian Science 111
coherence theory 130-132
common grace 23, 102, 193
conscience 102
conservative evangelicals 13, 17, 18
contemplation 95, 154, 159
conversion 46, 64, 104, 129, 199
correspondence theory 128-130
culture-religion 156, 170

death of God 167
deductive method 69, 90, 132
deism 167

democracy 20, 21, 65, 175
demonic, the 108, 109, 115, 116, 120, 121
demythologizing 162, 174, 175
dialectical materialism 66, 169
diastasis 23, 26
divine-human encounter 70, 152
doubt 194, 195, 199
dualism 49, 98, 105ff., 118, 129, 143

Ecumenical Institute 111
empirical theology 20, 70
empiricism 69, 70, 129, 135
Enlightenment 40, 87, 167, 182, 185, 186
Epicureanism 26, 124
epistemology 14, 31, 69
Eros 34, 96, 142, 172
eschatology 48, 55, 85, 114, 202
estrangement 108
eternal truths 34, 98
Evangelicalism 39, 97, 140, 151f., 176
evolution 7, 111, 124, 165, 175
existentialism 7, 14, 44, 87, 88, 98, 136, 138, 171, 172, 187

faith 12, 13, 19, 21, 22, 30, 33, 35, 41, 46, 58, 62, 68, 71, 73, 77, 81, 89, 103, 124, 138, 140, 142, 144, 145, 146, 147, 148, 149, 157, 173, 176, 177, 179, 181, 187ff., 202, 203
fanaticism 67, 166
Fate 115, 165
federal theory 122
fideism 35, 178, 179, 187
forgiveness 86, 95, 152
Free University of Amsterdam 79
freedom 32, 37, 44, 48, 99, 115, 122, 137, 186
fundamentalism 40, 176

German Christians 17
God
  holiness of 15

204

Index of Subjects

impassibility of 15, 37
reconciling work of 70
sovereignty of 15, 154
transcendence of 19, 97, 172
Gnosticism 30, 106
grace 36, 44, 45, 96, 113, 138, 177, 186, 187, 192, 193

hedonism 174
heresy 30, 61
Hinduism 106, 110, 141
history of religions 203
Holy Spirit 37, 39, 70, 71, 77, 90, 100, 103, 187, 188, 193, 198, 201

idealism 53, 69, 98, 99, 107, 112, 113, 120, 129, 130, 132, 135, 137, 183, 189
ideology 17, 102, 142, 158, 202, 203
idolatry 79, 98, 174
image of God 100
immortality of the soul 32
inductive method 69, 90
innate ideas 183
intuitionism 69
irrationalism 7, 86, 122, 180, 183
irresistible grace 36

Jainism 106
Jesus Christ
  cross of 14, 28, 76, 96, 97, 124, 150
  example of 153
  incarnation of 29, 147
  love of 39, 138
  resurrection of 28, 75, 76, 123, 150
  revelation of 12, 48, 100
justification 86, 137, 152

Kantian philosophy 48, 102
kerygmatic theology 13, 60
kingdom of God 8, 27, 65, 77, 81, 112, 123

Law of God 13, 33, 181
liberal theology 7, 16, 22, 40, 41, 52
logical analysis 55, 57
love 34, 37, 80, 81, 93, 96, 138, 146, 152

Manichaeism 106

Marxism 14, 17, 24, 102, 117, 169, 175
Marxist-Christian dialogue 25
materialism 98, 136
metaphysics 12, 16, 22, 33, 53, 57, 83, 90, 167, 195, 196, 203
method of correlation 43, 45
Mithraism 108
monads 97, 166
monism 49, 69, 98, 107, 110, 112, 113, 118, 120, 130, 143
Mormonism 112
mysticism 7, 15, 30, 34, 43, 52, 69, 80, 82, 96, 133, 134, 135, 140ff., 170, 172, 186, 197
myth 40, 101, 156ff.
mythology 80, 160, 162, 164, 165

National Socialism 19
nationalism 174
natural law 33, 177, 181
natural theology 7, 27, 28, 31, 39, 43, 47, 60, 186, 193
naturalism 7, 20, 69, 80, 97, 107, 111, 117, 135, 170
neo-evangelicalism 17, 18
neo-liberalism 16, 17
neo-naturalism 22, 53
neo-orthodoxy 15, 16, 52, 201
Neo-Platonism 109, 141, 142
neo-Protestantism 22, 193
new birth 77, 103
New Left 17
nihilism 43
nominalism 34, 35

ontology 57, 121
original sin 44, 122
orthodoxy, Protestant 17, 38, 52, 176, 202

panentheism 97, 116, 143
pantheism 79, 80, 97, 140
peace of God 148
personalism 30, 43, 53, 113, 143, 155
phenomenology of religion 203
philosophical theology 7, 31, 41, 53, 60
philosophy of religion 7, 23, 26, 27, 28, 31, 43, 47, 51ff.
Pietism 39, 40, 176, 183

piety 140, 141, 152, 153
Platonism 26, 30, 37, 48, 106, 107, 108, 109, 141
pluralism 109
Positivism 168
pragmatism 132, 133, 136
prayer 94, 95, 143, 144
predestination 37
pre-established harmony 113
prevenient grace 193
primal horde, myth of 168
process philosophy 20, 114, 116, 170, 171
progress, ideology of 16, 166, 167
prophecy, biblical 40
Puritanism 39, 176

racism 174
radical evil 102, 121
radical theology 16, 17
rationalism 22, 24, 34, 38, 42, 69, 82, 155, 176, 196
recollection 86
reconciliation 94
Reformation, Protestant 35, 78, 186
regeneration 77, 139
reincarnation 166
relativism 43
religionless Christianity 46
religious experience 7, 95, 142, 144, 149
Renaissance 87
repentance 86, 118
revelation 8, 13, 20, 21, 22, 24, 34, 46, 47, 52, 60, 67, 70, 71, 81, 88, 135, 139, 142, 149, 162, 174, 182, 183, 184, 185, 191, 192, 193, 194
revelational positivism 45

sacraments 74, 186
sacred history 89
saga 159, 161, 173
salvation 29, 30, 37, 66, 71, 91, 94, 95, 96, 137, 141, 186, 192, 193, 194, 198, 201

secular theology 16
sexual revolution 43
scholastic theology 24, 31, 32, 38, 51, 176, 184, 190
scientism 57, 174, 175
sin 24, 26, 33, 39, 44, 49, 52, 86, 96, 102, 113, 118, 120, 121, 122, 123, 138, 139, 196
skepticism 22
social holiness 93
soteriology 94
spiritualism 155
spirituality 24, 95, 112, 140, 153
Stoicism 26, 29, 37, 110, 112
subjectivism 18, 56
supernaturalism 41, 53, 98
supralapsarianism 112
syncretism 7, 142
synergism 192

theism 53, 59
theocracy 65
theodicy 117, 124
theologia crucis 152
theologia gloriae 152
theologia viatorum 85
theology of hope 16
theology of revolution 16
Thomism 44, 51, 56
Trinity 29

universalism 13, 50
unbelief 13, 60

Weltanschauung 47, 200, 202
Weltbild 200
white supremacy 175
Word of God 11, 12, 13, 45, 47, 66, 74, 85, 92, 131, 138, 174, 199, 201, 202
World Soul 134, 163
world view 12, 36, 47, 49, 175, 195, 196, 200ff.

Zoroastrianism 106, 108, 109

INDEX OF NAMES

Abelard 33
Abraham 80
Adams, George 53
Adams, James Luther 127, 160
Albertus Magnus 51
Allen, Diogenes 24
Altizer, Thomas J. J. 16, 17
Ames, Edward Scribner 97
Anselm 31, 32, 48, 90, 185
Aquinas, Thomas 31, 32, 33, 34, 78, 106, 107, 146, 177, 178, 185, 188
Aristotle 32, 33, 37, 38, 62, 83, 87, 93, 105, 153, 164, 165, 184
Ashen, Ruth 20
Athanasius 29
Augustine 30, 32, 61, 93, 106, 107, 122, 152, 177, 178, 183, 188
Aulén, Gustaf 120, 144
Ayer, A. J. 55

Bach, Johann Sebastian 185
Bailey, Page 22
Bainton, Roland 147
Barber, W. H. 110
Barth, Karl 13, 15, 25, 31, 45, 46f., 59, 61, 63, 75, 84, 85, 91, 92, 98, 101, 106, 108, 120, 122, 136, 140, 147, 159, 160, 161, 162, 171, 185f., 188, 189, 197
Bartsch, Hans-Werner 81
Bavinck, H. 122
Becker, Carl 166
Beckett, Samuel 43, 87
Berdyaev, Nicolas 88, 105, 115
Berkouwer, G. C. 61
Bernard of Clairvaux 93, 187, 189
Bixler, Julius 160
Bizer, Ernst 144
Blackney, Raymond B. 143
Blamires, Harry 24
Bloch, Ernst 17
Blondel, Maurice 189
Boehme, Jacob 115
Böhler, Peter 39

Bonhoeffer, Dietrich 45, 46, 64, 121, 138, 139, 147
Bouillard, Henri 31, 190
Braaten, Carl 16
Braithwaite, R. B. 55, 57
Brightman, Edgar 53, 83, 87, 115
Brock, Werner 127
Bromiley, G. W. 85
Brown, Colin 18, 24, 75, 76, 193
Brunner, Emil 15, 43, 54, 55, 80, 93, 94, 95, 120, 135, 140, 173, 187, 192, 193
Buddha, Gautama 94
Bultmann, Rudolf 16, 19, 44, 46, 186
Burnet, John 91

Cailliet, Emile 175
Calvin, John 35, 36, 37, 38, 62, 68, 78, 79, 101, 146, 155
Carnell, Edward J. 18, 52
Case, Shirley Jackson 119
Casserley, J. V. Langmead 195
Cassirer, Ernst 159, 164, 167
Chardin, Teilhard de 17
Cherry, Conrad 18
Clark, Gordon 100, 183, 184
Clement of Alexandria 28, 29, 78
Cobb, John 16, 19
Cochrane, Arthur 19, 24, 187, 200
Comte, Auguste 168
Confucius 116
Cornford, F. M. 156, 163
Cox, Harvey 16, 17
Cullmann, Oscar 162

Daane, James 18
Damian, Peter 34
Descartes, René 69, 83, 89, 184
Dewart, Leslie 16
Dewey, John 20, 21, 69, 157
Dionysius, the pseudo-Areopagite 106
Dooyeweerd, Herman 54, 55

Dulles, Avery 162
Dunn, John 165, 170
Duns Scotus, John 34

Eckhart, Meister 34, 143
Eddy, Mary Baker 111
Edwards, Jonathan 18, 40, 115
Eliade, Mircea 166, 169
Ellul, Jacques 24
Emmet, Dorothy 86, 87
Engels, Friedrich 91
Epictetus 95
Epicurus 93

Fairweather, Eugene R. 31
Ferré, Frederick 55
Ferré, Nels 55, 92, 112, 113, 114
Feuerbach, Ludwig 81
Fichte, Johann Gottlieb 82
Forsyth, Peter T. 29, 59, 72, 76, 77, 89, 97, 124, 131, 187, 191, 199
Frankfort, H. A. 159
Frankfort, Henri 159
Freeman, David 54, 157
Freud, Sigmund 21, 91, 116, 168, 169
Fromm, Erich 116
Fuller, Reginald 81

Garnett, A. C. 116
Garrigou-Lagrange, Reginald 146
Gilkey, Langdon 124
Gilson, Etienne 164, 165
Godsey, John D. 47
Gordon, Ernest 79
Groff, Warren 18
Guardini, Romano 192

Hamilton, Kenneth 24, 80
Hamilton, William 16
Harnack, Adolf 29
Haroutunian, Joseph 11
Hart, Jeffrey 176
Hartshorne, Charles 21, 53, 115, 170
Hegel, Georg Wilhelm Friedrich 40, 70, 82, 91, 92, 97, 105, 107, 111, 167
Heidegger, Martin 19, 44, 63, 64, 83, 105, 127, 171, 172, 174
Heiler, Friedrich 95, 98, 140, 151
Heim, Karl 79, 80
Hengstenberg, Ernst Wilhelm 176

Henley, William 94
Henry, Carl 18, 22
Heppe, Heinrich 144
Heraclitus 91, 110, 127
Hick, John 114
High, Dallas 102
Hocking, William 53
Hodge, Charles 182, 183, 190
Holloway, M. R. 128
Hollaz, David 38, 39
Holmer, Paul L. 102
Holmes, Arthur 101, 132
Homrighausen, Elmer 23
Hordern, William 57
Horrobin, David 175
Hosea 123
Huegel, Baron Friedrich von 140
Hugo of St. Victor 194
Hume, David 69, 182
Hunter, Alan 119

Irenaeus 30, 45, 112
Isaac 80

Jacob 80
James, William 94, 113, 132, 138
Jaspers, Karl 19, 20, 81, 87, 88, 91, 93, 94, 96, 105, 138, 157, 159, 160, 172
Jeremiah 119
Joachim of Floris 166
John, St. 137
John of the Cross 187, 192
Jonas, Hans 171, 174
Jowett, B. 102
Judas 112

Kant, Immanuel 18, 19, 23, 40, 48, 50, 56, 69, 82, 83, 87, 94, 95, 96, 98, 102, 166, 167, 180, 181, 182, 185, 191
Kaufman, Gordon D. 16, 160
Kaufman, Walter 157
Kepler, Thomas 179
Kierkegaard, Soren 18, 38, 41, 42, 68, 70, 79, 138, 181, 184, 190, 199
Knudson, Albert 53
Köberle, Adolf 141
Kuitert, H. M. 18, 24, 191
Küng, Hans 118, 136, 140

Index of Names

Kuyper, Abraham 79, 194

Ladd, George Eldon 18
Langer, Susanne 159, 160
Lawrence, D. H. 172, 173
Lean, Garth 172
Leibniz, Gottfried Wilhelm 22, 34, 38, 97, 112, 113, 166, 184, 189, 190
Lessing, Gotthold Ephraim 40, 82, 86, 166
Lewis, C. S. 160
Lewis, Edwin 109, 120
Lloyd-Jones, D. Martyn 187
Locke, John 18, 69, 87
Lucretius 124
Lunn, Arnold 172
Luther, Martin 24, 35, 36, 37, 38, 45, 62, 68, 72, 78, 98, 121, 144, 145, 147, 155, 165, 178, 179, 184, 189, 191

Mackay, John 89
Mackintosh, H. R. 196
Macquarrie, John 16, 171
Manheim, Ralph 64, 83
Marcuse, Herbert 169
Maritain, Jacques 88
Marty, Martin E. 162
Martyr, Justin 28
Marx, Karl 14, 17, 21, 25, 81, 102, 117, 169
Mathews, Joseph 111
Mathews, Shailer 119
McGann, Thomas F. 20
McNally, Arthur 111
McNeill, John T. 146
Melanchthon, Philip 37
Meland, Bernard 20, 53, 158, 171
Metz, Johannes 16
Miller, Donald E. 18
Moltmann, Jürgen 16
Montgomery, John W. 70
Mozart, Wolfgang A. 185
Murray, Henry 173

Nash, Ronald 101, 183
Niebuhr, H. Richard 17, 153, 154, 161
Niebuhr, Reinhold 15, 43, 44, 45, 52, 99, 140, 160

Nietzsche, Friedrich Wilhelm 21, 25, 81, 94, 157, 167
Novak, Michael 16
Nygren, Anders 140

Occam, William of 34
Ogden, Schubert 16
Origen 111
Orr, James 197
Ott, Heinrich 19
Otto, Rudolf 82
Owen, John 39, 79, 101

Pascal, Blaise 79, 150, 179, 180, 182, 187
Patrick, G. T. W. 129
Pauck, Wilhelm 189
Paul, St. 21, 22, 23, 26, 27, 28, 45, 61, 77, 78, 88, 119, 188
Peerman, Dean 162
Pegis, A. C. 177
Pelikan, Jaroslav 38, 71, 78
Peter, St. 27, 72
Pike, James 16
Plantinga, Alvin 84
Plato 23, 31, 33, 62, 69, 86, 87, 91, 94, 95, 102, 105, 106, 107, 109, 110, 153, 163, 164, 165, 184
Plotinus 105, 106, 153, 165
Pope, Alexander 110
Price, Lucien 21
Protagoras 87
Przywara, Erich 177

Rahner, Karl 44, 45, 51, 52
Ramm, Bernard 18, 24
Ramsey, Ian T. 55, 57
Ramsey, Paul 100
Reese, William 115
Renard, Henri 128
Rich, Arthur 16
Richmond, James 84
Ricoeur, Paul 115, 163
Rieff, Philip 173
Ritschl, Albrecht 41, 118, 195
Robinson, J. A. T. 16, 115, 143
Robinson, James 19
Robinson, Paul 169
Rogers, Jack 24
Rosenberg, Alfred 170
Rousseau, Jean-Jacques 116, 166

Royce, Josiah 69, 112, 113
Rushdoony, Rousas J. 175
Russell, Bertrand 21

Santayana, George 21, 92, 94
Sartre, Jean-Paul 91
Schelling, Friedrich W. J. 115
Schillebeeckx, Edward 16
Schleiermacher, Friedrich 7, 41, 52, 53, 106, 112, 113, 143
Schutz, Roger 154
Seneca 90
Shestov, Lev 83, 98, 157, 174, 181
Smedes, Lewis 24, 155
Smith, Earl 16
Smith, R. Gregor 16
Socrates 93
Sölle, Dorothee 16
Sontag, Frederick 16, 22
Speirs, E. B. 94
Spencer, Sidney 142
Spener, Philip Jacob 39
Spinoza, Benedict 40, 69, 87, 91, 110, 111, 112
Spurgeon, Charles 176
Stace, Walter T. 142
Standen, Anthony 175
Stevenson, W. Taylor 161
Stuermann, Walter 116
Suso, Henry 34
Swenson, David 42

Tatian 28, 78
Tauler, Johann 34, 152
Tertullian 29, 78
Thales 165
Thielicke, Helmut 23, 49, 187
Tillich, Paul 7, 16, 43, 45, 52, 69, 75, 80, 92, 106, 107, 108, 121, 127, 134, 135, 152, 158, 160, 167
Tolstoy, Leo 116

Torrance, Thomas 24, 57, 85
Torres, Camilo 16
Troeltsch, Ernst 41
Trueblood, D. Elton 24
Tucker, Robert C. 81, 159, 169
Turretin, Francis 144

Van Buren, Paul 55, 57
Versényi, Laszlo 127
Voltaire, François-Marie Arouet 25

Warfield, Benjamin 140
Watson, Philip 24, 35
Wesley, John 39, 40, 93, 140
Whitehead, Alfred North 14, 17, 20, 53, 62, 69, 82, 83, 84, 97, 99, 105, 107, 112, 130, 170, 171
Wieman, Henry Nelson 16, 53, 69, 98, 129
Wiener, Philip 112
Williams, Daniel D. 16, 20, 53, 112, 114
Williams, J. Rodman 19, 138
Wingren, Gustaf 187
Winter, Gibson 16
Wisdom, John 129
Wittgenstein, Ludwig Josef J. 55, 80, 95, 102
Wolff, Christian von 38
Wolters, Clifton 146
Wolterstorff, Nicholas 83, 84
Woolf, Bertram Lee 54, 147
Wright, William Kelly 136

Young, William 54

Zarathustra 168
Zeno 93
Zinzendorf, Count Nicolaus Ludwig von 39
Zuurdeeg, Willem F. 55, 57

INDEX OF SCRIPTURES

Genesis
  3 92

Psalms
  36:9 130
  51:10 137
  76:10 115
  119:160 126
  145:13 123

Proverbs
  2:6 92
  3:5, 7 92

Isaiah
  14:12-20 121
  14:24 137
  40:8 137
  57:15 154

Jeremiah
  17:9 119

Ezekiel
  11:19 193
  36:26 193

Hosea
  6:1 123

Matthew
  4:1-11 121
  4:8, 9 90
  5:45 27
  7:11 27
  7:16 133
  8:12 8
  11:25 27
  13:41, 42 8
  16:17 73
  16:25, 26 90, 133

Mark
  4:11, 12 27

Luke
  6:43-44 133
  10:18 121
  10:21 27
  12:47, 48 7
  16:8 62

John
  1:4 184
  1:5 125
  3:19, 20 26
  4:42 73
  5:39, 40 73
  8:31, 32 27, 137
  8:43 26
  8:43f. 27
  12:35 146, 195
  14:6 27, 128
  14:20 147
  15:1-6 144
  16:8 199
  21:24 137

Acts
  17:22f. 28

Romans
  1:20, 21, 32 193
  1:21 26
  5:8 152
  8:16 39
  10:17 75, 188
  14:23 27

I Corinthians
  1:21 75, 188, 199
  1:30 86
  2 92
  2:2 28
  2:4, 5 28
  2:7-10 28
  2:9, 10 197
  2:11 28
  2:14 76
  2:16 22
  3:16 154
  9:21, 22 28
  12:3 199
  13:12 23, 55, 202
  16:15 28

II Corinthians
  3:1-3 133
  3:18 193
  4:7 173
  5:17 193
  5:19 13, 124
  6:14-16 26
  13:5 154

Galatians
  1:11, 12 89
  1:12 161
  3:2, 5 199
  4:9 68

Ephesians
  1:13 199
  2:1-5 77
  2:3 119
  2:22 154
  3:17 154
  4:18 119
  4:18, 19 123
  4:21 128
  4:22-24 193
  5:29 119
  6:12 121

Philippians
  3:12 23

Colossians
  1:9 23
  1:27 154
  2:2, 3 23
  2:8 27, 61, 78
  3:1 23

I Timothy
  1:4 161
  4:7 161

II Timothy
  1:12 138
  4:4 161

Titus
  1:9 61
  1:14 161

Hebrews
  11:1 68
  12:14 153

James
  3:17 24
  4:4 26

I Peter
  5:8, 9 121

II Peter
  1:4 193
  1:16 27, 161, 173

I John
  1:7 146
  4:10 97
  5:7 128
  5:7-10 73
  5:10 73

III John
  12 137

Jude
  6 121

Revelation
  2:10 120
  3:20 139
  4:8 90
  11:7 120
  12:7-12 121
  13:7 120

www.ingramcontent.com/pod-product-compliance
Lightning Source LLC
Chambersburg PA
CBHW060607230426
43670CB00011B/2013